Caring Well

CARING WELL

Religion, Narrative, and Health Care Ethics

Edited by
David H. Smith

Westminster John Knox Press
Louisville, Kentucky

Scripture quotations are from the New Revised Standard Version
of the Bible, copyright © 1989
by the Division of Christian Education of the National Council
of the Churches of Christ in the U.S.A.,
and are used by permission.
Permission to quote excerpts from copyrighted works
has been granted by the following publishers:
Yale University Press. Excerpts from *The Patient as Person* by Paul Ramsey.
Copyright © 1970 by Paul Ramsey.
Putnam Berkley, a division of Penguin Putnam Inc. Excerpts from *Dying Well*
by Ira Byock. Copyright © 1997 by Ira Byock.
Johns Hopkins University Press. Excerpts from *A Midwife Through the Dying Process*
by Timothy E. Quill. Copyright © 1996 by Timothy E. Quill.
Viking Penguin, a division of Penguin Putnam Inc. Excerpts from *Measure of Our Days*
by Jerome E. Groopman. Copyright © 1997 by Jerome E. Groopman.

Book design by Sharon Adams
Cover design by Mark Abrams

First edition
Published by Westminster John Knox Press
Louisville, Kentucky

This book is printed on acid-free paper that meets the
American National Standards Institute Z39.48 standard. ∞

PRINTED IN THE UNITED STATES OF AMERICA

00 01 02 03 04 05 06 07 08 09 — 10 9 8 7 6 5 4 3 2 1

Library of Congress Cataloging-in-Publication Data
Caring Well: Religion, Narrative, and Health Care Ethics / David H. Smith, editor.
   p. cm.
Includes bibliographical references and index.
ISBN 0-664-22256-0 (pbk. : alk. paper)
   1. Medical ethics. 2. Medicine—Religious aspects. I. Smith, David H., 1939–
R725.55 .R446 2000
174'.2—dc21   00-036671

CONTENTS

CONTRIBUTORS

JOHN D. BARBOUR
Professor of Religion
St. Olaf College, Northfield, MN

COURTNEY S. CAMPBELL
Director of the Program for Ethics, Science, and the Environment and
Associate Professor of Philosophy
Oregon State University, Corvalis, OR

PAUL LAURITZEN
Director of the Program in Applied Ethics and Professor of Religious Studies
John Carroll University, University Heights, OH

GILBERT MEILAENDER
Board of Directors Professor of Christian Ethics
Valparaiso University, Valparaiso, IN

RICHARD B. MILLER
Director of Graduate Studies and Professor of Religious Studies
Indiana University, Bloomington, IN

MARGARET E. MOHRMANN
Associate Professor of Pediatrics and Medical Education
University of Virginia, Charlottesville, VA

ANN MONGOVEN
Assistant Professor of Religious Studies
Indiana University, Bloomington, IN

LOUIS E. NEWMAN
Professor of Religion
Carleton College, Northfield, MN

DAVID H. SMITH
Director of the Poynter Center for the Study of Ethics and American
Institutions and Professor of Religious Studies
Indiana University, Bloomington, IN

ALLEN D. VERHEY
Professor of Religion
Hope College, Holland, MI

EDITOR'S ACKNOWLEDGMENTS

I owe many debts of thanks for this book, but the most important is to the Lilly Endowment, Inc. and Craig Dykstra, its Vice President for Religion. Years ago, the Endowment committed itself to support study of the role of religion in American culture and, from the beginning, insisted that that research must include attention to the lives and work of professionals. This book represents the first formal publication of the Poynter Center's work on this topic.

The Endowment's assistance enabled us to convene a seminar comprising the authors of the papers in this volume. They engaged themselves intellectually in the enterprise, and together we explored the issues examined here in a true spirit of collaboration and collegiality. The essays they have produced will speak for themselves.

This project builds on prior work supported by the Endowment. William Meyer, now at Maryville College, was an invaluable collaborator in those endeavors, and his stamp remains on what is best in this project. My Indiana University colleague Richard B. Miller has been collaborator, adviser, and friend on all of our work in this area. Graduate students Lisa Sideris and Morna Brothers provided invaluable assistance, and Judith A. Granbois has transformed my prose, and that of some others, into something readable. Beverly Davis and Kathy Jacobson took charge of the heavy lifting associated with the project, helping with the complicated logistics and the inevitable paperwork.

To all, my thanks.

INTRODUCTION

The Importance of Listening
and the Pertinence of Religion

DAVID H. SMITH

INTRODUCTION

This book is premised on the assumption that we should reexamine the approach of scholars interested in bioethics. Individuals' religious commitments and religious institutions' actual and potential roles should be part of the data considered as we draw moral inferences about character, objectives, and obligations. We think that if we begin by listening to health professionals and patients talk reflectively about their work, religious loyalties and concerns will surface, and we think that there are several interesting ways of listening. We want to encourage an approach that is more dialogical than those used before: one that seeks insight from many sources on normative premises, on interpretations of fact, and on the role of religion in the lives of health professionals and patients.

We mean to argue for a close connection between moral reflection and study of the actual lives and life stories of persons who provide or receive health care. We claim that when bioethics (and professional ethics generally) distances itself from those stories and experiences, it sacrifices its vitality and that religious particularity—personal loyalties, ideas, and institutions—is lost from view. We want to try to recover that particularity without losing sight of a larger perspective.

BACKGROUND

Over the past quarter century, most of the scholarly work that has attempted to relate religion to medical ethics has treated religious ideas, metaphors, or theological concepts as the major premise of a moral syllogism. The idea has been that religion contributes a distinctive moral perspective from which a religiously committed moralist can draw inferences. For example, religion might serve as a rationale for defending the importance of respect for persons' rights to make their own decisions, or of a concept of justice requiring that all persons be treated equally, or of a set of goods that all persons should pursue. A key concept may be *agape,* or "covenant loyalty," or natural law. But the interaction between religion and whatever is not religious occurs at the conceptual level. A normative web of concepts is produced, and then one or more of those concepts serves as the basis for moral reasoning.

The assumption that religion might set background premises has gone hand in hand with the idea that professionals must take the religious commitments of patients or clients seriously. Indeed, the widely held conviction that one must respect religious difference is arguably the founding principle of the more general idea of respect for persons.

Some scholars have ventured a bolder alternative, however. For example, William F. May has insightfully analyzed social structures, practices, and loyalties as forms of faith. In his book, *The Patient's Ordeal,* May focuses attention on the changes in identity that persons experience in the course of illness or other trauma. He compares these changes with those associated with religious initiation or conversion. In other writing, notably *The Physician's Covenant,* May shows how professional communities appear as secular analogues of religious communities. In effect, categories useful in understanding religion are applied to loyalties and social structures that we do not usually think of as religious. The religious perspective provides what May has called "corrective vision," and the effect is to open a wide range of professional practices and cultural assumptions to theological critique.

This strategy is not as tidy epistemically as the more common approach. How the facts are seen or construed becomes problematical. Even if we could all agree on the normative frame of concepts to be brought to bear, there would still be a problem of interpretation. For example, was the forced treatment of Dax Cowart, a burn victim, best seen as overriding his choices or a forced change in identity? Arguably, both alternatives are bad, but one's discussion of what should have happened will be shaped by which of these interpretations one accepts. For some, the focus on the interpretive angle of vision is refreshing; for others, the richer insight seems purchased at the risk of bias. Some of the most important religious ethics contributors to the medical ethics literature in the past quarter century (for example, James F. Childress, Ronald M. Green, and Richard McCormick, S.J.) have worried about that bias. In their analyses of specific situations or problems, therefore, distinctively religious perspectives or categories are kept quite far in the background, serving as shapers of fundamental moral principles.

The outstanding exception to this generalization has been Stanley Hauerwas, who limits his commentary in biomedical ethics to what his construal of Christian tradition allows him to say. Others' definitions of "the issue" are to him irrelevant. His entire focus is on articulating the self-understanding and discernment, the vision and virtue that the Christian church is called to be and have in this time. Hauerwas does not attempt to solve general social problems. Instead, he wants to focus on the church's failure to sustain people as they confront patients' or physicians' problems in their lives or families. The effect is to change the subject, to raise a whole new set of issues, and to throw new light on the problem as originally perceived. But an obvious corollary of the strategy is that Hauerwas has nothing directly to say to the larger cultural debate.

THE PROBLEM

What are the results of all this work in medical ethics? Some of them are impressive. On the one hand, there is a rich theoretical literature, and the community of scholars who contribute to that literature has consistently included persons who take religion seriously and are known to do so. Scholars in religious ethics and theologians have not been marginalized but have been accepted to the extent justified by the merits of their work. But the degree of success enjoyed by individual scholars should not obscure another problem: that the resources of religious communities have been only partially engaged in the bioethics discussions. That is strange, as religion centrally concerns itself with events surrounding the beginning and ending of life, not to mention questions of love and justice among persons throughout the life span. Those issues are at the very heart of bioethics. Yet the bioethics literature has had very little impact on parochial or seminary education, or even homiletic practice, in American religious communities.

This phenomenon might concern only a small group of religious bioethicists, were it not for another fact: The social problems and prospects that have fueled bioethics debate show no sign of being solved. Take the problem of compassionate care for the dying as an example. Recent studies suggest that despite decades of elegant philosophical and legal argument and imaginative reform proposals, many Americans still die with inadequate pain or symptom control and with their wishes for their last days either unknown or unheeded. If this intolerable situation is to be addressed, it makes sense to ask what new resources might be utilized.

A first and obvious resource is the organized religious communities of the United States. They are shapers of opinion, formers of attitudes, and (to a degree) determiners of behavior. Many of them have invested resources in the establishment of hospitals and medical schools, where they provide chaplains. Persons who staff our health care system worship in their temples, buildings and congregations. These communities clearly do not speak with one voice, but they can be powerful forces for social change—or reaction. Religious communities should be taken seriously, at least as a political force, and that means learning to speak their distinctive religious languages.

Furthermore, health care professionals who take their religion seriously naturally look to the rituals and concepts of their faith traditions for support, consolation, and guidance. Engaging the religious dimension of their lives helps them and enables them to be of more help to others. Of course, not all health professionals are religious in any traditional sense. But some are, and more may be religious in a traditional way than is at first supposed. A larger number may describe themselves as "spiritual," signaling their recognition of their own finitude and their locus in some larger reality. In any case, someone who wants to improve care for the dying should listen to the religious views and concerns of health care professionals and should attempt to see issues as the professionals see them from their own religious or spiritual perspectives.

Finally, religious approaches and interpretations may illuminate points that others downplay or ignore. The medical ethics work of Paul Ramsey, to take one obvious example, was deeply informed by his Christian theological commitments, but secular scholars respected the light Ramsey shed on issues such as use of human subjects in experimentation, care for the dying, or organ transplantation. The same point can be made about the work of James M. Gustafson and William F. May, discussed by Richard Miller in the first essay in this collection. The fact that we do not share a starting point does not mean that we cannot learn from what others have to say.

Bioethics must attend to religious insights, religious institutions, and the perspectives of religious professionals if it is to be more than a theoretical enterprise. This fact may have been obscured by the tendency of bioethics to focus on issues of public policy and implicitly to assume that theoretical arguments should model the debate in a state or federal legislature or court. But, as Courtney Campbell has pointed out, bioethics concerns itself with questions that are often, indeed most typically, discussed in other contexts: clinical encounters, or family discussions, or times of pastoral conversation, or professional interactions.[1] Major policy decisions may well have to be made about questions such as cloning or physician-assisted suicide; a nation may have to set some general parameters. But, whatever those parameters are, much of the decision making—and the living with the results of decisions—occurs on other levels.

Moreover, engagement with the questions of bioethics may benefit religious communities, insofar as they have drifted away from focus on issues of fundamental importance to Americans. The central concerns of bioethics—the generation and nurture of new life; care for the dying; justice among persons—are concerns that religious communities dare not abandon. Vigorous internal dialogue on those questions might contribute to a renewal of concern with essentials in many a congregation or larger faith community.

LISTENING AS A KEY COMPONENT OF METHOD

These reflections have implications for the way scholars of bioethics should proceed. We should adopt a catholic vision of the multiple contexts or levels of bioethics discussion and give at least as much attention to the variables at play in clinical and institutional reality as to constraints on forms of public argument. In particular, a preoccupation with state or national policy has led scholars to avoid asking questions about professionals' religious commitments. From the point of view of the most widely used paradigms, those commitments are irrelevant because the appropriate value premises are set by "public reasons." For Hauerwas, they are equally irrelevant, as his main concern is with the vision and virtue that *should* inform Christian life and community. But a bioethics that is serious about social reform must inquire about the religious lives of actual people, and it must address the questions or issues with which they struggle. Without this engagement, it will be impossible to enlist religious communities in the reform effort.

Students of religious and theological ethics should be attentive to the real lives and religious commitments of patients and professionals; they should be asking how and in what ways professional identities are formed and about the ways in which those identities are either nurturing or destructive of persons; they should be students of the moral worlds—the perceptions, language, and judgments—of professionals, for these moral worlds are not only targets of criticism but can be sources of normative insight.

In fact, the bases for a more inductive dimension in professional ethics than that of the reigning paradigms has been familiar territory for students of religious ethics for half a century. Obvious roots lie in Tillich's theology of culture and H. Richard Niebuhr's analysis of forms of faith in *Radical Monotheism and Western Culture.* More recently, a renaissance in interpretive social science has stressed the various ways in which normative commitments and descriptive analyses are inseparably linked.[2] Certainly the best known of these endeavors was *Habits of the Heart,* a powerful analysis of one important segment of American society that identified competing normative traditions within the American body politic and suggested the moral poverty of some and the richness of others.[3] The authors based part of their methodological stance on the work of Alasdair MacIntyre who, in *After Virtue,* argued for an understanding of virtues as "goods internal to practices."[4] Setting aside the trajectory of MacIntyre's own subsequent work, this conception of virtue would seem to mandate the study of actual practices as one important component of the study of virtues. The excellence of a painter or cricket bowler will change with time and the evolution of the practice; a virtuoso athlete or artist will reconfigure those parameters. The same thing may be said about the virtues of doctors, lawyers, and merchant chiefs. One could never recognize excellence in any of these endeavors without study of the practices involved, nor would one be able to recognize a saint without familiarity with the practical world she inhabits and against which her virtue is radiant.

Michael Walzer's social philosophy provides another way of explaining the importance of study of people's moral perceptions and sense of self. He argues that "goods come into our heads before they come into our hands," and that once we really understand a good we will understand the principles that should control its distribution. He argues that different goods—money, educational opportunity, and health care—should be distributed according to different principles. If we get those principles right, we will have a society with "complex equality." Walzer then cites a wide range of historical and anthropological data to illuminate the meaning of diverse forms of goods. A more pedestrian way to go about the task would be seriously to study the perceptions of a given good held by persons deeply concerned with it. One can acknowledge that thoughtful politicians know something distinctive and important about politics, or that nurses or physicians know something distinctive and important about health care, without implying that those groups as a power bloc should determine the content of justice in politics or health care.

We want to argue for an ethic that begins on the ground in the sense that accurate characterization of the perceptions and moral evaluations of participants in clinical encounters is an important component in moral analysis. We want to hold open the possibility that these perceptions and evaluations have legitimate and independent moral weight. They are not simply to be *replaced* by a different moral vocabulary, whether that vocabulary be religious or secular, although they may well be challenged and displaced. Most of the essays in this collection engage in the task of presentation, analysis, and critique of diverse participant perceptions.

Thus we think that it is important to begin by listening, but listening is no panacea. Indeed, the great power of the bioethics revival of the past quarter century arises from the fact that it represented a willingness of academic ethics to turn outside academic argument and listen. But listening may be analyzed on several axes, and on each of them we mean to take a stand.

A first question is: To whom should we listen? On this point, the characteristic answer of professional ethics of the recent past is: to the patient or client. That focus has been liberating, and it has served the cause of justice; it has challenged entrenched professional dominance. But it has had the unfortunate effect of implying that professionals' perceptions have no independent moral weight. We resist that inference, and we intend to take the perceptions of professionals seriously and as potentially revealing the nature of the goods with which they are concerned.

A second question of listening is: What should we listen for? What sort of things might strike us as relevant? Of what kinds of comments and actions should we take note? We think that serious listening to patients and professionals concerned with health care will show that many of them talk about religion, that one cannot both listen and "bleach out" religion[5] from what is said. In fact, we think religion is inescapable in two senses. The first is obvious: Many patients and professionals naturally articulate their moral concerns and sense of self in traditional religious terms. We do not allege that "there are no atheists in foxholes," nor do we mean to imply that religious traditions should hold a preferred place. We simply assert that many real people—patients and professionals—are religious and that seriously listening to them is an important component on the agenda of professional ethics.

Yet religion is present in a more subtle way as well. Professional identities serve as forms of faith that sustain persons and determine to significant degrees the way they see and understand themselves in the world. Professional groups and institutions may serve as functional analogues of religious communities. Again, we do not argue that this claim is true for all, or even most, professionals. Just how many it applies to, just how professional identity may be affected, to say nothing of whether this manifestation of "religion" is a good or bad thing—all of these questions are open to analysis. We mean only to assert that religion is not confined to established and acknowledged traditions, and that we should listen for its presence elsewhere.

Finally there is the question of what is listened to, or how one goes about listening. At one extreme are major ethnographic studies such as Charles Bosk's *Forgive and Remember,* Daniel Chambliss' *Beyond Caring,* or Fred Frohock's *Special Care;* at the other, patient or participants' own narratives such as Arthur Frank's *At the Will of the Body.* There are many stopping points in between. While none of the essays in this collection represents a major ethnographic study, real differences can be seen. For example, John Barbour comments on a series of literary narratives while Paul Lauritzen, Allen Verhey, and Gilbert Meilaender make heavy use of life stories presented by commentators. In contrast, Louis Newman, Margaret Mohrmann, Ann Mongoven, Courtney Campbell, and David Smith base their work on interviews with practicing professionals. These are certainly differing modes of work, each with its distinctive advantages and liabilities. All stand in contrast to a method that proceeds with less concern for listening, narrative, and participant accounts.

THIS BOOK

Our book opens with three essays that explore some of these methodological issues and, in different ways, suggest the importance of listening before speaking.

Richard Miller argues that three of the religious leaders of the late twentieth-century bioethics renewal sought "intimate familiarity with medical contexts" and that "a legacy of clinical immersion has been lost" (19). Miller points to dangers that arise from heavy immersion in one particular kind of clinical setting; the moralist must avoid both co-optation and overcompensation. He stresses the importance of nuanced, insightful description and points out the oversimplifications and distortions that can be imposed by restrictive fundamental commitments. He values imaginative or conjectural immersion in the experience of others and argues that this immersion should lead to changes in theoretical commitments on occasion.

John Barbour shifts our focus to the autobiographical statements of patients and physicians. He asks, in effect, "If we are going to listen, why not ask people who have already tried to tell us?" Autobiographies are not always truthful, but they do provide us with rich resources of pertinent data. "Reading," Barbour writes, "can help develop those moral capacities without which the ideals of medical practice . . . cannot be achieved" (48). To be sure, the authors of polished autobiography are in some ways unrepresentative and untypical, but their capacity to articulate experience remains instructive.

Religious themes recur in these accounts. For example, many patient autobiographies recount a period or time of conversion analogous to religious experiences of conversion. A new identity is accepted or adopted. Physician autobiographies complement these patient accounts; sometimes physicians can tell their patients' stories with striking moral power. Narrative ethics depends crucially on one form of listening.

Paul Lauritzen shows how an analysis of experience might relate to a specific moral question: the legitimacy of physician-assisted suicide. According to Lauritzen, we need to maintain both a vital connection with experience and a somewhat detached perspective; narrative or ethnographic accounts are not sufficient as sources of moral insight. Instead, we must have criteria for sorting stories and ethnographies. "[W]e must move dialectically between the detailed stories and the theoretical accounts that frame the moral debate on assisted suicide" (67). Lauritzen shows how Timothy Quill and Ira Byock have carried out such a dialectical process in their arguments over physician-assisted suicide. Quill and Byock move back and forth between recounting cases and theoretical argument. Yet these physicians disagree about physician-assisted suicide. Who has the better of the argument? Lauritzen thinks we should make this decision using what the literary critic Wayne Booth has described as "coduction," a process in which we attempt a comparative assessment of parallel narratives. When the issue is physician-assisted suicide, we must ask which description of barbiturate infusions is more accurate: a description that suggests they are meant to kill, or one that says they are not. Which description fits best with the larger American community's understanding of the issue?

All of these essays suggest the importance of disciplined uses of experience in medical ethics. Miller makes the case for actual engagement with persons who suffer and those who care for them. He suggests that openness to such engagement explains some of the power and influence of some of the first serious religious writers on medical ethics in the second half of this century; Barbour describes the value and pitfalls of using structured and insightful polished narratives; Lauritzen shows how narrative can strengthen a moral argument.

The remaining chapters of the book focus these considerations on specific kinds of situations. Part Two, following a lead in Miller's essay, relates to pediatric care and its distinctive problems. Interestingly enough, the pediatricians that Margaret Mohrmann interviewed are most concerned with problems and limits in the lives of their patients that stand in the way of effective health maintenance or care. The issues they lose sleep about are not obviously medical—whether to perform a certain procedure—but concern about the social facts of their patients' lives. "These pediatricians associate their professional ethics very closely with their ability to form and maintain strong and healing alliances with patients and parents," Mohrmann writes (97). Those healing alliances push toward a broader definition of the physician's role than the common attitude of residents: "That's not my job." Breadth of discernment wasn't learned in medical training. Some of it has been learned in practice; much of it relates to the diverse religious traditions in which these pediatricians were raised. Mohrmann's experience was that any serious discussion of ethical issues "led each interview further into matters of religion" (108).

Religion does set some moral boundaries for the practices of these physicians, but just what they are—and how flexibly they are enforced—varies. Some have a faith that fits hand in glove with the necessities of their practice; some modify their principles to enable their patients to choose courses of action they do not themselves support. Religious belief also provides them with personal support. The religious influence in their lives is "embedded" (113), and it determines "what pediatricians are supposed to do" (114).

Louis Newman interviewed a group of Jewish pediatricians to try to learn if "a more religious orientation toward medicine continue[d] to play a role in the lives of some contemporary physicians" (118). Modern medical science has given them great power, and they like the trust and appreciation that comes from effective use of that power. But they make mistakes, and parents may push them to try things the doctors know nothing about. Some patients die despite their best efforts. Powerful—and aware of their powerlessness—they cope by developing three virtues: compassion, humility, and hope.

For these physicians, God has a role in the healing process. They see a miraculous aspect to human life, they see themselves playing a pastoral role, and they look on medicine as a calling. Although they do not pray with patients, they pray. They naturally use religious language to describe many aspects of their professional lives. Are these religious perceptions related to the virtues they think they need? Newman thinks that they fit together, and there may be a causal relationship: They stress these virtues because of their religious sensibility. But he concludes that we can't be sure of causation, only of affinity. The moral worlds of these physicians' professional lives shape their religious sensibility as well as being its product. Religious belief is one, but only one, determinant of who they are. As Newman writes, "medical practice itself may have tutored their sense of religiosity" (139). At the end of the day, relating the religious aspect of their professional lives to their traditional religious observance is not easy for Newman—or for the pediatricians.

What is very clear about both Mohrmann's and Newman's subjects is that the standard list of questions in biomedical ethics scarcely scratches the surface of their religious and moral concerns. These physicians' professional life pushes beyond normal professional parameters—either religious or political. Their professional education has not prepared them for the pastoral dimensions of professional life, nor do their current religious engagements help to sustain them in the difficulties they encounter professionally.

Allen Verhey opens Part Three on organ transplantation with a meditation on Richard Selzer's story "Whither Thou Goest." The story captures the "messiness" and ambiguity of defining persons as dead when they appear to be alive. Policy criteria may be conceptually tidy, he writes, "but the experience is confusing" (150). In fact, public response to transplant practice shows major ambivalence; the physicians involved are only "ambiguous heroes" (156). The relation of self and body is complicated, and the dead body remains a significant part of whatever communities shaped and informed the life of the person. What treatment of the body coheres with appropriate respect for the grieving? Giving the organs of a loved one cannot be routinized.

Verhey argues that religion is obviously pertinent to these complex issues and that the religious response to organ transplantation should be worked out in the theological contexts of particular communities, not as an adjunct to transplant programs. In fact, various religious groups have passed resolutions, but the pastoral help they offer is uncertain. Rather, appropriate rituals are needed to help persons cope with the ambiguities of transplantation. These rituals might make use of scriptural dirge and psalms of lament to suggest the dependence of all upon God. Verhey argues that these rituals acknowledge that "the organ donors and organ recipients are not trapped as benefactors or recipients into a creditor-debtor relationship; they are both recipients, bound together by their common indebtedness to God, and giving and sharing are mere tokens of community" (166).

Ann Mongoven explores the insights and problems of hospital chaplains who are involved in the transplant process. How do they see the ambiguous and religiously potent process that Verhey discusses? Organ donation issues for these chaplains are part of a larger complex of issues related to support of the grieving. The chaplains insist on "decoupling" the act of telling family members that their loved one has died from a second act of asking about organ donation. They note the problems created for families by medical staff members' inconsistent usage of terms like "dead" and "brain-dead."

Mongoven's chaplains share widely held concerns for respecting the wishes of the deceased, and they support Verhey's point about the need for meaningful ritual. They stand ready to discuss theological concepts or religious metaphors with families, but generally do not initiate those discussions. While all of these chaplains believe that organ donation is supported by theological principle and scriptural imagery, they are very aware that that is not the case for all religions or even for all Christians, and they worry that policies designed to encourage donation may place some persons in difficult situations.

These chaplains' concern with helping the family through a process of grieving contrasts with the Organ Procurement Organizations' (OPO) focus on a desired outcome—maximizing the supply of organs for transplantation. The chaplains define failure as family regret or feelings of guilt; the Organ Procurement Organizations define it as failure to get the organs. The chaplains face the tension of working with both patients who need organs and potential donors' families. Some are even involved with OPOs. But they disagree on whether they should be the ones to initiate discussion with a family about a possible donation.

These chapters suggest that the practice of organ transplantation is fraught with ambiguity, that many of the issues involved are religiously important, that clergy can play a significant role in the process, and that religious institutions should attend to the needs of donors and recipients.

The book concludes with a focus on care for the dying. The hospice professionals interviewed by Courtney Campbell regularly speak of "boundaries" and the crossing of boundaries, including the boundary between life and death. They agree on some basic values that care for the dying should embody, and some of them appreciate the religious dimensions of the process. They seem to favor a stance toward death like the one Meilaender ascribes to Kass, but holding to that perspective is not easy. Further, hospice caregivers find themselves torn between overly personal and too distant relationships with patients. They maintain the boundary of identity by maintaining a level of involvement they characterize as "empathetic distance" (208). Hospice caregivers, patients, and families are involved in actions and settings that inevitably raise issues of boundaries of intimacy, as much of the care is provided through "touch rather than technology" (212).

Particularly vexing are boundary struggles that arise when the patient's values conflict with the caregiver's values or those of the hospice program. Religion remains a powerful motivator and source of support for many hospice workers. Religious arguments for minimal pain control—for example, so that the patient may experience suffering as redemption—can be particularly difficult for them. Of course, the positions may be reversed, and the patient or family may request physician-assisted suicide (now legal in Oregon), a practice that hospices have traditionally opposed. Campbell traces the lines of conflict and compromise. Hospice caregivers provide attention to the religious or spiritual dimension of things *when the patient signals its importance*. But at least one person Campbell interviewed initiates conversations about religious matters with her patients.

Smith interviewed a group of ten nurses who care for dying persons. Making use of the work of the sociologist Daniel Chambliss, he argues that they are able to cope with this apparently trying situation because they have routinized the experience and taken on a new identity, constructing a moral world in which technical competence and provision of personalized care are highly valued. The commitment to personal care underscores the importance of the "empathetic distance" that Campbell identified, but it also challenges nurses who see dysfunctional family processes. Whether, how much, and when to intervene in such families are difficult issues.

These issues become particularly complicated when suffering seems to be religious or spiritual. Smith argues for provision of spiritual support on request from patients or families, but he opposes the practice of nurses volunteering to engage the religious dimension without some sort of explicit signal or request.

The final chapter is Gilbert Meilaender's discussion of the debate over death with dignity. Meilaender stresses the importance of the religious and metaphysical beliefs that inform our perspective on a case or narrative. He contrasts the perspectives that Paul Ramsey and Leon Kass brought to a debate over death with dignity, and he compares Ramsey's and Kass's perspectives with that of Ira Byock, arguing that Byock's perspective seems inadequate to his own narratives. The stories also suggest the limits of Kass's Aristotelianism and the associated idea that dying can always be dignified. Against Byock and Kass, Ramsey suggested that the real problem was not dying but death itself. Meilaender offers an Augustinian perspective on death that provides, he argues, a more adequate perspective for analyzing Byock's narratives of death than the one Byock himself embraces. In effect, Meilaender uses a dialogical method of the sort that Lauritzen proposed in Chapter 3.

CONCLUSION

Religion has not occupied the space it should in the serious discussion of bioethics. That may be because of a fear of dogmatism or an identification of religion with obscurantism. Because persons and communities need to come to closure on issues, religious communities and persons may appear in public with some issues apparently settled. Serious writing and teaching about issues of biomedical ethics must open some issues that some religious communities and persons think should remain closed. To avoid dissonance, it is tempting simply to rule religion off the table. But the effect is to cut off conversation and to purchase consensus at too high a price. The fact that religion can be and often remains divisive is not a good reason for excluding it from the conversation.

PART ONE

WAYS OF LISTENING

1

RELIGION, ETHICS, AND CLINICAL IMMERSION

An Appraisal of Three Pioneers

RICHARD B. MILLER

ETHICS AND EXPERIENCE

That fieldwork might contribute positively to theology and medicine is a novel and perhaps experimental idea, running against the grain of much research in medical ethics today. Despite the frequent claim that experience is an important source for theological and ethical reflection,[1] few scholars have immersed themselves in the lives of medical professionals or have familiarized themselves with the contexts in which health care providers carry out their work.[2] Ethicists who have immersed themselves in clinical settings often omit that fact from the fruits of their research. Medical ethics is more philosophical than ethnographic, requiring powers of argumentation rather than observation and evaluative description.

Medical sociologists and anthropologists often lament that fact. In their view, conventional bioethics fails to explore the social contours and experiential complexities of professional life. Excluded from the standard account of bioethics are medical professionals' moral idioms, personal challenges, logistical obstacles, religious commitments, and interpersonal interactions with patients and families. Instead, medical ethics is often abstract, deductive, and/or highly rationalistic, detached from the anguishing empirical realities and power struggles in which medical professionals find themselves. Daniel F. Chambliss writes, for example, that "much of bioethics assumes that people are autonomous decision makers sitting in a fairly comfortable room trying logically to fit problems to given solution-making patterns. The whole business is almost deliberately unreal—intellectually challenging but not very useful." Experience is different, Chambliss observes: "Inside hospitals . . . decisions are driven not by academic problem-solving techniques but by the routines of life in a professional bureaucracy."[3]

Medical decision making is collective, not individual, involving a clash of social interests and perspectives. With lawyers, legislatures, family members, and various medical specialists involved in medical cases, "individual dilemmas have ballooned into political and legal controversies; the lone practitioner has been absorbed into the large and amorphous 'health care team'; and the logical derivation of answers from principles (if it ever occurred) has certainly given way to a mélange of standard operating procedures, stopgap measures, and tortuous political compromises."[4] Chambliss thus argues for a reconfiguration of bioethics along organizational lines, focusing less on individuals' ethical dilemmas than on conflicts between occupational interest groups and the moral contours of the social milieu in which those conflicts materialize.

For Arthur Kleinman, the problem with conventional bioethics is not that it is untutored by sociological realities but that it fails to capture the existential challenges of patient suffering. Kleinman thus writes that "by and large the contextually rich, experience-near illness narrative is not privileged" in bioethics. Patients' experience is "reinterpreted (also thinned out) from the professional bioethical standpoint in order to focus exclusively on the value conflicts that it is held to instantiate."[5] As a result, bioethics is beholden to "medicocentrism," which focuses on "the professionally approved institutional structures of biomedicine, such as hospitals or clinical research." Lost in the bargain are "lay perspectives and everyday life experiences that might generate a deeper critique of that medical-moral domain and the economic interests with which it is inextricably held."[6]

According to Chambliss and Kleinman, participant observation can make a salutary contribution to medical ethics by illuminating the organizational features of professional work and the personal trials of patient suffering. In their minds, traditional bioethics has failed to capture the infrastructural and experiential aspects of modern medicine. Whatever one might make of their sense that medical sociology and anthropology can offer up profound social commentary, the truth is that ethnography remains outside the dominant paradigms in religion and biomedical ethics today.[7]

Chambliss and Kleinman pose an important challenge to bioethicists. Partly in response to that challenge, I immersed myself in the moral world of two pediatric intensive care units, seeking to develop an experience-near approach to pediatric medical ethics.[8] In Indianapolis in 1993, I rounded for five weeks with attendings and residents at a city hospital, leading to an article that commented on the professional practices and identities of those with whom I rounded and the challenges of coordinating care in a theater of tragedy.[9] In Boston in 1997–98, I spent a year in a large children's research hospital, participating in the ethics committee; rounding in one of its intensive care units for six months; initiating countless conversations with physicians, nurses, chaplains, counselors, parents, and patients; and discussing some of my ideas and arguments with hospital personnel.

During that time, I also reread some of the early writers in biomedical ethics—Paul Ramsey, James Gustafson, and William F. May—in order to reacquaint myself with the discipline's origins. In different ways, these authors have been important teachers: Ramsey as the topic of a graduate thesis and subsequent writings; Gustafson as my dissertation director; and May as the founder of the diverse and energetic Religious Studies Department in which I work. In revisiting these authors, I discovered a fact that might surprise many readers: *Early pioneering work in bioethics emerged from or gestures toward intimate familiarity with medical contexts.* A legacy of immersion has been lost or obscured in standard accounts of religion and medicine, which generally fail to probe the circumstances out of which path-breaking work in medical ethics developed. That fact might be explained by the reluctance of each pioneer to advocate for participant observation as a resource for medical ethics. But however suppressed the legacy might be, it is vital to early and influential work in the field.

In this chapter I would like to revisit some of that work by assessing the contributions of theology to medicine by Ramsey, Gustafson, and May. Of special importance is the fact that these authors draw from or rely on an experience-near methodology for medical ethics, however much they fail to promote that methodology's virtues as a research program. Here I want to explore that methodology and its place in their writings. I will not summarize or evaluate their views on theology and medicine in toto; I will critically examine the place of experience and/or clinical immersion in their respective programs. I will then conclude by identifying some of the merits and perils to which their work calls our attention, especially for those doing ethics in an ethnographic vein.

With that critical appreciation in place, the essays in this volume might be better understood. That is, we might be able to see them not as novel or experimental, but as developing a muted legacy in a more open and critical way. Moreover, I hope to broaden the reader's perception of bioethics so that it avoids the challenges (and caricatures) found in Chambliss's and Kleinman's writings. Modern bioethics is no stranger to clinical immersion, empirical observation, and attention to patient suffering. On the contrary, it is its offspring.

SPECIFYING THE MEANING OF CARE

Ramsey's path-breaking work, *The Patient as Person,* deploys the model of defining and applying the principle of care to medical practice. Ramsey outlined religious contours of that principle in an earlier book, *Basic Christian Ethics,* in which he places the idea of "God's steadfast love" at the center of his research project. For Ramsey, steadfast love is expressed in Jewish and Christian narratives of God's faithful covenant with humanity, to which all persons are called to consent in faithful obedience and in loving actions toward the neighbor. The language of covenant emphasizes steadfast commitment and stubborn faithfulness; it is enshrined in the idea of *agape,* or loyal, unreciprocated care. Considerations of merit, benefit, or social utility are beside the point; individuals should never be instrumentalized for society's benefit. Ramsey thus develops a deontological approach to religious ethics, focusing on the integrity of deeds and rules rather than on beneficial consequences.

Extending these convictions to the context of medical care and research, Ramsey states his chief goal in *The Patient as Person* as seeking "to explore the meaning of *care,* to find the actions and abstentions that come from adherence to *covenant,* to ask the meaning of *sanctity* of life, to articulate the requirements of steadfast *faithfulness* to fellow man."[10] The deontic implications of these ideas are explicit from the outset in this book, and Ramsey held stubbornly to those ideas throughout his career. He states, "Medical ethics has not its sole basis in the over-all benefits to be produced. It is not a consequence-ethics alone." Instead, there is an additional consideration: "What constitutes right action in medical practice?" For Ramsey, the answer is "the requirement of reasonably free and adequately informed consent." Deontic considerations that derive from religious convictions limit what can be done for the patient's or society's good. The sanctity of life, Ramsey writes, "prevents ultimate trespass upon [another] even for the sake of treating his bodily life, or for the sake of others who are also only a sacredness in their bodily lives."[11] Armed with these commitments and a prodigious body of technical and philosophical knowledge, Ramsey proceeds headlong into a series of controversies: research on children, definitions of death, care for the dying, organ transplantation, and resource allocation.

Ramsey sees himself as deliberating about medical problems "as competently and exhaustively as possible with the concrete features of actual moral decisions of life and death in medical care."[12] His arguments proceed in large part by *specifying* the implications of religious principles for practical reasoning.[13] Following Henry S. Richardson, we can say that specification is a way of qualifying normative commitments by "qualitatively tailoring . . . norms to cases."[14] To specify is to take a general norm or value and circumscribe its applicability. Richardson writes, "Specification proceeds by setting out substantive qualifications that add information about the scope of applicability of the norm or the nature of the act or end enjoined or proscribed."[15] As a qualitative inference, a specification does not generally follow from a more general norm or value in a deductive way. Rather, it interprets a broad norm or value and indicates the conditions according to which it absolutely pertains to a problem.[16] In a similar vein, Ramsey develops basic principles of medical ethics by specifying broad theological ideas about covenant, the sacredness of life, and steadfast loyalty.[17] His goal is to indicate what these values mean in practice by tightening up their pertinence to specific cases. In this way, Ramsey writes, "medical ethics . . . must, indeed, be 'casuistry'; it must deal as competently and exhaustively as possible with the concrete features of actual moral decisions of life and death and medical care."[18]

When Ramsey specifies the demands of covenant, faithfulness, and care, his main goal is to surround patients with moral immunity from medical and research imperatives, among other forms of impersonal treatment. In this way, Ramsey exhibits a deep existential concern about the illness experiences and trials of patients and research subjects. At the heart of his argument is the conviction that medical providers should remain steadfastly committed to respecting the patient as person and to guarding each person's inviolable dignity. When discussing withdrawing medical care from the incurably ill, for example, he insists that decisions be developed under "the *categorical* imperative: 'Never abandon care!' "[19] Doctors who wish to withdraw treatment from incurably ill patients may justifiably do so, but they are never permitted to abandon patients to impersonal care or neglect: "Upon ceasing to try to rescue the perishing, one then is free to care for the dying. . . . An attitude toward the dying premised upon mature and profoundly religious convictions will display an indefectible charity that never ceases to go about the business of caring for the dying neighbor."[20] Specifications further enable Ramsey to prohibit nontherapeutic pediatric research, to resist redefining death so as to make organs more readily available for transplantation, and to consider when it is permissible directly to take human life without violating the requirements of care as a deontic principle.[21] One aim is to ensure that the concrete needs of individual patients are not subsumed by or subordinated to collective demands, research imperatives, or considerations of medical utility. Covenant is generally a social metaphor, but Ramsey's specifications produce an ethic that seeks to protect individuals against collective goals.[22]

Ramsey's work was informed by a year's worth of interaction with health care providers and medical researchers. As the Joseph P. Kennedy, Jr. Foundation Visiting Professor of Genetic Ethics at the Medical School of Georgetown University during the spring semesters of 1968 and 1969, he directly engaged physicians and researchers on various topics. His appointment, Ramsey writes, "enabled me, a Protestant Christian ethicist, to be located in the middle of a medical school faculty—not on its periphery—and to begin some serious study of the moral issues in medical research and practice."[23] At biweekly conferences, members of the Georgetown Medical School presented their views on a medical and moral topic to Ramsey and other theologians from the Washington area. Ramsey was free to question faculty members, "overhear discussions among them, and begin to learn how teachers of medicine, researchers, and practitioners themselves understand the moral aspects of their practice."[24] Summarizing the daunting challenge of these sessions, Ramsey states that he came away from each meeting "with a year's worth of work to do before I, a layman, could venture to say anything about a single medical question."[25]

The impact of that experience is not made explicit in Ramsey's writings on medicine, but it appears to inform his work in several ways. First, it led him to admire medicine's commitment to ethics and to see considerable overlap between the ethics internal to medicine and his own theological program. On learning how professionals understand the moral aspects of their practice, Ramsey argued for a parallel between his idea of covenant and the proper professional relationship between physicians and patients, and researchers and subjects. Clinical immersion enabled Ramsey to conclude that medical and research relationships are a subset of his more general religious and ethical vision, that "the moral requirements governing the relationship of a physician to patients and researcher to subjects are only a special case of the moral requirements between man and man."[26]

Ramsey thus sets out to examine "the covenant between physician and patient, the covenant between researcher and 'subject' in experiments with human beings, the covenant between men and a child in need of care, the covenant between the living and the dying, the covenant between the well and the ill or with those in need of some extraordinary therapy."[27] In his view, medical and scientific relationships are irreducibly covenantal, and they impose on practitioners the same demands of faithfulness, loyalty, and respect for persons that should be found in social life more generally. Ramsey's experience enabled him to speak confidently as a Christian ethicist without worrying about imposing alien ideas or formulas on medical controversies. That is to say, the overlap between the metaphor of covenant and ideal relationships in medicine and scientific research allowed Ramsey to see himself as developing a form of connected criticism.

One result of this overlap is that it enabled Ramsey to enter confidently into debates about medical practice and policy without worrying about whether his overall outlook was appropriate to the profession. The parallel between covenantal theology and the ethics internal to medicine freed him from having to work back to theological foundations to justify his claims; often his theological ideas are barely evident. That is, Ramsey writes as a Christian ethicist confident that his views were not exclusively Christian; in his mind, they have a wider public plausibility. As Albert R. Jonsen remarks about Ramsey's writing, "Although theological style occasionally dominates, the religious skeptic or the theological illiterate can usually appreciate the force of his ethical argumentation."[28]

Another outcome of Ramsey's interactions with physicians is that it prompted him to adjust some of the substantive values of a care-centered ethic in light of medicine's attention to the good of embodiment. As a result, he qualifies the voluntaristic implications of consent with considerations about duties to the body. In his discussion of donating organs for transplantation, for example, Ramsey argues that selfless love along the lines of *agape* would suggest that healthy individuals should donate their organs to the needy. But he is quick to observe that such a requirement would violate potential donors' bodily integrity. In a more theological vein, the idea is that the requirements of covenantal love must be weighed against the goods of creation.[29] Ramsey finds the good of the body to be an integral feature of the ethics of medical professionals. He remarks,

> I have discovered only one physician who, in allowing the self-giving of organs by living donors, proposes merely this additional test: "in all cases the advantage to the recipient has to be greater than the disadvantage or danger to the donor." Other physicians say that, in respecting the desire of one person to risk his life for another, the doctor must "be sure that the risk to the donor is very much less than the probability of success to the patient."[30]

For Ramsey, physicians' concern for embodiment "is the only way to conceive of charity as the action of creaturely men, of men of flesh, and not as the action of disembodied spirits."[31] In this way, experience produced moral insights that bubbled up into his theological ideas, leading him to amend his understanding (and specification) of charity. The result is a more sensible recommendation than a system of heedless giving: Donations from living persons must promise greater benefit to the recipient than risk to the donor.[32]

Ramsey's respect for and familiarity with medical practice also sharpened his understanding of how to delegate expectations of practical reasoning in hospital and laboratory contexts. Moral reasoning involves a division of labor, which limits an ethicist's authority and claim to competence. Ramsey saw his work as clarifying the principles of medical ethics, leaving medical practitioners to apply those principles to specific cases. Ethicists like himself are responsible for deepening our understanding of basic values and norms, but they are to do so without "trespassing upon the competence of medical men."[33] For example, about determining what the principle of informed consent requires in practice, Ramsey writes, "This, physicians and investigators and boards of their peers must do."[34] In short, familiarity with clinical contexts helped Ramsey specify the meaning and requirements of moral expertise.

Access to a research hospital likewise fueled Ramsey's anxieties about "the omnivorous appetite of scientific research" and the "therapeutic technology that has a momentum and life of its own."[35] These concerns took Ramsey into deeper and more controversial topics, and unfortunately skewed his angle of vision regarding loyalty, consent, and the first issue he tackles in *The Patient as Person,* namely, medical experimentation with children. In this respect, Ramsey's work exhibits a potential drawback to clinical immersion: Institutional life can distort an ethicist's perspective by subtly tailoring it to the contours of professional circumstances and exigency.

In Ramsey's case, that distortion occurs when he attempts to apply a canon of adult medical ethics to cases involving children. He mistakenly assumes that the covenantal requirements of adult care can be extended to children and other noncompetent patients. As a result, Ramsey overlooks some of the distinctive features of my principal interest here, namely, pediatric care and its covenantal obligations. Indeed, Ramsey's logic about pediatric care exhibits a tension of which he seemed unaware.

At the heart of *The Patient as Person* is the following claim:

> Any human being is more than a patient or experimental subject; he is a *personal* subject—every bit as much a man as the physician-investigator. Fidelity is between man and man in these procedures. Consent expresses or establishes this relationship, and the requirement of consent sustains it. Fidelity is the bond between consenting man and consenting man in these procedures. The principle of informed consent is the cardinal *canon of loyalty* joining men together in medical practice and investigation. In this requirement, faithfulness among men—the faithfulness that is normative for all the covenants or moral bonds of life with life—gains specification for the primary relations peculiar to medical practice.[36]

The effect of this argument is to impose a clear and unbreachable side-constraint on all medical experimentation: Experiments may not violate a subject's autonomy. Without reasonably free and informed consent, "experimentation and medicine itself would speedily become inhumane."[37]

From this claim Ramsey argues that all nontherapeutic research with children is impermissible because they are unable to provide consent. Moreover, a proxy is eligible to consent for his or her child only when treatment promises to be therapeutic for that child: "No parent is morally competent to consent that his child shall be submitted to hazardous or other experiments having no diagnostic or therapeutic significance for this child himself."[38]

But in this apparently simple inference from the general requirement of consent, Ramsey conflates several concerns that ought to be distinguished. His real, unstated conviction has less to do with autonomy than with beneficence as a basic principle of pediatric care. Parents are rendered ineligible as proxies if their decisions do not promise to benefit their children. Respect for their autonomy is secondary to a more fundamental test, namely, patient benefit.

Ramsey fails to see this point, arguing at length that nontherapeutic experimentation on children is wrong because it cannot meet the standards of true and informed consent. He writes, "No child or adult incompetent can choose to become a participating member of medical undertakings, and no one else on earth should decide to subject these people to investigations having no relation to their own treatment."[39] But in stating that children cannot choose to become participants in nontherapeutic medical trials, Ramsey proves too much, for children (or at least very young children) cannot competently choose to become participants in *any* medical trials, beneficial or nonbeneficial.[40] Children's incompetence would exclude them from medical experimentation *tout court*, that is, experimentation that is therapeutic or nontherapeutic.

Ramsey sees no problem with parents consenting to experimentation on their child in cases that might prove medically beneficial for that child.[41] His claim that "no parent is morally competent to consent that his child shall be submitted to hazardous or other experiments having no diagnostic or therapeutic significance for this child himself"[42] leaves open the moral possibility of proxies consenting to potentially therapeutic experimentation on children. That fact indicates that beneficence and the corresponding requirement to provide therapeutic treatment specifies the first criterion or canon of loyalty in Ramsey's pediatric ethic, not the criterion of informed consent. *Consent may be secured only for treatment that has passed a prior test, namely, that it is therapeutic.* On his logic, proxy representation and informed consent should become important *after* the treatment's aims are evaluated.

Here we see the potentially distorting effects that clinical immersion can have on an ethicist's logic. Situated in a research setting, Ramsey was understandably concerned that individuals would be instrumentalized by research and technological imperatives. He thus sought to define restrictions that are implied by informed consent. Such restrictions work to protect noncompetent persons from exploitation in research settings. But Ramsey's canon of loyalty for protecting noncompetent patients is too broad, for it excludes all young children from any experimentation, which is not his aim or final position. The fact that Ramsey accepts parental consent to therapeutic experimentation with children indicates that beneficence—not autonomy—defines the basis for protecting children from instrumentalization in medical and research contexts. His argument on behalf of protecting children is internally gnarled because it presumes that respect for autonomy rather than beneficence can provide a discriminating basis for protecting the interests of pediatric patients.

Stated differently, Ramsey mistakenly uses the criterion of *patient benefit* as a test for determining the *competence* of parents or guardians who are asked to provide proxy consent for pediatric experimentation. Such a test is irrelevant in cases of competent adults; these patients may refuse potentially therapeutic treatment for themselves. That is because competence, properly understood, calls attention to the *process of deliberation* rather than to the skill in *reasoning correctly.* Competence is not a matter of producing the correct answer when making decisions about biomedical treatment or experimentation. It is rather a matter of integrating information, weighing and judging its implications, and communicating one's reasons to relevant health care professionals. On that general account, parents can competently refuse treatment that could benefit their child.

Had Ramsey seen matters more clearly, he would have argued that canons of loyalty to a child in research settings must begin not with determining competence when professionals secure proxy consent, but with determining whether treatment is in that child's basic medical interest.[43] Beneficence is a norm that can stand independently of autonomy; each norm is subject to different tests. Ramsey's preoccupation with consent as the "cardinal canon of loyalty" in research contexts involving children prevents him from recognizing those facts and distinctions.

The concrete implications of this problem bear directly on how (and to whom) canons of loyalty ought to apply in the treatment of children. Ramsey's theory is designed to assess the competence of parents as proxies: They are ineligible to represent their child if they assent to nontherapeutic treatment. *But that line of argument places the onus on parents without first examining the moral merits of professionals' experiments.* If Ramsey had properly understood his own argument about pediatric ethics, with beneficence as the first moral consideration, responsibility would have been placed first on researchers rather than on parents.[44] On his terms, researchers who propose nontherapeutic experimentation commit a moral wrong. That is not to say that parents are free of moral responsibility in considering the interests of their child, only that the first line of normative inquiry should target the nontherapeutic proposals of medical professionals rather than the decisions of parents or guardians. By focusing on proxy consent rather than on the norm of beneficence in the treatment of children, Ramsey fails properly to develop the implications of care as a resource for social and professional criticism.[45]

Beyond this problem, a final point deserves brief discussion, namely, Ramsey's general moral focus. Ramsey accomplishes many tasks in *The Patient as Person* and his subsequent writings in medical ethics, but he does not help us to understand the cultural parameters, division of labor, and logistical challenges of medical treatment and research. Instead, his aim is to use religious ethics to produce dispositional- and action-guides for medical and research practitioners. Convinced of the overlap between the idea of covenant and the proper relationship between physicians and patients, Ramsey argues that resources from the former can be developed to instruct and discipline the latter. Those resources usually take the form of moral principles that could be applied to cases in clinical or research practice. A precursor to secular medical ethics that relies on fundamental or mid-level principles, *The Patient as Person* eschews reference to the culture of professionals whose practices and policies Ramsey seeks to evaluate. For that task, a more expansive model is needed.

THEOCENTRIC VALUES

A more diffuse but more promising alternative to Ramsey's approach is defended by James M. Gustafson. According to Gustafson, theology is "reflection on human experience with reference to a particular dimension of the human experience denoted 'religious.' "[46] By *religious*, Gustafson means that "dimension of experience . . . that senses a relationship to an ultimate power that sustains and stands over humans and the world."[47] The goal of the theologian or religious critic is not to provide a set of theologically informed first principles but to draw inferences "from those dimensions of experience with reference to the power that is experienced."[48] Theologians are to mine symbols and their general moral implications for human agency; theology is less prescriptive of specific action than it is normatively interpretive of human experience.

According to Gustafson, theological inferences must begin from the belief that God wills the well-being of creation, a belief that should provide a fundamental moral perspective, a set of ordering attitudes toward life, and a basic intentionality that directs human interventions in biological processes.[49] On his view, human decisions must be shaped by an understanding of the common good of creation and the belief that God acts to preserve life and to furnish the conditions of creative action that advances the well-being of creation. Specific dictates for professional practice or policy are not produced as necessary conclusions from theological beliefs. Rather, dictates for action must be coherent with the common good of creation as that is conceived according to cultural data, religious tradition, and scientific information.

For Gustafson, theology's contribution to medical ethics has less to do with generating specific dispositional- or action-guides than with providing a general horizon for interpreting human activity. That horizon is largely informed by the idea that human beings must first situate themselves within a wider biological and scientific order, an order that includes goods that may supersede human desires and well-being. Central to Gustafson's theological program is the idea of finitude: our dependence on natural forces and cultural institutions, and our limited power to direct the course of human life. Human agents must understand themselves as parts of a larger whole; theologically informed medical ethics must operate within a wider set of time and space coordinates than is conventionally the case in moral philosophy. Placing human well-being within a wider compass of the creation's well-being may mean that we must sometimes sacrifice the former for the sake of the latter; theological ethics is theocentric, not anthropocentric.[50] So conceived, theology leads less to a specific set of ethical recommendations than to an understanding of competing goods and rival demands that human agents must consider as they ponder medical and scientific activity.

The key feature of this model is that theology functions to *qualify* rather than generate ethical prescriptions.[51] Theology reorders certain values, especially the conventional understanding of the priority of human to nonhuman goods. Rather than proceed with theologically informed ideas like care as a deontic principle, Gustafson begins by identifying specific variables that bear on medical practice or policy and then comments on those variables in light of relevant theological and ethical ideas.

Gustafson's methodology is informed in part by his Reformed heritage, in which the creative activity of God is reformed by God's judging and redemptive work.[52] Natural processes, including social life and common reason, have relative goodness. Whatever reform is recommended generally involves incremental rather than revolutionary change. The religiously informed critic must therefore probe processes and reasons already at work in social life as a prelude to developing religious and ethical commentary. The overall effect is a theology of culture and practical reasoning that is more inductive, hermeneutical, and contextual than Ramsey's.

Gustafson did little to deploy this model in actual practice. Despite the fact that he was an active and astute observer of bioethics in its nascent years, his contributions to theology, medicine, and culture are more programmatic and theoretical than practical.[53] Unlike Ramsey, he was not inclined to enter into specific debates about individual conduct or professional policy. But in one important essay we can see the distinctive contours of Gustafson's model and the kind of practical requirements that it imposes on medical ethics in an ethnographic vein.

That essay, "Mongolism, Parental Desires, and the Right to Life," focuses on the famous "Johns Hopkins Case" of 1963, in which an infant who was born with duodenal atresia and Down's syndrome was deliberately left untreated. Surgery of nominal risk and virtually certain benefit would have been recommended for a non-Down's child. Owing to the child's disabilities, however, the parents refused permission for the surgery, and the child was left in the hospital to starve to death over a two-week period.[54] Gustafson disagrees with this decision, and the way he develops his views presents in condensed form many of his theological and methodological commitments.

Gustafson begins his analysis not by stating his theological convictions or ethical principles, but by first articulating the parents' reasons for refusing treatment and then surmising how those reasons might be justified. He starts from the agent's presumed perspective.[55] This approach appears to differ from Ramsey's, but a closer look reveals a point they share. Like Ramsey, Gustafson is aware of the limited authority of ethical competence and is alert to the problem of making pronouncements that sound moralistic or self-righteous to those anguishing about a case. He expresses his understanding of such limits by avoiding an analysis that proceeds from "on high," detached from existential drama. Distinguishing between different kinds of perspectives in moral analysis, he writes,

> There is a tradition that says that ethical reflection by an ideal external observer can bring morally right answers. I have an observer's perspective, though not that of an "ideal observer." But I believe that it is both charitable and intellectually important to try to view the events as the major participants viewed them. The events remain closer to the confusions of the raw experience that way; the passions, feelings, and emotions have some echo of vitality remaining.[56]

The goal is to lend voice to those who were involved in the case—the parents, the physicians, and the nurses—and to infer how their views might find rational support. Gustafson thus enters into a deep, empathetic analysis, seeking to ascertain the plausibility of the parents' decision, their pattern of moral reasoning, and the cultural sources of their values. Justice to the parents' other children, the value of intelligence in American society, the importance of being born into a welcoming family, the claims of family autonomy, and the limits of a physician's moral competence provide reasons that explain why the parents made their decision and why the health care providers did not seek to override it.

Only after presenting those views and exhibiting the parents' conscientiousness does Gustafson develop his own comments. He places the case in a different perspective by qualifying the relevant moral values in light of his ethical and religious convictions. He thus practices a form of connected criticism that goes beyond the connected criticism we see in Ramsey. Gustafson's commentary is connected not only to the views and values of the professionals involved in the case but also to the parents' perspective, for they must shoulder the consequences of the decision.

Central to this case, Gustafson notes, are two "reference points": the desires of the parents and the fact that the child has Down's syndrome. If the parents had desired otherwise, the physicians would have carried out the surgery. If the child had not had Down's syndrome, the physicians would have sought a court order to authorize surgery in the absence of parental consent. Neither of these reference points is sufficient to justify withholding treatment but taken together they explain why the physicians chose not to override the parents' decision against surgery.

Gustafson then takes issue with each of these points, arguing that 1) desires are insufficient to override duties to dependent parties, 2) Down's syndrome does not justify denying the infant the basic right to life, and (3) the care of a Down's child—with outside support—does not impose disproportionate hardships on the family. Rather than develop this argument in terms of a standard schedule of rights and duties, however, Gustafson draws out implications of our experience of dependence and suffering, themes that he would develop later and more systematically in his theological understanding of human finitude.

According to Gustafson, those who are dependent place claims over and against us. "The fact that we brought our children into being lays a moral obligation on my wife and me to sustain and care for them to the best of our ability. They did not choose to be; and their very being is dependent, both causally and in other ways, upon us. . . . Their claims are independent of our desires to fulfill them."[57] The existence of a child, regardless of intelligence, beauty, and personality, requires parents to consent to his or her being and to respond appropriately to his or her needs. Family responsibility is a microcosm of humanity's place within the larger natural universe and, formally speaking, generates an analogous set of duties. As Gustafson would argue in his mature theology, we must act responsibly toward the larger goods of creation, even if these goods do not coincide with our perceptions of our own well-being.

Gustafson then turns to matters of suffering, a venerable theme in religious ethics and theological reflection. Without seeking to valorize the experience of hardship, he surmises that basic questions about inconvenience were not sufficiently broached in this case and tend to be downplayed in ethical debates about social responsibility. Weighing the harms involved, he notes that "the avoidance of potential suffering at the cost of that life was not warranted."[58] Moreover, no evidence suggests that the parents would have found raising the child unbearably burdensome should outside assistance have been made available.[59] In general, Jewish and Christian traditions require adherents to be for others at least as much as for themselves. As a general orientation, this requirement makes it more difficult to privilege the avoidance of suffering at the expense of others than is evident in the moral reasoning of the parents and professionals. Being for others does not settle all practical problems, but it "shapes a bias, gives a weight, toward the well-being of the other against inconvenience or cost to oneself."[60] The claims of the parents are not entirely discounted, but they are qualified, enabling Gustafson to assign lesser weight to them when compared with the claims of the infant.

Here we see a feature of Gustafson's pattern of reasoning that differs from Ramsey's: Gustafson is inclined to think that practical reasoning involves weighing and balancing conflicting claims, whereas Ramsey tends to approach concrete problems by specifying the principle of care. One aim of Gustafson's painstaking analysis is to uncover different perspectives and the values that animate them.

Theological and ethical commentary is to sift through these values, understand their place in practical decision making, and ensure that they have been assigned their due weight. Ramsey is confident that care as a deontic principle can do considerable work to resolve moral controversies, and he worries about the vagueness, subjectivity, and possible consequentialism that might plague weighing and balancing rival values.[61] Gustafson is a pluralist who sees moral experience in more complex terms; he could rejoin that qualitatively specifying norms is no less interpretive than weighing and balancing them.

Of course, appreciation for moral complexity does not ensure correctness of judgment. No less than Ramsey's, Gustafson's efforts to resolve a difficult case involve him in potentially controversial claims. Most notable is an oblique suggestion that appears in his discussion of the physicians' decision, namely, that they might have considered directly taking the infant's life after deciding to forgo corrective surgery. Gustafson asks,

> Once a decision is made not to engage in a life-sustaining and life-saving procedure, has not the crucial corner been turned? If that is a reasonable and moral thing to do, on what grounds would one argue that it is wrong to hasten death? . . . [Euthanasia] goes against the grain of the fundamental vocation of the medical professional to maintain life. But, of course, the decision not to operate also goes against that grain. If the first decision was justifiable, why was it not justifiable to hasten the death of the infant? We can only assume at this point traditional arguments against euthanasia would have been made.[62]

It is not clear how Gustafson wishes us to interpret his queries. On one reading, he is taking the physicians' logic to a *reductio ad absurdum* in order to criticize it, showing that their failure to operate on the infant would lead to a permission to take the child's life. If that prospect seems offensive to them, then perhaps they should have reconsidered their decision not to operate. On another reading, Gustafson's disapproval of euthanizing the child is not so obvious. Here the idea is that the decision not to operate should have been followed up by decisions to shorten the child's anguish. And that reading raises concerns. Euthanizing handicapped children hardly coheres with a vision that emphasizes human finitude and the importance of consenting to wider powers and purposes of nature. Gustafson might respond that *forcing* someone to suffer differs from consenting to conditions of finitude, and that the infant is being forced to suffer a cruel fate by starving to death. But the infant's pain and discomfort could be alleviated with palliative measures without raising the specter of euthanasia. Deciding against low-risk surgery with lifesaving benefits for a handicapped person, and then using that decision to justify killing the patient, establishes a chilling precedent, the symbolic importance of which is hard to understate. That said, I must add that Gustafson's attitude is not entirely clear. About euthanizing the infant, he is either indirect in stating his disapproval or not entirely disapproving. In either case, it is striking that Gustafson does not raise this objection bluntly and directly.[63]

Beyond this difficulty, I should note that Gustafson did little to bring his model to bear on professional culture and practice. Indeed, his experience was more imaginative than empirical, more empathetic than observational. His analysis of the Johns Hopkins case reveals many pastoral sensitivities; it did not develop from directly encountering the parents and medical professionals who were involved in the case, but from viewing a film about the controversy.[64] Nor did it borrow from sustained engagement with the professional culture of medicine—its daily rhythms, division of labor, institutional routines, and individual personalities. Gustafson's immersion might best be understood as conjectural, a kind of experience-near methodology that invokes lessons from common experience and religious sensibilities to connect vicariously with the (real) participants.

In this respect Gustafson's essay points to a feature of "immersion ethics" that is missing from Ramsey's work: the need imaginatively to engage the individuals and the larger contours of the case at hand, and to think carefully about how the case is represented. Gustafson is self-conscious about this requirement of an inductive approach. At the outset of his essay he observes, "One of the points under discussion is how we should view it. What elements are in the accounts that the participants give to it? What elements were left out? What 'values' did they seem to consider, and which did they seem to ignore? Perhaps if one made a different montage of the raw experience, one would have different choices and outcomes."[65] He notes that his reconstruction of the case involves a creative reordering of relevant values, requiring him to "redraw the picture."[66] One item that Gustafson contributes to our understanding of practical ethics is its poetic, demiurgic aspect: Ethics draws on imaginative skills and demands that writers think carefully about matters of representation as they confront moral and cultural complexity. Writing in ethics involves not only a methodology but a style.

Seen together, Ramsey's and Gustafson's efforts point to an enormous paradox: Ramsey's method provides little help in addressing the professional culture in which he learned medical ethics, while Gustafson did little to deploy his method to assess the subject matter—medical culture—for which his model seems well-suited. Although each author gestures toward an experience-near methodology, each eschewed medical ethics in a fully ethnographic vein. That bold step was taken by William F. May, whose work represents a religiously informed medical ethics that critically heeds the corporate culture of professional practice and the voices of those who endure the tribulations of medical treatment.

IMAGES OF COVENANT AND REBIRTH

Developing a third model, May draws on Ramsey's interest in covenant fidelity and Gustafson's interpretive, interdisciplinary understanding of theology's relation to culture. Those commitments shape and are shaped by clinical immersion in various contexts that directly inform May's work. After a year's observation at the Cornell Medical College in New York City in 1976–77 and five summers of teaching ethics to health care providers, May produced his first book in medical ethics, *The Physician's Covenant*. His various interactions with professionals who work with the profoundly retarded, recovering alcoholics, and victims of domestic violence and molestation contributed to a subsequent book, *The Patient's Ordeal*. May's third book in medical ethics, *Testing the Medical Covenant*, develops themes that grow out of his previous works. The overall program is a theology of culture whose interdisciplinary aspects comment on the moral world of medical professionals and the suffering of those they serve.

May begins by identifying features of experience that invite religious analysis. Fateful events that accompany "sickness, suffering, and death . . . shatter or suspend the ordinary resources that people trust for managing their lives and send them to the doctor in hope of rescue."[67] Like Ramsey, May uses the notion of covenant to shape his analysis of how physicians should respond to such fateful occurrences. Medicine as a kind of covenant involves trustworthiness and commitment to the patient's health and has a donative, selfless dimension. These ideals, he argues, are superior to images of the physician as parent, fighter, and technician, which are flawed by paternalistic, militaristic, and/or instrumentalist visions of professional responsibility. For May the idea of covenant serves less to stipulate norms for practice and policy than to frame how we are to understand the moral qualities of the relationships between health care providers and patients. Covenant is more of a social, intersubjective image for May than for Ramsey, and it is more hermeneutical than directly prescriptive. This desire to use interpretive images to qualify experience thus puts May closer to Gustafson than to Ramsey, despite the fact that Ramsey and May share a substantive interest in covenantal ethics.

A key point is that May conceives of covenant as a metaphor rather than as a norm—although it has important ramifications for how norms should be applied to professional experience. Following Paul Ricoeur, he argues that metaphors structure our ways of seeing and lend coherence to our experience. When used in ethics, metaphors provide grounds for framing experience in a certain way by articulating a corrective vision. May believes that ethics has a creative, demiurgic quality.[68] He thus conceives of ethics less in terms of fashioning victorious disputations than in constructing moral representations that challenge our modes of perception. So conceived, ethics "may not always eliminate moral quandaries, but it opens up a wider horizon in which they may be seen for what they are and thus become other than what they were. It helps correct our perceptions of the world as it appears to the myopia of timidity and the astigmatism of vice."[69]

May sharpens this line of thought by considering the metaphoric and moral differences between covenants and contracts. In his mind, the idea of covenant "provides a more spacious framework for interpreting the professional's full obligation to a patient and the nation's needs in a health care system."[70] Both covenants and contracts depend on a promise and an exchange. But a contract governs buying and selling on the basis of each party's self-interest, whereas a covenant is ruled by "disinterested giving and receiving that may carry the parties beyond the partial and limited terms of a contact."[71] According to May, a covenanted professional exchange must

> transcend the marketplace transaction of buying and selling. The professional professes something (the art of healing) on behalf of someone (the patient). This double fidelity to the art of healing and to the patient generates trust. This is why we call the professional relationship *fiduciary*. For healing to work, the patient must assume that the professional will not merely treat him as a profit opportunity. . . . Something else besides a piece of paper must hold self-interest in check and let the disinterested work of healing take place. The name for this additional ingredient of good faith that binds persons and communities together is *covenant*.[72]

On this model, theologically informed medical ethics defines the virtues that ought to shape the professional identity of health care practitioners and examines the moral climate in which professional and patients interact. For May, the idea of covenant prescribes not deeds and rules for resolving cases, but the terms of professional self-interpretation and intersubjective interaction between medical practitioners and patients.

Interpreting covenant in this way informs an influential distinction that May has defined, namely, the distinction between "transactional" and "transformational" relationships in professional life.[73] Contracts mark transactional relationships, whereas covenants provide a space for transformative, interpersonal relationships. A transactional approach involves an exchange of information and the guarantee that practitioners will provide adequate goods and services to their clients. Transactions do not require doctors to instruct patients about how to decrease the likelihood of future illness or how to improve their health-related habits. Echoing recent critiques of professionalism, May argues that a transactional approach privatizes professional responsibility by reducing it to a commodity to be bought and sold in the marketplace.[74]

A transformational approach, in contrast, requires physicians to get to the bottom of their patients' problems and envisions professional life as part of the larger commonweal. A doctor confronted by an insomniac patient, for example, may be asked to provide the quick remedy of a sleeping pill. But in a transformational approach, a physician "may have to challenge the patient to transform the habits that led to the symptom of sleeplessness."[75] May thus encourages something like "soft paternalism," in which physicians are to act on behalf of values that patients are presumed (or led) to embrace.[76] The aim is not to satisfy patients' preferences, but to address patients' long-term problems with an eye to prevention and public health.

A transformationist approach to medical responsibility generates more robust moral expectations than those of transactional dealings. It informs May's approach to practical reasoning, for he is concerned with how background assumptions inform the application of moral norms to professional practice. In this vein, he remarks that "images . . . do not operate as a manual for getting the decision maker out of an exceptional moral bind in which he or she does not know what to do. Rather, they provide a comprehensive ordering of life—an interpretation of role, metaphysical setting, and institutional context—that makes moral behavior seem more like a rite repeated than a puzzle solved."[77]

That is to say, our interpretation and application of moral norms rely in part on unarticulated, background assumptions.[78] For May, social responsibility acquires an expanded set of implications for health care practitioners given what we should infer from transformational dynamics. In this respect, the demands of biomedical ethics—especially the norm of beneficence—are amplified; their range of application is broadened owing to background assumptions regarding the proper responsibilities of health care providers.

Amplifying the range of a norm's meaning or its concrete implications is one pattern of reasoning that is rarely noted in discussions of practical ethics. With Ramsey and Gustafson, we see more familiar models of practical reasoning: specifying norms, and weighing and balancing norms after they have been specified. Amplifying norms is a pattern of moral reasoning that stands apart from the reigning models, and May's understanding of covenant and transformational dynamics is noteworthy in its attempt to broaden our understanding of the social responsibility of health care providers.

May adds that his method is defined only partially by theological terms, that the traditions that inform him are "partly literary, partly phenomenological, and partly religious."[79] A virtuoso at moral poetics, he successfully coordinates numerous sources, ranging across drama, literature, history of religions, Christian theology, and medical data in constructing compelling portraits of his subjects. In this regard, one distinctive feature of May's work is his attention to what patients must undergo in the course of their treatment. Arguing that illness is an assault on a patient's identity, May insists that health care providers must attend not only to bodily but also psychological and social well-being.

Indeed, May's concern for patient suffering and the challenges it poses to professional responsibility came after his initial immersion in medical culture, and he developed that concern in part as a corrective to the angle of vision that informed his initial foray into the field. At the opening of *The Patient's Ordeal,* he writes,

> [W]hile rereading my field notes from that year [of observation], I realized how readily I adopted the doctor's angle of vision on the hospital scene. I focused largely on the doctor's practice rather than on the patient's sense of medical crisis, on the rhythms and tempo with which professionals deliver their services rather than on the ordeals which patients suffer. My own personal focus on the doctor, moreover, largely reflected and repeated the broader preoccupation of the field of medical ethics. Moralists have concentrated chiefly on the ethics of the professional, not on the ethics of the patient and the patient's family.[80]

As in his earlier work, May focuses on fateful events that "shatter or suspend the ordinary resources that people trust for managing their lives," but his focus shifts to the kinds of challenges that patients face in rebuilding their lives. Those challenges imply a broader set of social responsibilities for professionals than May delineates in *The Physician's Covenant,* requiring him to consider patients' ordeals and to solicit the voices of those whose medical challenges touch directly on identity. He thus writes about the burned, retarded, gestated and sold, battered, molested, aged, and addicted.

To understand these patient populations, a new set of interpretive categories is needed. May notes that catastrophic illness touches the core of identity and confronts the patient with death. Victims of such illnesses move "through a kind of death into some sort of new identity";[81] the challenge they confront is as metaphysical as it is physical. That is, recovery bears on the fundamentals of patients' self-understanding as well as bodily rejuvenation. Patients do not move from a relatively worse to better quality of life on a linear trajectory. Rather, their lives are dramatically interrupted and forever changed. It is therefore necessary to see their experiences according to the sequence of life/death/rebirth.

Such challenges require special professional virtues—not only wisdom, courage, and justice but also the commitment to "make good" on one's original decision to care for a patient. The ordeal of patient suffering bids us to recall and broaden the requirements of covenantal care. Physicians should not only educate and transform patient habits with an eye toward contributing to the commonweal but also respond to the psychological burdens of patient suffering and the need to empower patients who face devastating loss or injury.

May's analysis of various patient ordeals is powerful and unique. He deploys a great body of cultural knowledge in his writings, and his sensitivity to human suffering is compelling. Much of his work is interpretive and suggestive rather than apodictically prescriptive. Yet, no less than Ramsey and Gustafson, May enters into controversial matters of interpretation and judgment. Owing to his emphasis on metaphor and vision, disagreements with May are likely to focus less on differences about specific opinions than on broader interpretive matters. About such issues I wish to record two concerns.

First, the theme of life/death/rebirth requires some additional distinctions in order to capture the range of experiences to which May applies it. As it stands, it remains too coarse an interpretive grid to sift through various features of patients' ordeals and the challenges of recovery. At times May uses the theme to describe external tragedy, for example, in his analysis of the burned or battered. In these cases, individuals must undergo changes to overcome hardships that have descended on them from without. The burned or the battered would have enjoyed more favorable circumstances had they not been visited by misfortune. They are conscious of a "before and after" in their personal narratives. Their recovery leaves them with a condition of second-best when compared with the life that would have been, free from the assaults of fire or domestic violence. Other patients in May's analysis should be seen differently, however. For them, rebirth is not a matter of producing a second-best condition. With recovering alcoholics, for example, the life/death/rebirth sequence captures *necessary* and *desirable* changes that individuals must undergo. Dying to the past, far from being a tragedy, is a desideratum. With recovering alcoholics, the "before" is less desirable than what rebirth promises "on the other side."

This phenomenological difference suggests alternative challenges for individuals who work in the helping professions. Some cases involve deeper setbacks. In cases of the burned or battered, victims must deal with images of themselves that are lost and regrettably cannot be recovered. In cases of alcoholism (or other addictions), however, victims must deal with images of themselves that they want to lose, or images of themselves *from which* they seek to recover. In the first set of cases, the desideratum of rebirth is a shadow of the former self. In the second set of cases, victims seek to overcome the shadows of the past rather than to (feebly) recapture them. May's uniform use of the life/death/rebirth sequence fails to sort through the different challenges in these ordeals.

Nor is it true that the life/death/rebirth sequence applies to all of the populations that May discusses. His chapter on the institutionalized retarded, for example, focuses largely on the medical professionals at a state institution in North

Carolina, not on the patients or the patients' families and their ordeals. Although May's analysis is characteristically interesting and instructive, his subject shifts from patients and families to health care providers.

Second, it is not clear whom we are to privilege when the ordeals of patients conflict. Consider one example from *The Patient's Ordeal:* the discussion of the ethics of fetal tissue transplantation. May situates his analysis in an overall account of the ethics of organ donation. His general point is that routine salvaging of organs fails to heed our culture's general revulsion from death and that purchasing organs involves an unwarranted commercialization of the body. He adds that religious symbols and rites can discipline that general revulsion and, far from preventing organ procurement, can encourage a system of giving. May turns from that argument to a discussion of fetal tissue transplantation, in which he provides a qualified permission for using previable abortuses so long as they are not bought and sold in the marketplace. His argument is controlled in part by concerns about the ethics of terminating fetal life. One important question for May is whether using fetal tissue puts transplantation in an alliance with abortion.

While these concerns are doubtless important to ethics and policy regarding fetal tissue transplantation, it is striking that May does not devote much attention to the ordeals of those who might benefit from receiving fetal tissue: victims of Parkinson's or Alzheimer's disease. They are natural candidates to consider in May's program, for surely they die to their past and retain only a shadow of themselves. Interestingly, in May's chapter on the aged in *The Patient's Ordeal,* those ordeals are not described. That oversight is carried over into his analysis of fetal tissue transplantation, where the benefits of transplantation for the aged receive only brief mention.[82] It remains unclear why abortuses, and not victims of the aging process, ought to be privileged among the ordeals that May considers.

Herein lies a problem with research that immerses itself in medical contexts: When ordeals conflict, it is necessary to determine whose problems should control the analysis. Soliciting voices or securing the perspectives of different participants (real or presumed) is a crucial feature of ethnographic analysis. But when relative weight is assigned to those voices and interests, independent justifications are necessary in order to make sense of priorities.

OBSERVERS OBSERVED

If, as Jonsen remarks, *The Patient as Person* is "the first truly modern study of the new ethics of science and medicine,"[83] then clinical immersion has a foundational role in the development of modern bioethics. That legacy now spans three decades, ranging from Ramsey's work in the late 1960s through Gustafson's writings in the 1970s and 1980s to May's publications in the 1980s and 1990s.

As that legacy has progressed, the challenge of an experience-near methodology has become more refined as that methodology has become more self-reflexive and sophisticated. At a minimum, each of our pioneers, in his own way, has tried to resist the idea (as Chambliss asserts) that bioethics is a matter of assuming "that people are autonomous decision makers sitting in a fairly comfortable room trying logically to fit problems to given solution-making patterns."[84] Rather, each of our authors has fashioned his approach to bioethics in a dialogical way, focusing on groups and their interactions within institutional settings, and learning from what Gustafson calls the "confusions of raw experience." Nor would these pioneers want to contribute to a field in which, as Kleinman writes, "the contextually rich, experience-near illness narrative is not privileged." Gustafson and May have explicitly sought to avoid the charge that patients' experiences are "reinterpreted (also thinned out) from the professional bioethical standpoint in order to focus exclusively on the value conflicts that it is held to instantiate."[85] For May and Gustafson, patients' and families' voices emerge as an authority for moral and religious reflection. Moreover, Ramsey's attention to the demands of steadfast care speaks directly to Kleinman's existential concerns about patient suffering in that Ramsey is keenly sensitive to the problems of patient instrumentalization and abandonment. For that matter, May's assessment of his early forays into the field and his idea of transformational as opposed to transactional relationships seek to draw on lay experience and to critique medical professionals' inability to "transcend the marketplace transaction of buying and selling."[86] His program thus accepts Kleinman's call to build on "lay perspectives and everyday life experiences" and to provide resources that "might generate a deeper critique of [the] medical-moral domain and the economic interests with which it is inextricably held."[87]

That is not to say that each of these pioneers teaches us the same lesson about an experience-near approach to bioethics or that their work yields a polished research paradigm. I rather think that we should look to each of them as contributors to a more general legacy, still in a nascent stage, and not without internal tensions and distinct emphases. What do these authors say about the merits, challenges, and limits of an experience-near methodology for bioethics? What can we garner from my survey of their ideas? By way of conclusion, four issues suggest themselves: the dangers of power, the challenge of moral poetics, the requirements of practical reasoning, and the formation of moral priorities.

First are the issues of power and perspective. In this respect both Ramsey and May are instructive, although in different (and mutually correcting) ways. May's admission that his first major contribution to medical ethics tracked professionals rather than patients suggests that the effects of power on an ethicist's point of view cannot be discounted. Access to medical contexts usually requires deference to institutional gatekeepers. Adopting a sharply critical stance can seem disloyal and ungrateful, and disloyalty is a real problem for those like May whose convictions are informed by a covenantal ethic. Seen against this backdrop, the fact that he subsequently adopts the perspective of a patient, even if that effort is inconsistent, is no small achievement.

If May warns us about the danger of co-optation, then Ramsey's work points to the opposite danger, namely, that of overcorrection. Ramsey's concern about the problem of exploitation in a research setting led him to emphasize some values in pediatric care at the expense of others. As a result, his argument is internally flawed by a confusion between protecting pediatric noncompetents against exploitation out of respect for autonomy instead of respect for patient benefit. Resisting co-optation can lead to overcompensation. Striking a proper balance between the two is the challenge that May and Ramsey put before us.

Second is the issue of representation and moral poetics, what I have called the demiurgic quality of ethical writing. Here Gustafson's and May's work is instructive. Recall that Gustafson's key move in his analysis of the Johns Hopkins case is to "redraw the picture" and that May's work emphasizes the importance of metaphor and vision. These authors remind us that moral problems scarcely come prepackaged for moral analysis and resolution. Rather, we meet moral experience as unruly contingency, unrefined and unprocessed. Central to the task of moral deliberation is the need to sort through messy particulars of experience, to identify what is at stake in those particulars, and to argue on behalf of seeing a problem one way rather than another. Social critics are, among other things, producers of meaning, engaged in a sense-making endeavor.[88] Conceived as a representative practice, ethics requires interpretive insight and seeks to deepen our moral perceptions. The key to moral representations, then, is to make manifest moral properties of experience, bringing them to light in perspicuous ways.

Descriptions themselves are not morally neutral, and I am not suggesting that ethnographers or ethicists enable others to grasp the facts of a problem before turning to the normative task of evaluating them.[89] Rather, the point concerns the constructive, creative dimension of practical reasoning as an essential ingredient in the process of moral deliberation. Gustafson and May suggest that, when medical ethicists set out to address a moral dispute, they implicate themselves in problems pertaining to the imagination and the need for strong readings of moral issues.

Related to this point about ethical creativity is the fact that there are artisanal and poetic aspects of ethical writing.[90] By *poetic* I do not mean something analogous to the literary convention of using verse. Rather, I mean that there are literary and narrative conventions to moral representations and that writing requires what John Van Maanen aptly describes as "wordsmithing."[91] In this respect May's work is exemplary. That his style is "partly literary, partly phenomenological, and partly religious"[92] suggests that his work involves artful configurations of moral experience, thereby involving him in the difficult task of reflecting carefully about which strategies to deploy in the attempt to persuade audiences to conceive of moral problems in a certain way. An ethics of immersion involves the skillful fashioning of cultural artifacts, symbols, statements, interests, values, and convictions, enabling readers not only to judge rightly, but to see correctly. No less in medical ethics than elsewhere, practical reasoning depends on optical skills.

Third is the matter of practical reasoning and the relation between norm and context. Here, Ramsey and May are instructive once again in mutually correcting ways. May reminds us of the importance of background beliefs and assumptions in the application of norms to cases. In his case, the metaphor of covenant amplifies our understanding of beneficence by emphasizing the responsibility of empowering patients to begin their lives anew. The more general point is that we do not approach moral problems in a value-neutral way, but with preunderstandings that shape our interpretation of norms when connecting them to cases. In this respect, May's work bids ethnographers and ethicists to make explicit the values that they bring to their fieldwork or casework.

Yet we should also note that the traffic between norm and context is not unilateral, for experience can contribute to our understanding of values and background beliefs. Here Ramsey's discussion of the ethics of organ transplantation, and his initial emphasis on selfless giving, are instructive. He reminds us of the moral values that he was led to revise on hearing physicians affirm the value of embodiment. That affirmation enabled him to modify the voluntaristic implications of *agape* to include not only informed consent but also the good of bodily life. The outcome is a position that understands caring activity to include a consideration of one's own bodily integrity.

I cite May's and Ramsey's examples of practical reasoning for methodological reasons: Together they suggest that the relation between norm and context is bilateral, requiring both to coexist in what is now famously known as a reflective equilibrium.[93] Preunderstandings shape our interpretation of local contexts and vernacular traditions, and those traditions and contexts can help sharpen the meaning of broader background beliefs. Ethics in an ethnographic vein suggests that moral expertise and lay experience, far from being separate departments of knowledge, belong in a creative synergism.

The fourth point concerns the challenge of moral conflicts in the formulation of moral priorities. Naturally, conflicts arise in all facets of medical ethics; the problem is not unique to medical ethics and ethnography. But given the fact that "immersion ethics" may solicit a variety of voices and perspectives, the problem can be especially acute. We see the relevance of conflicts to Ramsey's concerns about nontherapeutic experiments with children, Gustafson's attempt to adopt the parents' and physicians' perspectives in the Johns Hopkins case, and May's discussion of fetal tissue transplantation. Drawing out various perspectives and the values that animate them deepens our understanding of the moral stakes of an issue. In the final analysis, however, there are difficult second-order questions: What role *should* such values have, and how *should* they be ranked? Answering these queries may require moral argumentation that is independent of the participants' (real or presumed) convictions.

In calling attention to the features of an experience-near methodology in the works of Ramsey, Gustafson, and May, I do not mean to suggest that immersion in a clinical setting is sufficient for doing good research in medical ethics. Nor is it true that such experiences guarantee accuracy of judgment when deliberating about moral particulars, as my criticisms of these authors suggest. Yet I should add that all of my judgments are informed in no small way by my immersion in pediatric medical settings, and I doubt that I could have raised objections about Ramsey's, Gustafson's, and May's views without the kind of experience that their work exemplifies for ethics. Intimate and empathetic knowledge of medical cases, professionals, and patients, based on firsthand familiarity or imagined possibilities, contributes significantly to the power and effectiveness of their writing. It seems safe to infer that such immersions, while not sufficient, help to explain their success in generating an interested and informed public. That immersion also points toward a paradigm of bioethics that solicits lay and professional perspectives, requires attention to individual experience and corporate culture, and deploys interdisciplinary resources for (future) research in the field.[94]

2

THE BIOS OF BIOETHICS
AND THE BIOS OF AUTOBIOGRAPHY

JOHN D. BARBOUR

Bioethics is ailing, according to the diagnosis of recent critiques, for a variety of reasons. The principles-based paradigm of ethical reflection that has dominated the field since the 1960s is said to isolate the quandary, the moment of difficult ethical choice, from the larger temporal context of a patient's life. A second criticism is that the concern to protect patient autonomy severs our understanding of persons from the communities and relationships that give their lives meaning. Current paradigms of bioethics also obscure both the bodily basis of self-identity and the soul—patients' deepest sense of their lives' meaning. And the religious values that should guide ethical reflection are slighted when the overriding goal is to formulate a public policy or procedure that everyone in a pluralistic society can agree on.

Many contemporary thinkers agree that bioethics must extend its concerns beyond individual decisions—and beyond the formulation of public policies regulating medical practice and research—in order to raise fundamental questions about the ways we understand life and death, gender roles, aging, embodiment, human community, and other values that shape reflections on illness and health. Moral reflection on medicine must not only consider dilemmas involved in restoring patients to physical health but also ill persons' and their caregivers' understanding of the meaning of life and death. The roles and the concerns of patients and physicians are more complex, ongoing, and religiously informed than most bioethical theory has acknowledged.[1] We might summarize these various criticisms by asserting that bioethics needs to recover the larger meanings of *bios* (life) that are rooted in history, the body, communities, and the sacred.

While there is no panacea for these diverse criticisms and concerns, I propose

that autobiography yields the sorts of insights called for. At the heart of autobiography—"self-life writing"—lies *bios*. *Bios* in autobiography does not mean
simply the temporal span of organic existence, but the "sense of life" of an individual: all that gives meaning and purpose to a person's existence in time. In the
most compelling and powerful autobiographies, the subject's *bios* is not simply a
chronology of significant events, but the disclosure of what *gives life,* what animates her being, what she lives for.

To articulate this meaning of *bios,* the author explores those dimensions of
human existence stressed by recent critiques of bioethics. The autobiographer
depicts the temporal unfolding of personal life, the continuities and disjunctures
in her sense of identity at different ages. Autobiography may examine the relationship between identity and one's bodily nature and experience, especially
when they are drastically altered by disability or illness. To express one's sense
of *bios* often means reflecting on the spiritual dimensions of life, the ultimate
powers that sustain, bear down on, and transform the individual. Persons' sense
of life is what it is, as well, because of the relationships and communities that
have formed them and to which they have become committed. And when autobiographers reflect on how their social context enhances or diminishes their vitality, and on this basis affirm or challenge particular beliefs and practices, they
engage in a compelling act of cultural criticism. All of these aspects of the *bios*
of autobiography should inform bioethics, enriching our sense of the temporal,
communal, and spiritual contexts of both patients and their caregivers.

In this essay I explore the relevance of autobiography for medical ethics by
interpreting narratives about illness by patients and physicians. I am especially
interested in the ways that patients and doctors understand the role of religion in
the healing process. Before turning to these works, I discuss several theoretical
issues related to the use of narratives in moral reflection.

AUTOBIOGRAPHY AND NARRATIVE ETHICS

Two areas of theoretical reflection converge with my advocacy of attention to
autobiography. First, a growing body of scholarship within the fields of the medical humanities and social sciences discerns the important role that narratives may
play in medical ethics.

For instance, Arthur Kleinman's groundbreaking work *The Illness Narratives*
analyzes cases of chronic illness in terms of how patients' cultural backgrounds
affect their experiences of illness. Kleinman's work is not directly autobiographical, but biographical and ethnographic, summarizing patients' oral reports and
interpreting them from the perspective of a cultural anthropologist. Kleinman
makes a crucial distinction between disease, which is the suffering of physical

pain, and illness, which "refers to how the sick person and the members of the family or wider social network perceive, live with, and respond to symptoms and disability."[2] Cultural beliefs and values shape understandings of illness, especially by determining the stigma associated with most forms of disease. Kleinman proposes that sick persons develop a narrative that significantly affects their experiences of being ill. Often such illness narratives are extremely detrimental, keeping patients trapped in guilty, self-destructive, fatalistic, or blaming attitudes. A crucial aspect of the healing process involves "remoralization": patients' construction of a new narrative that helps them come to terms with disease, threatening emotions, changed family and work situations, and sometimes death.

Physicians can play a crucial role in patients' construction of these narratives. Kleinman reconceptualizes the physician's role by stressing the need for active listening, empathy, the translation of medical discourse into everyday language, and emotional support as patients try to discern meaning in the illness experience. In the final two chapters, Kleinman proposes "a method for the care of the chronically ill" that would require significant changes in medical education and practice. He calls for—and his own example demonstrates—skills of moral reflection, literary insight, and ethnographic interpretation of the ways culture shapes experience.

Kleinman's work has influenced many thinkers who see patients' reconstruction of a narrative, and doctors' influence on this process, as a crucially significant act of healing and a topic for ethical reflection.[3] Some thinkers advocate not simply the traditional "case study" but extended narratives that reveal the details of an individual life. Howard Brody proposes that a model of "the joint construction of narrative" by patients and their physicians focuses many current moral concerns about medical practice and indicates the direction of necessary reforms.[4] Exploring autobiographies of illness would be a good way to test these proposals, for we could discern in the lives of patients and doctors the ways that the joint construction of an illness narrative involves moral skills.

A second group of scholarly studies of illness narratives is by literary critics and humanities scholars who are not directly concerned with ethical issues, but rather with the different forms taken by writing about illness and the reasons for conventions and innovation in the depiction of illness. Anne Hunsaker Hawkins's *Reconstructing Illness: Studies in Pathography*, Lucy Bregman and Sara Thiermann's *First Person Mortal: Personal Narratives of Illness, Dying and Grief*, and Thomas Couser's *Recovering Bodies: Illness, Disability, and Life Writing*, in spite of very different theoretical orientations and ways of categorizing illness narratives, all interpret writing about illness as cultural criticism.[5] As autobiographers try to understand illness, they sometimes realize that its stigma reflects their culture's beliefs about the body, gender, death, community, autonomy, and many other things. The more insightful autobiographers discern that to understand illness one must broaden one's focus to evaluate those cultural values that make a person experience the suffering of disease as a particular form of "illness." What threatens and diminishes patients' vitality is not only physical symptoms but their culture's attitude toward a particular disease. Couser, for example, discusses how attitudes toward sexuality affect narratives about breast cancer and AIDS; Bregman assesses the degree to which religious beliefs provide consolation to the dying and the bereaved; and Hawkins interprets similarities between certain alternative therapies and "New Age" religion, discerning in both areas contemporary versions of the peculiarly American mind/body dualism, optimism, and denial of the reality of death that William James called "healthy-mindedness."

These works are important resources for bioethics, showing how attitudes toward medical treatment reflect cultural conflicts about basic values. While none of these literary studies claims to be ethnography in the strict social scientific sense, they understand both autobiography and their own interpretive work as forms of writing about culture that raise fundamental questions of evaluation. I, too, see autobiography dealing with illness as ethnography with a normative dimension, as an assessment of how cultural beliefs help or harm persons struggling with illness.

These literary studies provide helpful models for discerning and assessing the norms implicit in illness narratives. Some autobiographies affirm values a critic may find questionable. For instance, Couser discusses several AIDS narratives by conservative Christians who interpret that illness as God's punishment for homosexuality. In narratives by a family member related to the AIDS sufferer, the resolution of the plot often involves accepting the dying gay person back into the family of origin. "As 'family narratives' these books quite literally represent the family's 'terms': they tend to encode or enact family values that are sometimes at odds with those of the member being reassimilated. Sometimes, then, these narratives of reaffiliation reveal residual blind spots in the way they appropriate and recount the lives of gay men with AIDS."[6] The underlying plot of such narratives is a variant of the parable of the Prodigal Son. However, it is at least debatable whether a life of homosexuality involves "sin" needing to be forgiven. Such narratives by family members often seem to wrench the meaning of a dying gay man's life away from his own choices, in effect returning him to childlike dependence on his family.

Another instructive example of a critic's evaluative role is Hawkins's analysis of the values governing "healthy-minded" autobiographies. The virtues of positive thinking, belief in the healing powers of nature, and emphasis on the patient's will to live can become a denial of the reality of death and of the need for acceptance, letting go of life, and coming to terms with the end of relationships and projects. Forced optimism and positive thinking may promote self-deception. Hawkins discusses in these terms the pathos of Gilda Radner's *It's Always Something,* in which Radner, suffering from ovarian cancer, confesses herself a "hope addict" and reveals a desperate, obsessive desire to go on living that can lead to devastating disappointment.

These examples remind us that simply turning to narrative does not resolve basic questions about which norms should guide bioethics. Autobiographies reflect the authors' normative views, and they need to be evaluated according to all the norms that readers use to assess experience. In my view, this task is not a simple matter of judging narratives according to whether they measure up to some predetermined moral theory, Kantian or utilitarian, Christian or Muslim, feminist or social-contractarian. The problems of bioethics become if anything more complex and methodologically unsystematic when we recognize the dialectical interplay in moral reflection between general theories and particular cases, abstract principles and specific narratives, individual experience and appeals to impersonal criteria for public policy. All of these considerations may be relevant to the question of how best to interpret and respond to suffering. Autobiography is an invaluable source of insights for narrative ethics, superior to other forms of discourse in reminding us of certain aspects of life, but it must be synthesized with other ways of thinking about ethics.

Narrative approaches to bioethics and studies of illness narratives agree that composing one's own story of illness is itself a healing and therapeutic action. Part of the suffering brought by illness is due to patients' feeling that their uniqueness and humanity have been lost as they become medical cases described in impersonal technical language. While this discourse is necessary for medical practitioners, its focus on the pathology of particular organs or bodily systems does not begin to account for patients' subjective experience of illness, their fears, hopes, and emotional vacillations. It may alienate patients from their physicians, their bodies, and their previous understanding of their lives.

Arthur Frank has described storytelling as resistance to "medical colonization" and as a refusal to be "reduced to clinical material."[7] Since illness is terrifying partly because it interrupts one's anticipated course in life and thwarts self-control, reclaiming one's "voice" by interpreting experience in one's own terms brings a significant recovery of freedom. Narrating one's story is also a moral act insofar as patients realize their personal responsibility for understanding illness, offer testimony to others, and build community among fellow sufferers. "Ill people's storytelling is informed by a sense of responsibility to the commonsense world and represents one way of living *for* the other. . . . The idea of telling one's story as a responsibility to the commonsense world reflects what I understand as the core morality of the postmodern. Storytelling is *for* an other just as much as it is for oneself."[8]

"Going public" with one's story may represent an attempt to overcome the shame and stigma associated with illness, which isolate the ill person from others. Illness wrecks healthy persons' narratives of their lives; by becoming autobiographers, ill persons seek meaning and purpose in what was first experienced only as defeat, diminishment, and the threat of destruction. Frank's belief in the healing power of storytelling is shared by advocates of narrative ethics and is echoed in many autobiographical stories of illness, such as Frank's *At the Will of the Body,* his reflections on a heart attack and treatment for cancer.[9]

Reading and reflecting on autobiographies can help restore the *bios* to bioethics. Such activity helps us to imagine the inner lives of ill persons, especially the ways they undergo suffering and the ways they struggle to rebuild their lives by constructing new narratives that interpret disability, illness, or looming death. Autobiography reveals how well religious beliefs sustain people in crisis, and it shows the potential impact physicians may have beyond diagnosing and treating physical symptoms.

To be sure, reading autobiographies will not resolve every vexed normative question of medical ethics. The guidance offered by narrative ethics often seems uncertain and ambiguous. Arthur Frank acknowledges this: "Thinking with stories means that narrative ethics cannot offer people clear guidelines or principles for making decisions. Instead, what is offered is permission to *allow the story to lead in certain directions.* Medical workers need this permission. When physicians in an intensive care unit present a case to me, I can only ask questions about who their patients are, how the present illness fits into the pattern of these people's lives, and where both the physicians and the patients' families see their pattern leading."[10]

Narrative adds a necessary dimension to overly rationalistic or mechanistic models of moral reflection, but by itself a particular story is usually insufficient to give necessary guidance to those concerned with illness, partly because the richest stories are open to conflicting interpretations. Personal narratives do not readily yield public policies applicable to a broad range of individuals from differing value systems and religious traditions.

Yet if narrative ethics is not a formula producing ready answers for every moral question, it provides indispensable insights that should play a role in any ethical theory. Reading can help develop those moral capacities without which the ideals of medical practice, however conceived, cannot be achieved. The reader's discernment of the role of circumstances in making an action what it is, of the significance of motivations and intentions in individual character, and of the ways the remembered past and anticipated future shape a person's decision making are skills of practical wisdom, Aristotle's phronesis. The moral capacities nurtured in reading overlap with the skills necessary in moral casuistry; both processes of interpretation require a synthetic act of judgment integrating principles and ideals, the particular features of a singular case, and comparison with analogous moral situations encountered previously. Reading and ethical reflection alike require the imagination and intelligence to discern how individuals' self-interpretations affect the quality of their lives and how alternative interpretations would stress other values.

Among the genres of narrative, autobiography has a special kind of power and persuasiveness because of its claim to truthfulness, its capacity for detail, its expansive temporal context, its interest in revealing both individual character and the cultural forces that shape character, and its freedom to encompass both plotted events and topical or thematic discussion of ideas. Autobiography is singularly suited to demonstrate and test the theory that by reconceiving one's personal narrative a person can come to terms with illness and, whether one recovers from disease or not, find healing. First-person writing discloses insights that should guide bioethics, revealing the sense of life that animates individuals and the cultural values that diminish or augment their sense of vitality.

How does this assertion of the promise of autobiography for bioethics hold up when we turn to particular narratives? I will assess narratives about illness by patients and doctors, specifiying more precisely both the ethical guidance they offer and their limitations.

ILLNESS NARRATIVES BY PATIENTS: THREE ISSUES

Patients' illness narratives demonstrate the promise of autobiography for bioethics and also raise three issues needing discussion: the representativeness of illness narratives, the ideal of conversion, and the role of physicians in the construction of narratives. Hawkins, Couser, and Bregman and Thiermann discuss more than one hundred first-person works about illness. Most of these are not complete autobiographies recounting the author's entire life, but narratives focusing on a particular experience of illness and, usually, either recovery or a new kind of life adapted to disability or chronic illness.

Representativeness

The most compelling and insightful illness narratives that I have read are Frank's *At the Will of the Body;* William Styron's *Darkness Visible,* which deals with severe depression; Nancy Mairs' *Ordinary Time* and *Waist-High in the*

World, which are collections of essays that discuss, among other things, her multiple sclerosis; and Reynolds Price's *A Whole New Life,* a work describing his spinal tumor, chronic pain and paralysis, and renewed sense of the value of his life despite the lack of physical recovery.[11] These works do most of the things called for by advocates of narrative ethics, including exploring the spiritual resources that helped the author, assessing the performance of medical practitioners, and reflecting on how American cultural values affect a person trying to come to terms with incapacitating illness. Apart from their value for medical ethics, these books are all rich and rewarding texts by gifted professional writers, well worth reading for their literary qualities and their depiction of complex personalities.

Yet the very expressiveness and insight of these works raises several questions about their role in bioethics. Those who choose to write autobiographically about their illness are extraordinarily articulate about their experience. Not only have these writers survived their illnesses, but they have come to terms with and found meaning in them. They have attained sufficient composure and self-confidence to undertake the many tasks involved in creating a book. While these four authors hold that all must find their own way to respond to illness, they are in many ways ideal exemplars of how to survive and cope with illness. They model many of the virtues that patients need. Autobiographers can be compelling moral examples for other people and significant sources of insight for doctors, family members, and other caregivers. But is their example the only or even the best one for every kind of illness, every sort of person?

Mairs, Styron, Price, and Frank are professional writers, teachers, and intellectuals. For each of them, facility in the use of language is central to the vocation that gives their life meaning. Illness threatens their ongoing work, and writing a narrative about that threat restores their sense of meaningful work, their feelings of self-confidence, their ability to direct their lives, their income, and their connections with other people. These four individuals are unusually resourceful in terms of imagination, introspection, and creativity; they have a vast experience of different ways of organizing human experience in narrative terms, and they can reinterpret their lives with new metaphors. This pattern is an ideal that perhaps all patients should strive toward, but it is not easily achieved by many individuals, and it is only partially applicable for some kinds of disability: for a farmer or manual laborer whose occupation is permanently lost because of injury, for an airline pilot who loses his vision, or for persons whose cancer is felt to be so shameful that they cannot bear to speak of it to others. These persons can and should learn to articulate their experience, I think, but the meaning of self-expression will not be the same for them as for a professional writer. Is the autobiographer an ethical exemplar for those mute, terrified sufferers who, like characters in some of Flannery O'Connor's stories, can only bear their pain in silence, hoping to outlast an illness? For some people, grim endurance may be not only the best survival tactic but the most relevant moral norm.

Like the advocates of narrative ethics, Frank, Mairs, Styron, and Price value supremely the written and spoken word. Their ability to appreciate and create well-wrought language is their primary vehicle for religious experience. Other individuals' religious sustenance comes in different forms: through ritual action, communion with the natural world, the beauty of music, the ministrations of a priest or rabbi, or simple human touch, as compassionate hands hold on to them in their pain. Even among those whose primary religious resource is language, there is a significant difference between the sort of person who feels the need to create a new personal narrative and the individual who finds solace in repeated readings of the Psalms. The forging of a creative and highly individualized spiritual path is probably not possible for a person with Alzheimer's disease, who may still be comforted by the familiar traditions of his faith.

Writers are atypical of patient populations in other ways. Bregman and Couser point out several ways in which autobiographies about illness and death are not representative. Nearly all autobiographies dealing with illness are by white authors, for only a few racial minorities have published accounts of illness. The autobiographers are usually well-educated, upper-middle-class persons who, when their lives are disrupted by illness, have medical insurance, access to high-quality medical care, and financial resources and family relationships that provide support during the illness. These resources make their situation very different from those for whom poverty or isolation are major issues.

Notice, too, that autobiographers tend to be middle-aged: those for whom disability or the threat of death comes as a shock that requires a major reorientation of their adult plans and self-conception. Illness disrupts their sense of autonomy, independence, and self-control. These are not the same circumstances as those of an elderly person for whom physical diminishment causes pain but not surprise, or a young person with neither a clearly formulated life trajectory nor the intellectual resources to reconstruct a coherent life narrative. When we draw conclusions about illness and recovery from narratives, we need to recognize their limited applicability to very different kinds of patients.

According to Thomas Couser, autobiographies about illness are "best-case scenarios" not only because of the resources of the person who writes them but because the publishing business tends to select stories with an upbeat ending. There are very few AIDS narratives by those suffering from this disease: "Autopathography is rarely begun until and unless the remission of illness and/or the resolution of related life issues allows for a comic plot. With AIDS, however, both the virulence of the illness . . . and the early age at which many are infected militate against the writing of autobiographical illness narratives."[12] There are, however, many narratives about AIDS by the children, parents, siblings, spouses, or lovers of persons who died of AIDS, and in these works the writer's reconciliation with or response to bereavement, especially the working through of conflicting emotions, is as much the focus of the narrative as illness and death.

While I think Couser's use of the term "comic" is misleading in its application to these wrenching accounts of agonizing death, he points out an important consideration regarding the selectivity not only of what gets written but of what gets published. If the reading public is looking for uplifting, "heartwarming," and basically affirmative works, then those illness narratives that meet this expectation will be most marketable. Certain kinds of illness and individual experience are difficult to organize in these terms: "Those with chronic disability or illness may have difficulty reconciling their experience of illness with the comic plot expected of autobiography; in many cases the culturally validated narrative of triumph over adversity may simply not be available."[13]

The issue of the representativeness of autobiographies of illness needs to be kept in mind, then, when we consider these texts as ethically normative for other persons. Since any norm points to an ideal, the fact that an autobiographer is a best-case scenario is not necessarily a weakness, but it must be reckoned with. Bioethics needs models of struggle and recovery that can inspire or guide others, even as the ideal must be translated into terms applicable to other lives. Certain illness narratives provide examples of virtues that are desirable in almost any case: honesty, responsibility to others, hope, courage, wisdom in balancing concern for oneself and the wider world, spiritual searching for the meaning of one's life, and, sometimes, renewed commitment to one's faith. Whether or not I ever write an illness narrative, I can aspire to live by these values and practice these virtues as I face my own and others' illnesses.

Conversion

Let us turn from the issue of representativeness to another question about the role of illness narratives as an ethical norm. Many illness narratives dramatize a sort of conversion, as the writer arrives at, if not a new religious faith, "a whole new life." A whole new sense of life, that is—a new *bios*. Reynolds Price gives this advice to anyone undergoing an ordeal similar to his: "Your chance of rescue from any despair lies, if it lies anywhere, in your eventual decision to abandon the deathwatch by the corpse of your old self and to search out a new inhabitable body." In *A Whole New Life,* he "tried to map the lines of that change and the ways I traveled toward the reinvention and reassembly of a life that bears some relations with a now-dead life but is radically altered, trimmed for a whole new wind and route."[14]

The links between the idea of religious conversion and recovery from an illness are as old as Augustine's *Confessions.* Augustine's mother diagnoses his spiritual condition using a medical metaphor: "She had no doubt that I must pass through this condition, which would lead me from sickness to health, but not before I had surmounted a still graver danger, much like that which doctors call the crisis."[15] In Book 8, Augustine's account of "the nature of my sickness" reaches its turning point, the "crisis," and his spiritual condition is dramatically transformed as he turns to God.

This analogy between the Christian experience of conversion and a patient's recovery from illness shapes countless illness narratives. It also influences contemporary medical ethics in both religious and secular modes. For instance, Christian ethicist William May, interpreting "the patient's ordeal," stresses the need for a kind of religious conversion. May discusses how medical and social problems "assault identity," with chapters on the burned, the retarded, the battered, the aged, and other forms of ordeal for sufferers and their caregivers. In each case, health crises not only confront people with pressing decisions and practical demands, but also, "far more profoundly, as such crises assault identity, they force their victims to decide who and how they will be."[16] For May, ethics is more than resolving dilemmas; it requires reflection on identity. Particularly in the case of traumatic injury such as severe burns in "Dax's case," the patient "must reconstruct afresh, tap new power, and appropriate patterns that help define a new existence. One cannot talk simply of a new accessory here, a change of venue there, but—as one image puts it—of a new Phoenix that must emerge from the ashes."[17] May argues that an individual's recovery from severe illness involves a kind of death and rebirth of identity, and that this transformation needs to be articulated in narrative and ritual. While he does not pursue the significance of narrative, the normative thrust of May's ideas is that caregivers need to help a patient to reconstruct a new identity. This effort involves, along with other kinds of care, support in the process of devising a new life narrative.

Thus a deep premise of many versions of narrative ethics, in both its autobiographical and theoretical expressions, is the ideal of conversion. The focus on how patients reformulate their life stories assumes that the creation of a new narrative has a transformative effect on health that is analogous to a religious conversion. Let us call this the conversion paradigm for illness narratives and consider several implications.

Is the conversion paradigm valid for all patients? Should everyone go through a form of conversion by coming to a new understanding of life and of what gives it significance? There are other ways of responding to illness, and other forms of narrative may better express that response. For example, by writing a series of autobiographical essays, Nancy Mairs shows up-and-down episodes in her struggle with multiple sclerosis and depression without arriving at a climactic moment of insight or character transformation. Her essays are thematic rather than chronological, and they explore various dimensions of disability, such as lack of mobility, fear of the future, sexuality, and dependence on others. Mairs organizes her work to depict her day-to-day efforts to cope with physical deterioration and her interactions with the "nondisabled." Her essays are autobiographical, but her books are not autobiography in the traditional sense; she narrates personal experience but also engages in free-ranging cultural analysis; and she explores religious issues without seeking closure about the answers.

Yet certain aspects of the conversion paradigm influence Mairs' writing. In *Ordinary Time,* she stresses the need for continual conversion, repeated acts of "turning-towards" God and others: "At each instant I find myself here I must turn again, choose again, name myself again, anew, 'Catholic,' 'feminist,' struggle again to fathom the significance of affirming so provisional an identity, ask again the question I put during a period of excruciating loss to Father Ricardo: 'How is God here?' "[18] The conversion paradigm shapes Mairs' self-interpretation, but she makes it a constant possibility, an opportunity to affirm life at every time of trial. In the final passage of *Waist-High in the World,* she depicts a moment of choice about how to respond to limitations she faces while confined to a wheelchair as a tourist in England:

> At Knole, the 365-room ancestral home of the Sackvilles, only the oak-paneled Great Hall can be reached by wheelchair. I can huddle in it grieving over the rare and fabulous silver furniture the others will see upstairs in the King's Room without me. Or I can contemplate the ancestral portraits all around me, the elaborately ornamented oak screen at one end, and, when I've looked deeply enough, wheel out into the Green Court to bask in the rare bit of English sun, dreaming that Vita Sackville-West and Virginia Woolf once walked by this very spot, heads together, arms entwined, their laughter fluttering through the gate and out into the deer park beyond. Only one of these options will bring me joy.
> I choose joy.[19]

The desire to choose joy, to affirm life, and to respond to loss by appreciating what remains unites the four autobiographers. They present occasions when they are able to achieve this goal in terms that resemble the scene of conversion in spiritual autobiographies. For Arthur Frank, "the gift is our human capacity to choose how we use each day, however limited our choices."[20] However, these authors all emphasize the human ability to make this choice, as opposed to relying on God's transforming grace. And they differ from the classic Augustinian conversion story in dramatizing not a single climactic moment of crisis but many repeated acts of turning. These writers show us, then, the possibility of selectively adapting certain elements of the conversion paradigm but not others.

Another issue is the conversion paradigm's focus on the fate of one individual. Thomas Couser criticizes the individualism of conversion narratives. What he calls the "minority model" of disability, in contrast, emphasizes the solidarity of groups of ill persons and their resistance to the ways their society "constructs" illness. He sees the conversion paradigm as especially attractive to male professionals whose illness does not prevent them from working with their minds: "One significant pattern in their accounts is the redemptive shifting of emphasis from the body to the mind. Self-rehabilitation involves in large part redefining the self as more a function of mind and spirit than of the flesh."[21] Couser criticizes "the hegemonic narrative paradigm of transcendence over bodily injury" because it fails to criticize the cultural construction of illness, and he sees in this type of autobiography "a male pattern of concern with individual autonomy and freedom."[22] Price's *A Whole New Life,* he asserts, "inscribes the individual model of disability insofar as his emphasis is on overcoming his impairment—the way his injury affects his ego and his work—rather than with battling disability—marginalization in an 'ableist' society."[23]

I don't agree with Couser's claim that the conversion paradigm's supposed individualism is necessarily opposed to social criticism and solidarity with others. Traditionally, Christian conversion required the believer to learn the language of a church and to narrate a personal story using the terms of this community. Converts were to criticize their former way of life as sinful and reject the continuing temptations of the world. Similarly, illness narratives often involve socialization into a "community" of ill persons and a social critique of the society that ostracizes them. Even in a modern illness narrative that primarily emphasizes the author's individual struggle to recover, the act of writing seeks solidarity with readers, both those who suffer from a similar adversity and those invited to understand, imagine, and empathize.

Because the conversion paradigm is adaptable to a wide range of normative positions and many different kinds of illness, I find it a compelling model for thinking about patients' responses to illness. Still, it should not be seen as the only valid model for ill persons reconfiguring their life story and self-conception. Styron's *Darkness Visible* suggests an alternative way of interpreting a recovery from illness. A well-known image from Dante's *Divine Comedy* evokes the onset of his depression:

> In the middle of the journey of our life
> I found myself in a dark wood,
> For I had lost the right path.

In the final paragraph of his narrative, Styron uses another passage from Dante's work to articulate his sense of his journey out of depression:

> For those who have dwelt in depression's dark wood, and known its inexplicable agony, their return from the abyss is not unlike the ascent of the poet, trudging upward and upward out of hell's black depths and at last emerging into what he saw as "the shining world." There, whoever has been restored to health has almost always been restored to the capacity for serenity and joy, and this may be indemnity enough for having endured the despair beyond despair.
> *E quind uscimmo a reveder le stelle.*
> And so we came forth, and once again beheld the stars.[24]

This passage suggests that a return to one's former way of existence, when that is possible, is enough to give meaning to life. Illness need not bring redemptive meaning or self-transformation, and the goal of recovery and return to ordinary life is for some persons as valuable as compensatory spiritual gains. Yet is the world, and one's return to ordinary life in it, ever the same after severe illness? His ordeal has changed Styron, and emergence from darkness into a world with both darkness and a vision of the stars is experienced as a blessing reminiscent of religious ecstasy. The ill person who returns to a familiar world may have learned to appreciate it with new gratitude and wonder. There is a remote analogy to religious conversion in every affirmation that positive insights have emerged through an experience of illness.

I do not want to make any one form of narrative normative for everyone writing about illness, and I worry about a Christian bias in my attraction to the conversion paradigm. Yet I find that model to be extraordinarily influential and adaptable in shaping illness narratives. Perhaps every illness narrative should be considered as a potential story of conversion, raising the question of how illness transformed the writer and led to a new apprehension of what is ultimate. In the doctor's story to be discussed in the final part of this paper, we will see that this hermeneutical lens raises important issues even when a dying patient does not undergo a conversion.

The Physician's Role

One of the most interesting and appealing themes in narrative ethics is the idea of the joint construction of narrative by doctor and patient. This theory recommends a more active and empathetic involvement of physicians, as they listen, encourage, suggest alternatives, and challenge patients in the process of remoralization. Anatole Broyard, who died of prostate cancer in 1990, called for such involvement in "The Patient Examines the Doctor." Broyard wanted "a doctor who is not only a talented physician, but a bit of a metaphysician, too. Someone who can treat body and soul."[25] Broyard's ideal doctor would resemble Oliver Sacks:

> I can imagine Dr. Sacks *entering* my condition, looking around at it from the inside like a kind landlord, with a tenant, trying to see how he could make the premises more livable. He would look around, holding me by the hand, and he would figure out what it feels like to be me. Then he would try to find certain advantages in the situation. He can turn disadvantages into advantages. Dr. Sacks would see the *genius* of my illness. He would mingle his daemon with mine. We would wrestle with my fate together.[26]

But Broyard never finds such a doctor. And the autobiographies that seem to me most insightful about illness show a very limited role for physicians. For instance, Styron asserts that "while I would never question the potential efficacy of psychotherapy in the beginning manifestations or milder forms of the illness—or possibly even in the aftermath of a serious onslaught—its usefulness at the advanced stage I was in has to be virtually nil."[27]

Styron, Frank, Mairs, and Price all criticize insensitive physicians who aggravate their feelings of anxiety and aloneness. They do have positive interactions with doctors, and Price is emphatic in acknowledging gratitude for a doctor's personal involvement and support. But while all of them appreciate the felt concern of medical practitioners, they get very little if any specific guidance from them as to the content or form of their reconstructed life. Arthur Frank even warns fellow patients against expecting much in this way from doctors:

> After five years of dealing with medical professionals in the context of critical illness, as opposed to the routine problems I had had before, I have accepted their limits, even if I have never become comfortable with them. Perhaps medicine should reform itself and learn to share illness talk with patients instead of imposing disease talk on them. Or perhaps physicians and nurses should simply do what they already do well—treat the breakdowns—and not claim to do more. This book will not resolve that question. What I offer ill persons is more immediate. Recognize that more is happening to you than you can discuss with most physicians in most medical settings. To talk about illness you must go elsewhere.[28]

It is not surprising that these insightful, articulate, resourceful individuals do not rely much on medical professionals to compose their narratives. Most persons may be more willing to follow a doctor's suggestions in considering new ways to think about life in the wake of accident or disease. It is worth examining more closely the roles that physicians may play as patients rework their life stories. Let us look at the patient-physician interaction from the other side, asking what is revealed in autobiographical reflections by doctors.

A DOCTOR'S STORY

I have formulated three issues about the moral status of autobiographies, examining the extent to which autobiographers are representative of other patients, the conversion paradigm as the normative model for illness narratives, and the physician's role in the process of reconstructing a life story. I would expect physicians to raise a number of skeptical questions about the proposal that a significant part of their role should be to assist patients in constructing new life narratives. Does this theory confuse the distinct skills and roles of doctors with those of psychological counselors and therapists? Does it recognize the institutional constraints on physicians, such as the increasing demands on their time required by managed care health systems? Does an emphasis on the joint construction of narrative sufficiently respect patients' autonomy by recognizing that healing narratives should emerge primarily from patients' own efforts? Does the theory acknowledge the pluralism of values in contemporary society that often makes physicians' values very different from those of their patients? As a theory of professional ethics, does this approach overly exalt doctors' role, ignoring the dangers of domination or subtle manipulation? Do we want physicians to be a source of moral guidance for their patients, or is their ethical attention better focused on conscientious performance of strictly medical duties?

These questions do not undermine the value of a narrative approach to bioethics, but rather present important considerations involved in realizing its ideals in practice. At just this point—the translation of ideals into practice—autobiography may again prove instructive. Narratives about a physician's interaction with patients show both the potential for positive influence and the limitations of this relationship.

Of many illuminating recent autobiographies by physicians, I will focus on a compelling story by Jerome Groopman, a cancer specialist at Harvard's Beth Israel Deaconess Medical Center. The story of his encounter with "Kirk" is the first chapter of Groopman's *The Measure of Our Days*.[29] Kirk Bains (not his real name), a fifty-four-year-old Wall Street investor, comes to Groopman as his last hope after three other clinics have assessed his cancer as too far advanced for treatment. The clinical diagnosis: "Diffusely metastatic renal carcinoma. Multiple sites including liver, bones, and lungs involved. No effective therapy. Palliative care advised" (8). Groopman's initial response to this patient prior to the physical examination seems to me to model the empathy and communicative interaction advocated by narrative ethics:

> Even if I discovered no new fact or physical finding, there was a journey taken when I listened to a patient recount his history and when I palpated his body. It was a journey of the senses—hearing, touching, seeing—which carried me into another dimension, that of intuition.
>
> I planned to walk deliberately along the milestones of Kirk's life—the character of his parents and his siblings, the extent of his education, the nature of his occupation, the details of his travel, the status of his personal relationships, the vicissitudes of his prior and current illnesses and treatments—and for brief but illuminating moments I would become integrated into his experience (8–9).

Kirk responds to this encounter by interpreting it as he does everything in life, as an opportunity to take risks, to speculate, and to beat the odds. Kirk directed an independent investment company that specialized in international venture capital and commodities trading. Now he views his cancer as a chance once again to defy prudent common sense, to gamble, and to emerge a winner. Groopman thinks Kirk's remaining life span is probably only a few weeks. But there is a tiny chance that a highly experimental treatment might help him. Groopman devises a treatment schedule alternating three drugs that have never been mixed before: interleuken-2, vinblastine, and progesterone. He informs Kirk about the considerable risks involved, worrying about whether his patient can soberly assess them. Kirk's response reveals his consistent attitude to life: "Jerry, I'm a damn successful venture capitalist. And I know what a lousy investment I am. The time on my mortgage is almost up. I have no inventory left. And this fucking cancer is taking my market share, meaning my life" (21). Terrified of dying, Kirk commits himself to the treatment as his "last deal," his final gamble. He eagerly agrees to be "a guinea pig" in the clinical experiment: "I'll surprise you. There'll be a tenfold return on your investment" (27).

In a crucial passage, Groopman observes that patients often have a central metaphor with which they interpret their situation, and that Kirk's investment metaphor may prove useful in the struggle against cancer:

> When I care for a patient, I have noticed, a metaphor sometimes emerges that draws on a unique element in the patient's work or family or cultural heritage. Throughout the relationship, when we assess an option or embark upon it, when it succeeds or fails, when we enter

remission and resume living or acknowledge that our therapy has not succeeded and that the end is near—at each critical point, we invoke our metaphor. It becomes our intimate form of communication, drawing us closer, like children who invent a secret language, or siblings with special words and phrases that have resonance for them and no one else.

Kirk and I had created our metaphor after only two days, and I believed at this moment that it was a good one for his condition. He would gain strength from returning to the images that had spelled success in his life. He could again be the triumphant contrarian, betting against the market's prevailing wisdom, and proving to the world that the commodity of his life had a future (27).

Notice that Groopman tries to work with Kirk's metaphor in spite of his sense of its limitations. Asking Kirk about his religious faith, he learns that, although a nominal Episcopalian, Kirk has little commitment, for he "can't put much stock in a church founded because Henry VIII wanted a younger wife" (14). Another financial metaphor expresses Kirk's view of what lies beyond this life: "I'm not a long-term investor. I like quick returns. I don't believe in working for dividends paid only in Heaven" (14–15). Kirk sees everything in life as a matter of returns on investment; he has no commitment to what he buys: "For me, the product means nothing. It can be oil or platinum or software or widgets. It's all a shell game played for big money, and once I win enough I wave goodbye" (15).

Groopman's way of describing Kirk suggests his detachment from, and perhaps distaste for, Kirk's dominant metaphor. The doctor's involvement with Kirk elicits reflections on his own view of death and an afterlife, which are based on his father's Jewish belief that, although there is no heaven or hell, personal "existence is perpetuated in the hearts and minds of the people who remember those who are gone" (25). But Groopman doesn't try to convert his patient to a new story, or even encourage Kirk's halfhearted religious beliefs. He works with Kirk's financial metaphor, as if the ultimate truthfulness of a metaphor is less relevant at this point than whether it motivates and gives hope to a patient. The question of how to instill hope is at the heart of this story, as Groopman's experimental treatment offers Kirk an alternative to "another rejection, an exile into hopelessness and certain death" (20). What will give hope, make a patient want to live, animate his sense of vitality, his *bios?*

The rest of the story interprets the course of Kirk's treatment using his metaphor of speculative investment, as when doctor and patient, noticing a positive response, "sense a drift in the market" and "up the leverage" by increasing the dosage. Yet after his initial elation about his recovery, Kirk seems strangely depressed. The information in the financial papers no longer seems to him important. Finally his tumors recur and his prognosis is hopeless. In their last conversations, Kirk confesses that he sees "no reason to live, anyway." He realizes that he never really cared about or was committed to anything:

> "I was a short-term investor. Like I told you, Jerry, I had no patience for the long term. I had no interest in creating something—not a product in business or a partnership with a person. And now I have no equity. No dividends coming in. Nothing to show in my portfolio." Kirk grimaced in pain. "How do you like my great epiphany? No voice of God or holy star but a newspaper left unread in its wrapper" (36–37).

Groopman tries to get Kirk to see that he might still reach out to his family and friends. Facing his doomed patient, Groopman expresses his own faith in the continuing influence of our lives on the memories of those who survive us. Kirk could still make a difference to them with his words. But Kirk believes that it is too late, that there is no point in telling his family what they already know: "that I was a self-absorbed, uncaring shit." He dies soon after this conversation, and in the last paragraph of the story, Groopman offers a prayer and a eulogy:

> After Cathy's call I put aside the paperwork on my desk and took a moment to offer a prayer, as I always do when a patient of mine dies. I prayed that, before his passing, Kirk's soul had found some comfort, and that if there is a beyond it would be at peace. Then I composed in my mind a eulogy—addressed, as eulogies are, to the living. The words I chose were not from a holy text but from Kierkegaard: "It is perfectly true, as philosophers say, that life must be understood backward. But they forget the other proposition, that it must be lived forward" (38).

This powerful story concisely discloses how one physician's sense of *bios* affects his practice of medicine, and how a patient's *bios* affects his illness. Groopman witnesses a person struggling to recognize three failures: the failures of a course of medical treatment, of a metaphor for human life, and of the meaning of a life. Kirk admits that he has lived the wrong way. From our perspective, that is partly because he was captivated by an inadequate metaphor for life. To see every occasion as a chance for a quick profit does not allow for the care, concern, and commitment that make life meaningful. Kirk's *bios* is impoverished because he is isolated from other persons, from long-term engagements, from community, from a direction or purpose beyond making money, and from a sense of the sacred. By contrast, Groopman's own *bios*, although it remains in the background in his interactions with Kirk, is revealed in the way he narrates the story and reveals substantial commitments to his work, human relationships, and a religious context.

The situation of doctor and patient in this story is very different from those depicted in the illness narratives by Frank, Mairs, Styron, and Price. Groopman has deep convictions about the meaning of life and great sensitivity to the role of metaphor and narrative in human experience, above all in the healing process. Yet the doctor's wisdom and narrative skills do not help Kirk reconstruct his story or rebuild his life. Groopman's patient fails to make a narrative conversion.

Part of this story's power is the way that it expresses its author's sense of the individuality and mystery of each person's metaphors. As he deals with his patients, Groopman is highly conscious of the limitations of his own sense of the meaning of life and of the metaphors by which it is expressed. Rather than a jointly constructed narrative, this story depicts at least three distinct narratives that do not converge: Kirk's investment/gambling metaphor, the "disinterested clinical syntax" of the official medical record, and Groopman's own metaphors, which express his rich sense of *bios* and cannot be captured in a phrase. In their final conversations, he suggests to Kirk that there are other possible ways to understand his life, even as he recognizes that Kirk's identity limits his ability to transform his life story by finding a new metaphor to reinterpret it.

In a strange way, Kirk's failure emerges as a muted victory for both patient and doctor. By recognizing the moral bankruptcy of his life (to continue his metaphor), Kirk finally achieved an honest and insightful assessment of it. The relationship between Groopman and Kirk reminds us of Marlow's affirmation in Conrad's *Heart of Darkness* that Kurtz's final words—"The horror! The horror!"—represented "a moral victory."[30] Groopman discerns in Kirk's dying a lesson for the living. Kirk could not see that his memory might have helped to guide others and that this form of survival beyond death could be enough to give one's final days meaning. This, I take it, is part of the significance of the eulogy from Kierkegaard. Understanding Kirk's life story "backward," retrospectively, should help us— author and readers—in our living "forward." The doctor's witness to his patient's failed narrative reconstruction enriches his readers' sense of *bios* by making us think about our own dominant metaphors and about how we would confront illness and death.

Thus this autobiographical narrative contrasts with the patients' illness narratives in regard to the three issues I raised. It shows not a "best-case scenario" but in some ways a "worst-case scenario": not recovery but death, and not a conversion to a better narrative, but a patient's despair about his inadequate metaphor for life, with no embrace of an alternative metaphor. The physician is not able to midwife a new narrative but feels deep compassion for his patient's suffering even as he shares Kirk's final judgment that to view one's life as a series of business ventures is inadequate. Groopman both accepts and grieves for Kirk's inability to reinterpret his life or create a better metaphor for it. Yet in spite of its divergence from the patients' illness narratives we examined earlier, Groopman's account confirms several aspects of recent narrative ethics, demonstrating many of the virtues most of us would want in a doctor, in particular those related to understanding the role of metaphor and narrative in human life. It shows a doctor cautiously encouraging a patient to make a kind of conversion, yet respectful of Kirk's character and choices.

We already expect a great deal—probably too much—from doctors. Narrative ethics demands still more. Should we settle for less? A theory of medical ethics must both point toward an ideal and recognize the constraints of practice and human finitude. In both of these endeavors, bioethics can draw on insights that I think are best conveyed in autobiography.

We hope physicians will have, in addition to a great deal of technical knowledge, the capacities for imagination, understanding, communication, and compassion that are conveyed in Groopman's *The Measure of Our Days*. Our understanding of these virtues and our commitment to them can be nurtured through reading as we experience the sense of *bios* conveyed in illness narratives by patients and in physicians' accounts of their medical practice. Reading first-person accounts of illness can play a crucial role in developing the moral qualities that we will all need as we face illness in ourselves and in those we care for, whether professionally or because of personal relationships. Autobiography enriches our understanding of the sense of life of ill persons and their caregivers, and of the ways patient and doctor can transform and enrich each other's lives as their stories intertwine.

3

ADEQUATE IMAGES
AND EVIL IMAGINATIONS

Ethnography, Ethics, and the End of Life

PAUL LAURITZEN

In the spring of 1940, John Steinbeck embarked on a six-week expedition in the Gulf of California with his longtime friend and biologist Edward Ricketts. In describing the origins of this expedition in the book that grew out of the trip, Steinbeck and Ricketts offer the simple explanation that they undertook the trip because they were curious about marine life in the Gulf, and they wondered what might come from observing it together. They had little doubt that each would see a different reality, as the following passage attests:

> The Mexican sierra has "XVII-15-IX" spines in the dorsal fin. These can easily be counted. But if the sierra strikes hard on the line so that our hands are burned, if the fish sounds and nearly escapes and finally comes in over the rail, his colors pulsing and his tale beating the air, a whole new relational externality has come into being—an entity which is more than the sum of the fish plus the fisherman. The only way to count the spines of the sierra unaffected by this second relational reality is to sit in a laboratory, open an evil-smelling jar, remove a stiff colorless fish from formalin solution, count the spines, and write the truth "D.XVII-15-IX." There you have recorded a reality which cannot be assailed—probably the least important reality concerning either the fish or yourself.[1]

I begin with Steinbeck's remarks because this chapter will explore the importance of ethnography (broadly construed) for ethics, and I take this passage to show the mistake of abstracting from experience, even as it shows that we cannot avoid abstracting from experience in an effort to understand it.

One appeal of ethnographic work in ethics is evident in the contrast Steinbeck seeks to draw in this passage. On the one hand, we have conjured for us the specter of the dutiful scientist, as pale and lifeless as the fish he studies, counting spines and recording a truth that has no relation to any lived reality. On the other hand, we have the imagined fisherman and the immediacy of his experience: the smell of the salt water, the sweat on his brow as he fights to land the fish, the flailing fish fighting to be free and to live. In short, we have a stark contrast: a detached lifelessness or an engaged and abundant fullness of life. Even the structure of the paragraph reflects this choice. We have the sparse and anemic sentences that begin the paragraph and set out the detached reality of the scientist, followed by the forceful and full sentences that describe the reality of the fisherman.

In contrasting lifeless theory with concrete reality, Steinbeck could be speaking for any number of critics of contemporary moral philosophy who have complained about what H. A. Prichard once gently described as the "comparative remoteness of the discussions of moral philosophy from the facts of actual life."[2] This complaint, of course, has taken a variety of forms and has often been made far less gently. Following Carol Gilligan, many feminist writers have argued that moral philosophy is too abstract; that in focusing on justice, philosophers have neglected care; that in emphasizing justice at the expense of care, philosophers have not attended to the concrete lives of actual moral agents. Bernard Williams, Alasdair MacIntyre, and Charles Taylor have all questioned modern moral philosophy's preoccupation with impartiality and the picture of the self it appears to require.

In the spirit of Steinbeck, we might say that the critics' complaint is that reaching a moral decision is a whole lot more like feeling a line burning your hand than it is like counting dorsal spines in a lab. So I invoke Steinbeck at the start because I believe with him that the quest for objectivity can distort, or indeed eclipse altogether, the truth to be found in reality as it is lived, and because he draws the contrast between attention to lived experience and what might be called laboratory experience with such rhetorical force. Attending to lived experience, in my view, is crucial to ethics. It follows that ethnographical work of the sort that this volume contains and promotes is central.

There is, however, another reason for beginning with this passage, and it has to do with the unstated lesson to be taken from Steinbeck's remarks. I have already noted the way in which the paragraph itself appears structured to reinforce Steinbeck's point, as if the "But" that begins the third sentence signals, like the fish's first hard tug on the line, the imminent plunge into the depths of the paragraph, where we find a highly colorful, richly textured rendering of the fisherman's experience, an account by contrast to which the opening sentences are clearly meant to appear limp and lifeless. Notice, however, that in the middle of this sentence that calls us to the celebration of the concrete, in the middle of a description that, in its detail, renders the fisherman's experience almost palpable, we also find talk about "a whole new relational externality." What are we to make of this unlikely marriage of concreteness and abstraction? How are we to account for the apparent contradiction? The answer, it seems to me, is that Steinbeck here (perhaps unwittingly) undermines the very choice he appears to frame for us: either abstraction or experience. Indeed, in the very positing of the experience he attempts to make sense of it, and he does so, quite properly, by trying to get some distance on it. And this is the second lesson we must take away from this passage: Any ethnographic work in ethics must be a critical ethnography. We cannot accept the appeal to experience as self-verifying; we must develop criteria for assessing ethnographic work in ethics.

That brings me to a second passage that helps frame this chapter. Taken from H. Richard Niebuhr's *The Meaning of Revelation*, it is in some respects strikingly similar to the passage from Steinbeck. In a section entitled "History as Lived and as Seen," Niebuhr writes,

> Of a man who has been blind and who has come to see, two histories can be written. A scientific case history will describe what happened to his optic nerve or to the crystalline lens, what technique the surgeon used or by what medicines a physician wrought the cure, through what stages of recovery the patient passed. An autobiography, on the other hand, may barely mention these things but it will tell what happened to a self that had lived in darkness and now saw again trees and the sunrise, children's faces and the eyes of a friend.[3]

Whether we draw the contrast Niebuhr delineates here as that between history as lived and history as seen, as the title of this section of *The Meaning of Revelation* does, or (as Niebuhr does elsewhere in the volume) as the *difference* between the inner history of selves and the outer history of things, or again as the difference between internal and external history, the point is the same. There is a truth that is missed if we abstract from the lived experience of an individual life. This conviction Niebuhr appears to share with Steinbeck. But at least two further points, implicit in this passage, take Niebuhr beyond Steinbeck. First, according to Niebuhr, there must be a test of what he calls the "dramatic" truth of internal history. Second, that test is to be found in a community.

With these two suggestive passages as my point of departure, I turn to consider an issue that has received enormous attention of late and has generated a substantial body of ethnographic data—physician-assisted suicide (PAS). Following Steinbeck and Niebuhr, I want to insist on the importance of attending to the stories of dying patients as we reflect on the morality of PAS and active euthanasia.

And perhaps in no other area of recent moral debate has there been such a wealth of ethnographic materials on which to draw. Stories of dying patients, told by physicians, families, and friends have been pervasive in the public debate, even finding their way into the usually staid and discursive legal decisions in this area. Yet, as important as these stories are, we must acknowledge with Anne Hunsaker Hawkins that

> the narrative description of illness is both less and more than the actual experience: less, in that remembering and writing are selective processes—certain facts are dropped because they are forgotten or because they do not fit the author's narrative design; and more, in that the act of committing experience to narrative form inevitably confers upon it a particular sequence of events and endows it with a significance that was probably only latent in the original experience.[4]

So we have no choice but to evaluate the stories of death and dying that fuel the debate about PAS. Nor can we avoid the need to abstract from the particularities of the stories, as Steinbeck intuitively perceived. To appropriate the stories of death and dying in a morally useful way, we must engage in critical ethnography; we must move dialectically between the detailed stories and the theoretical accounts that frame the moral debate on assisted suicide. Unfortunately, we do not have much practice moving between the abstract and the concrete. In debates about euthanasia, we are uncertain how to move between what John Arras has called the conceptual skirmishes about PAS and the personal battles with death and dying so frequently found in the stories of terminally ill patients.[5] And there are clearly dangers here. As Yale Kamisar writes, "we should not let a compelling individual case blot out more general considerations." [6]

But how do we assure that general considerations do not blind us to the truths to be found in individual cases? In an effort to answer that question, I want to look at both the conceptual skirmishes and the personal battles. I will suggest that it is possible to move between the theoretical arguments and the ethnographic material in a way that illuminates both.

Although it may sometimes be best to begin with the concrete and particular and move to the abstract and general, I follow the reverse course here. In the first section of the paper, I discuss one of the central theoretical notions that frames the debate about assisted suicide: the distinction between killing and letting die. The question of whether there is a morally relevant difference or a rationally defensible distinction between killing and letting die is one of, if not the, most fundamental issue in the debate. As I will try to show, it is certainly the central issue in the recent court cases on the topic.

There is no paucity of theoretical material on this issue. Although no adequate treatment of this question can fail to take account of this literature, we must also ask whether there is something to be learned from the stories of dying patients. Thus, in the second section of the chapter I ask what light is shed on this theoretical question by the stories of dying patients and their families. In asking that question, I turn to two of the better-known advocates in this debate, Dr. Timothy Quill and Dr. Ira Byock. Although the ethnographic literature on death and dying is voluminous, I chose to focus on stories narrated by Quill and Byock because both are well-known, well-respected, and fair. They also disagree about the appropriateness of PAS. Juxtaposing Quill's book of stories of dying patients, *A Midwife Through the Dying Process,* with Byock's *Dying Well* offers a particularly rich set of ethnographic material on which to draw. If any stories are to be morally useful to the debate about PAS, it is likely to be those collected by Quill and Byock. Indeed, I will suggest that the stories confirm the validity of the distinction between killing and letting die.

THE THEORETICAL DEBATE

To understand current debates about physician-assisted suicide and active euthanasia, it is necessary to recall some of the history of moral and legal reasoning in this area. Although there has been debate about euthanasia in this country since at least the 1950s, most commentators point to the case of Karen Ann Quinlan as the first significant euthanasia case. Karen Quinlan was a twenty-one-year-old woman who lapsed into a persistent vegetative state in 1975. In the judgment of her doctors, there was no hope of recovery, but because she was hooked up to a respirator, she might continue to live in this vegetative state for many years. Perceiving the respirator as a form of futile treatment, her family sought to have the respirator removed so that she could be allowed to die. The case ultimately went to the New Jersey Supreme Court, which found that there is a fundamental difference between active euthanasia and withdrawing life support. In the words of the court, there is a "real distinction between the self-infliction of deadly harm and a self-determination against artificial life support."[7] The court thus ordered that the family could remove their daughter from the respirator.

By insisting on distinguishing between withdrawing treatment and actively killing, the New Jersey court drew attention to and reinforced a distinction between killing and letting die that has long served as the cornerstone of public policy. For nearly twenty-five years now, there has been a moral and legal consensus in this country that physicians may either withdraw life-sustaining treatment or not start such treatment, if the patient so desires. Sometimes referred to as passive euthanasia, the practice of forgoing life-sustaining treatment is accepted by the American Medical Association, by many religious groups, and by the law in every state. By contrast, active euthanasia has generally been condemned as unjustifiable killing.

The distinction between active and passive euthanasia, of course, has always been fiercely debated, as has the distinction between killing and letting die on which the active-passive contrast appears to rest. As early as 1975, James Rachels raised serious reservations about both distinctions in what was to become a classic essay in the debate over euthanasia,[8] and there has been a nearly steady stream of such articles ever since. Nevertheless, until quite recently both the distinction between killing and letting die and that between active and passive euthanasia were widely accepted both at law and in the popular imagination. Suddenly, however, the consensus that there is a fundamental moral and legal difference between killing and letting die seems to be disintegrating. Why?

The answer to this question can be seen by attending to the most famous euthanasia case in recent years, that of Nancy Cruzan. Nancy Cruzan was a twenty-five-year-old Missouri woman who was left in a persistent vegetative state as a result of injuries sustained in a car crash. Although irreversibly comatose, she was able to breathe on her own, and the only medical treatment she received was the delivery of nutrition and hydration through a feeding tube. Five years after the accident, the family sought to withdraw the feeding tube on the grounds that the patient herself had indicated that she would not want to continue existence if she were irreversibly comatose. Missouri fought the family's efforts to have the feeding tube removed, and the case ultimately ended up before the U.S. Supreme Court.

In a landmark decision, the Supreme Court inferred from past decisions that individuals have a constitutionally protected right to bodily integrity, which extends to the decision to refuse medical treatment, even treatment that is life-sustaining.[9] Moreover, they stated that a feeding tube was medical treatment, no different in kind from a respirator. Given the fact that the feeding tube is surgically placed, requires monitoring, and is considered treatment by the American Medical Association, this conclusion was certainly reasonable.

Thinking of the feeding tube as medical treatment, however, blurs the distinction between active and passive euthanasia. Given the social consensus about passive euthanasia noted above, withdrawing the feeding tube would be perfectly acceptable, for withdrawing the feeding tube is stopping treatment. Notice, however, that stopping treatment in this case is not obviously like turning off a respirator. If you turn off a respirator, the patient may breathe on her own, as Karen Quinlan in fact did. Not so with a feeding tube; if the tube is removed, the patient will die. In its simplest terms, that is the problem: In some ways, removing a feeding tube is like turning off a respirator; in other ways, it is like giving a (slow) lethal injection. Yet, if removing a feeding tube is like giving a lethal injection, can we honestly say that in disconnecting it we merely "let nature take its course"? Is letting die really so different from killing after all?

That this has become the central question in recent debates about euthanasia and PAS is evident from the fact that supporters of assisted suicide and active euthanasia now frame their case almost exclusively in terms of this issue. Consider, for example, the most recent Supreme Court cases on euthanasia and assisted suicide. In June 1997, the court handed down decisions in two cases it had accepted on appeal from federal circuit courts. Although both circuit courts rejected the distinction between withdrawing medical treatment and assisted suicide, I focus primarily on the case from the Second Circuit because that court's ruling turns decisively on this issue.

The case before the Second Circuit involved an action brought by three physicians who sought to have a New York law prohibiting assisted suicide declared unconstitutional. Although I am not qualified to offer a technical explication of the constitutional complexities of the case, the core legal claim is fairly clear. The physicians argued that by preventing doctors from prescribing lethal medications to help their terminal patients die, New York was violating the constitutional principle that requires that similarly situated people must be treated alike. The physicians reasoned that the state currently allows doctors to hasten some patients' death by discontinuing treatment. So to allow physicians to help hasten death in one case and not the other was a violation of the equal protection clause of the Constitution. In short, the state was treating similar cases differently.

It should not be supposed that the question of whether the New York law prohibiting assisted suicide violates the equal protection clause of the Constitution is merely a narrow legal issue. It is also a philosophical, moral, and religious issue, and the philosophical/moral/religious issues clearly bear on the legal ones. In this case, for example, it is clear that the Court took the arguments of Dr. Timothy Quill very seriously in reaching its decision. Quill, who was a plaintiff in this case, is an outspoken supporter of assisted suicide. He is also, by all accounts, an extraordinarily caring physician who is also a strong advocate for the hospice movement and for better palliative care at the end of life. In his supplemental declaration to the court, Quill makes the case for assisted suicide, and the Court quotes his argument at length in its decision. Quill writes,

> The removal of a life support system that directly results in the patient's death requires the direct involvement by the doctor, as well as other medical personnel. When such patients are mentally competent, they are consciously choosing death as preferable to life under the circumstances that they are forced to live. Their doctors do a careful clinical assessment, including a full exploration of the patient's prognosis, mental competence to make such decisions, and the treat-

ment alternatives to stopping treatment. It is legally and ethically permitted for physicians to actively assist patients to die who are dependent on life-sustaining treatments. . . . Unfortunately, some dying patients who are in agony that can no longer be relieved, yet are not dependent on life-sustaining treatment, have no such options under current legal restrictions. It seems unfair, discriminatory, and inhumane to deprive some dying patients of such vital choices because of arbitrary elements of their condition which determine whether they are on life-sustaining treatment that can be stopped.[10]

Here we see the core moral/philosophical argument for assisted suicide. It can be formalized more or less as follows:

1. Since competent patients may decide to hasten their own deaths by deciding to forgo life-sustaining medical treatments; and
2. Since physicians may assist competent patients to hasten their deaths by discontinuing life-sustaining medical treatment; and
3. Since there is no morally relevant difference between (A) terminally ill patients receiving life-sustaining treatments and (B) terminally ill patients not receiving life-sustaining treatments;

It follows that:

4. Physicians should be able to assist terminally ill patients not receiving life-sustaining treatment (Group B) to hasten their deaths, just as they assist terminally ill patients receiving life-sustaining treatment (Group A) to hasten their deaths.

Notice that in characterizing the difference between Group A and Group B as arbitrary and insignificant, Quill is also implicitly denying the distinction between killing and letting die. And what Quill implicitly denies, the Second Circuit Court explicitly rejects. Accepting Quill's analysis, the court concludes that New York's law banning assisted suicide does violate the equal protection rights of patients who are terminally ill but not on life support. The court writes,

In view of the foregoing, it seems clear that New York does not treat similarly circumstanced persons alike: those in the final stages of terminal illness who are on life-support systems are allowed to hasten their deaths by directing the removal of such systems; but those who are similarly situated, except for the previous attachment of life-sustaining equipment, are not allowed to hasten death by self-administering prescribed drugs.[11]

In reaching this conclusion, the court clearly relies on Quill's analysis, particularly his claim that because doctors are actively involved in hastening death when life-sustaining treatment is discontinued there is little reason to oppose the active involvement of doctors in prescribing lethal medication. According to the court,

> the writing of a prescription to hasten death, after consultation with a patient, involves a far less active role for the physician than is required in bringing about death through asphyxiation, starvation and/or dehydration. Withdrawal of life support requires physicians or those acting at their direction physically to remove equipment, and, often, to administer palliative drugs which may themselves contribute to death. The ending of life by these means is nothing more nor less than assisted suicide.[12]

The court thus equates the withdrawal of life-sustaining treatment with assisted suicide because it concludes that there is little sense in talk about letting nature take its course. A death that results from respiratory failure after the withdrawal of a respirator, the court emphatically insists, "is not natural in any sense."

What is particularly interesting here is that although very significant legal questions are at issue in this case (for example, questions about the appropriate level of judicial scrutiny of state-drawn classifications of differing groups), the circuit court's ruling turns largely on a nonlegal issue, namely, whether helping to withdraw treatment is a form of assisted suicide. Indeed, Chief Justice Rehnquist, writing for the Court, says exactly that in the U.S. Supreme Court decision in this case. The circuit court's conclusion that New York law treats similarly situated people differently, Rehnquist writes, "depends on the submission that ending or refusing lifesaving medical treatment 'is nothing more nor less than assisted suicide.' "[13] Unlike the Court of Appeals, however, the Supreme Court rejects the equation of treatment withdrawal and assisted suicide. According to the Court, there are many reasons for reaffirming the distinction between treatment withdrawal and assisted suicide, including the fact that the distinction is widely recognized and endorsed in the medical profession and in law and that it accords with traditional legal principles of causation and intent.

Perhaps more important, however, is the fact that the Supreme Court had already implicitly endorsed the distinction between killing and letting die in the Cruzan case. Chief Justice Rehnquist highlights this point in bringing the decision to a close. "This Court," writes Rehnquist,

> has also recognized, at least implicitly, the distinction between letting a patient die and making that patient die. In Cruzan v. Director, Mo. Dept. of Health, we concluded that "[t]he principle that a competent person has a constitutionally protected liberty interest in refusing

unwanted medical treatment may be inferred from our prior decisions," and we assumed the existence of such a right for purposes of that case. But our assumption of a right to refuse treatment was grounded not, as the Court of Appeals supposed, on the proposition that patients have a general and abstract "right to hasten death," but on well established, traditional rights to bodily integrity and freedom from unwanted touching. . . . Cruzan therefore provides no support for the notion that refusing life-sustaining medical treatment is "nothing more nor less than suicide."[14]

What divides these two courts is precisely what divides supporters and opponents of position assisted suicide generally. Supporters of PAS see very little difference between helping dying patients hasten their deaths by removing life-sustaining treatment and writing a prescription for medication by which they can take their own lives. For supporters, helping a patient stop life-sustaining treatment is in fact nothing more nor less than assisted suicide. To say that the former is allowing to die and the latter is killing is, to supporters of PAS, to invoke a distinction without a (moral) difference. By contrast, opponents of PAS insist that although the two actions are similar, helping to remove treatment is not the same as helping to die. For opponents, although the line between killing and letting die is sometimes razor thin, it nevertheless marks a genuine difference and is a line worth maintaining.

THE APPEAL TO EXPERIENCE

As the disagreement between the Circuit Court and the Supreme Court attests, people can disagree about whether refusing medical treatment is nothing more nor less than suicide. And the courts' disagreement here tracks the deep divide in the philosophical and theological literature on the significance of this distinction. Indeed, the disagreement is so long-standing and the arguments on both sides are by now so well known, that there seems to be little hope of progress if we restrict our attention to the philosophical and theological debate alone.

For that reason, I want to broaden the discussion to include some ethnographic data on PAS. In particular, I want to focus on two works that provide a rich experiential base for thinking about the distinction between stopping treatment and assisting a suicide. The first is Dr. Timothy Quill's book, *A Midwife Through the Dying Process: Stories of Healing and Hard Choices at the End of Life.*[15] The second is Dr. Ira Byock's, *Dying Well: Peace and Possibilities at the End of Life.*[16]

Although Quill supports PAS and Byock does not, there are a number of striking similarities between these authors and their works. First, both are caring physicians (and keen observers) who have worked with dying patients for many years; both have extensive experience with hospice care. Second, both insist on the importance of storytelling to understanding end-of-life issues and to assessing the morality of assisted suicide. According to Quill, "the best way to get beneath the surface of the personal and ethical challenges of dying is through real-life patient narratives." For Byock, "stories are the only satisfying way I know of explaining the paradox that people can become stronger and more whole as physical weakness becomes overwhelming and life itself wanes." Third, both insist that we need much better palliative care than we currently have in this country. Despite these similarities, however, Quill and Byock draw different conclusions from their experiences working with dying patients; pairing Quill and Byock promises to be instructive.

A Midwife Through the Dying Process tells the story of nine patients for whom Quill cared during their dying. As Quill indicates in the preface, friends and families helped him in telling these stories, for some of those who knew these patients were willing to provide details of the patients' lives unknown to Quill and to read and comment on drafts of Quill's work. With their cooperation and based on his long-term relationships with the majority of these patients, Quill is able to provide a richly textured rendering of his patients' lives and deaths. Moreover, because he has chosen a diverse group of patients who suffered from a wide variety of diseases, Quill is able to offer an impressive array of experiences.

Quill argues that although pain can be controlled in the vast majority of cases—perhaps 98 percent of the time—there are inevitably cases where pain cannot be controlled or where other intractable problems arise. Because the problems associated with pain or its treatment can be so vexing, Quill insists that it is not enough for physicians to assure their patients that they will not die alone or in pain. The promise that physicians must make to their dying patients, Quill says, "should have three parts: 'You won't die alone, you won't die in pain, and we will struggle together to face whatever has to be faced.' "[17] If physicians would only make this pledge to their patients, the enormous fear many patients experience with a terminal illness would be greatly lessened.

The problem with making this commitment, however, is that honoring the third part of the promise may well require physicians to assist in a patient's suicide. Although Quill makes it clear that assisting in a suicide should be a rare occurrence, physicians' unwillingness to help a patient die in this way means that they may not be able to keep the third part of their commitment to the patient. For Quill, this failure is tantamount to abandoning the patient. Unfortunately, he says, both the law and the ethos of traditional medicine work to encourage physicians to abandon patients just when they most need their physicians' support. Quill writes,

The absence of this commitment is part of our core problem in the care of the dying. Many dying patients do not feel that they can count on their doctors to be responsive when and if they begin to live out their worst nightmare, especially if it falls outside of rigidly prescribed legal and ethical boundaries. As the stories in this book illustrate, the complex realities of dying patients rarely remain entirely within these confines.[18]

As evidence for this claim, Quill cites the story of Jane Smith. Jane Smith was one of the six patients described in his book with whom Quill had a long-term relationship. Quill met Jane Smith early in his medical career and had worked with her over many years treating the asthma and emphysema that ultimately threatened her life. After many years, her breathing had deteriorated so dramatically that she required high-dose corticosteroids and constant oxygen to live. Although she had no wish to die, neither did she want to continue living in her diminished condition. And Quill is quite clear about the level of diminishment. "The steroids," he writes,

> were associated with all the predictable complications, including worsening hypertension, significant weight gain, edema in her legs, and diabetes mellitus. She lost her voice from the constant coughing, and she became fatigued and short of breath with minimal activity. . . . Her list of medications now numbered fifteen, totaling more than sixty doses each day. . . . She had developed pulmonary hypertension, and the right side of her heart was failing. She had to sleep sitting up, the veins in her neck were distended, and fluid was accumulating in her legs.[19]

Given her medical condition, how could Quill keep his three-part promise?

One answer, of course, is that he could certainly help her if she chose not to accept treatment. For example, at some point, she was going to need to be on a ventilator. If she chose not to go on the ventilator, then Quill could certainly help to facilitate that request and he could certainly give her morphine to ease the feeling of suffocation. And in fact he did help her to complete a DNR (Do Not Resuscitate) order, and he agreed to give her morphine if needed.

But she did not want to die slowly from asphyxiation in the hospital, and she did not want to risk ending up in the hospital at a time when Dr. Quill might be out of town and unavailable to help her. So she asked him for a prescription for Seconal, a barbiturate that can be used both to treat insomnia and to end a life. Although she asked him for the drug to treat her insomnia, it was clear to Quill that she planned to stockpile the drug in order to take an overdose. Once he was confident that she had thought carefully about her decision and understood the consequences, Quill prescribed the medication for her insomnia. Still, because the rigid legal and ethical boundaries prevented him from talking with her as openly and as honestly as he would have liked, and because these boundaries prevented him from being with her when she took the overdose of medication, Quill feels that he abandoned her.

Quill compares Jane Smith's death to that of another of his patients, Jules. Because Jules suffered from ALS—a degenerative nerve disease that ultimately deprives the patient of the ability to breathe on his own—and because he was respirator-dependent and no longer wanted to be, he was given heavy sedation, removed from a respirator, and allowed to die. "Unfortunately," Quill writes that

> because Jane did not have a life-sustaining treatment to discontinue, her act had to be carried out in secret. When things went wrong and it appeared that she might not have taken enough medicine to ensure her death, there was no doctor there to help her over the threshold. Her friends fulfilled their commitment to Jane, but their actions caused them considerable pain, undermining the love and caring that was otherwise demonstrated. I feel as if I abandoned Jane and her friends and that our years of partnership were severely compromised. Jane was allowed to maintain her integrity while completing her life story, but her friends and I remain haunted that she had to die with a plastic bag over her head. There is no place for such stark images in a humane system of caring for the dying.[20]

As the contrast between Jules and Jane is meant to signal, Quill believes that it is the distinctions between killing and letting die and between assisted suicide and withdrawing treatment that force such stark images on us. For Quill, the specific medical intervention that hastens death "is much less important than the process of caring, excellent palliative care, and joint decision making that precede it."[21] Because the traditional distinctions leave so little room for these considerations of care, relying on the distinctions to frame our moral and legal views of assisted suicide assures that the horrific spectacle of Jane Smith's death will be repeatedly reenacted.

Quill's experience with dying patients thus leads him to conclude that there really is no significant difference between allowing to die and killing, that what is important is that all medical interventions be directed to relieving the patient's suffering. The fact that one intervention involves removing a respirator and another involves a lethal injection is clinically meaningless and should be recognized as such by the law.

There is no disputing the forcefulness of Quill's case. The stories he tells provide powerful experiential support for those who have argued in far more abstract ways that there is little difference between killing and letting die. Before we assess Quill's argument, however, it is worth considering the other ethnographic work before us, Ira Byock's *Dying Well.*

Like Quill, Byock narrates the stories of his patients' lives and deaths, and like Quill, he uses the stories of individual patients to illustrate particular points he wishes to make in the ongoing debate about assisted suicide. Also like Quill, Byock insists on the importance of not painting either an overly pessimistic picture of palliative care or an overly romantic picture. Indeed, both Byock and Quill are remarkably fair in choosing stories that illustrate both peaceful deaths and extraordinarily difficult ones. And while Byock's narration is occasionally flawed by the inclusion of imagined dialogue or improbable detail, generally his account is both plausible and believable.

If there are these striking similarities between Byock and Quill, how then do they differ? One difference is particularly notable. Although Quill claims that pain is intractable in about 2 percent of cases, Byock emphatically insists that physical pain can always be alleviated. "With strong resolve from patient and doctor," Byock confidently writes, "relief of *physical* suffering is *always* possible."[22] Since Quill's argument for assisted suicide rests squarely on the need not to abandon patients when suffering is intractable, it is worth examining Byock's claim in some detail.

To see how Byock supports this claim, we need to look at one of his stories at some length. The story I have chosen is one of the most difficult in the book, the case of Michael Merseal, an eight-year-old boy with untreatable brain disease. Although the disease was similar to Fragile X syndrome, Michael's condition was not entirely consistent with this disorder. Although by the age of five Michael had learned to walk, speak a few words, and use the toilet, by age seven he had regressed to the mental age of a ten-month-old and was unable to feed himself or move around without help. By the time Dr. Byock became involved with his care, Michael's health was rapidly deteriorating. He had been hospitalized for persistent vomiting and choking, he was having frequent seizures, and he was often limp and listless. Because he was likely to die soon from complications of his neurological deterioration, and because his father, Mike, had already declined surgical interventions that he believed would only prolong the inevitable, Byock discussed the possibility of stopping Michael's tube feeding and fluids. In addition, Byock recommended lowering Michael's usual seizure medication and putting him on Versed, a fast-acting medication similar to Valium. Although large doses of Versed could suppress Michael's breathing and hasten his death, both Michael's father and Dr. Byock agreed that their first priority was eliminating the physical suffering brought on by the seizures.

To everyone's surprise, after Michael's fluid intake was significantly reduced and he was placed on around-the-clock Versed, his seizures stopped, and he emerged from the listless state into which his seizures had sent him. Suddenly and unexpectedly, his eyes began to track objects, he began to coo, and he was once again able to eat and drink without choking. Although Michael's recovery lasted for about five months, the seizures eventually returned, and he once again began to vomit frequently. In an effort to control Michael's suffering, Byock agreed to increase the Versed infusion and to provide bolus injections to be given at the onset of mild seizures in order to prevent major seizures from developing. Moreover, he offered to provide intravenous barbiturates, if the family wanted, and he agreed to stop the tube feeding as well. When Michael's father decided on this course of action, Byock sought and received the approval of his hospice's ethics committee, and Michael was given the sedation that allowed him peacefully to die.

There are several things to note about this case as we compare the respective positions of Quill and Byock on assisted suicide. First, although Byock acknowledges that Michael's case was agonizing and that both Michael and his family suffered a great deal, in the end, Byock would say that Michael's physical suffering was eliminated. To be sure, it took intravenous barbiturates to control the suffering, but from Byock's perspective the suffering was ultimately controlled. By contrast, Quill would almost certainly classify Michael's case as among the 2 percent of cases where pain is intractable. Indeed, Quill offers a similar case as evidence that physical suffering cannot always be eliminated, and it is instructive to consider this case.

Unlike most of the stories that Quill narrates, the case of Mr. Kline is one in which Quill became involved only toward the end of the patient's life. Mr. Kline was an eighty-year-old widower who suffered from lung cancer that had spread to his bones. By the time Quill became involved, Mr. Kline had developed severe pain in his neck. Although initially the pain was controlled with a combination of morphine and antidepressant medication, which also helped his neuropathic pain, eventually even round-the-clock morphine, antidepressants, antiseizure medication, and steroids failed to control the pain. With Mr. Kline's consent, Quill admitted the patient to the hospital and ordered the morphine infusion to be increased every thirty minutes with bolus doses in between, if necessary.

Unfortunately, although this regimen controlled the pain, it also induced paranoia and hallucinations that were resistant to changes in medication or treatment with tranquilizers or both. When the morphine was cut back, the hallucinations stopped, but the pain returned. With all other options exhausted, Quill approached the family about the possibility of using a barbiturate infusion to control the hallucinations. Although Mr. Kline would not be able to respond or to eat or drink in this condition, his pain and suffering would likely be controlled. The family accepted Dr. Quill's offer, Mr. Kline was sedated, and he died quietly five days later.

It is clear from Quill's commentary on this case that he does not consider this to be a case in which the medical team actually was able to control the patient's pain and suffering. And I think it is clear from Byock's discussion of Michael's case that he would likely treat Mr. Kline's situation as another agonizing case where extreme measures were needed, but where physical suffering was ultimately controlled. So although the initial disagreement between Quill and Byock—pain cannot always be controlled/pain can always be controlled—initially appeared irreconcilable, on closer inspection, the disagreement appears to be largely a matter of interpretation. Moreover, both agree that it is acceptable for physicians in rare cases to administer barbiturate sedation.

ASSESSING APPEALS TO EXPERIENCE

At the start of this chapter, I suggested both that in the absence of an experiential base theoretical debates about assisted suicide can distort the lived experience of death and dying and that any appeal to experience must itself be subject to critical scrutiny. I further suggested that reasoning on the basis of experiential narratives requires moving dialectically between detailed stories and theoretical accounts, making evaluations in both directions. At this point, we can see that one of the real merits of both Byock and Quill is that both move dialectically between the theoretical discussion on assisted suicide and their own experience in treating dying patients. For example, we can now see that Quill is offering an experientially based argument against the principle of double effect, which in turn is an argument against the distinction between killing and letting die.

We can see the form of Quill's argument by looking a bit more closely at the principle of double effect. Double effect is typically described in terms of four conditions:

1. The action performed must, at worst, be morally indifferent.
2. The evil effect of the action must not be the intended goal of the action.
3. The evil effect must not be the means by which the good effect is brought about.
4. The good effect and the evil effect must be roughly proportionate.

Quill's dispute with double effect is primarily with conditions 2 and 3 because these two conditions allow us to distinguish a) aiming at death when undertaking an action, from b) foreseeing that death will result from an action, but not aiming at death when undertaking that action. And it is precisely that distinction that Quill believes his experience with dying patients undermines.

Quill makes this point clear in his discussion of Mr. Kline. According to Quill, Mr. Kline's death forces us to ask whether death can really be said to be an unintended consequence when we give the barbiturate infusion or whether death can even be thought to be "bad" in such a case. Quill puts his point in very strong terms:

> Mr. Kline was treated with terminal sedation as a last resort to fulfill our promise that he would not die an agonizing death. He was put under the equivalent of general anesthesia and then "allowed to die" from dehydration. The difference between terminal sedation and euthanasia (when a lethal overdose is given at the terminally ill patient's request) is paper thin, requiring a highly intellectualized analysis and presentation of the physician's intentions. In both circumstances, the patient inevitably dies as result of the treatment. With terminal sedation, the wished-for death must be foreseen but not intended if it is to remain under the protective umbrella of the "double effect." The potential for self-deception in such justifications is substantial.[23]

So Quill's argument is that experience with patients like Mr. Kline undermines the very principle on which the distinction between killing and letting die is said to rest. However useful it may be in other contexts, or however useful it may have been to medicine in another era, the principle of double effect now interferes with the practice of compassionate medicine rather than supporting it. Attending to the experiences of physicians and their dying patients should thus lead us to jettison the principle of double effect and allow physicians to assist in suicides.

Is Quill's conclusion that double effect ought to be abandoned justified? Even though his experiential narratives are compelling, I do not think that Quill has made his case. But how exactly do we assess his case? How should we respond to Quill's argument, based as it is on the appeal to experience? There is no easy answer to this question, but let me suggest that just as we need to move between theory and experience, we need also to move dialectically between competing appeals to experience. And the caution we noted from Anne Hunsaker Hawkins's work that appeals to the experience of illness always have a storytelling quality is suggestive for how we might do that. I have argued elsewhere, for example, that the moral force of appeals to experience is in some ways like that of fictional literature, for they often function by engaging the reader's emotions and imagination, just as, say, a novel does. But if appeals to experience and fictional narratives share this similarity, then strategies for assessing fictional literature may be useful when evaluating appeals to experience.

Consider, for example, Wayne Booth's account of how we might begin to assess a literary narrative. According to Booth, we evaluate stories much as we evaluate persons. We evaluate in light of our past experiences with people (or books) that are like or unlike those in front of us. Thus our evaluations are always comparative. Our evaluations are also usually public, because we usually seek others' views and test our views against theirs. Indeed, says Booth, the comparative and public dimension of such reasoning suggests that evaluating a literary narrative is like what a judge does when she decides a case, for a judge must determine how the case before her is like or unlike previously settled cases, and then explain the similarities and differences in a public way.

Booth coins the term, "coduction," for this process of evaluation, and he describes it as follows:

> Coduction will be what we do whenever we say to the world (or prepare ourselves to say): "of the works of this general kind that I have experienced, comparing my experience with other more or less qualified observers, this one seems to me among the better, (or weaker) ones, or the best (or worst). Here are my reasons." Every such statement implicitly calls for continuing conversation: "How does my coduction compare with yours?"[24]

Booth's insistence that coduction is inescapably comparative reminds us that we cannot assess Quill's narratives in isolation from other narratives of this sort. Having Byock's narratives before us is thus enormously helpful to any assessment of Quill, just as having Quill's narratives would be helpful to any assessment of Byock. So how do the accounts of Byock and Quill stand up to the comparative process of coduction?

In my view, both stand up pretty well. Although it is not possible strictly to codify the process of coduction, we will certainly want to consider such matters as the narrator's attentiveness to the concrete details of the case, and his willingness to include the "inconvenient" facts of the case, his ability to elicit a compassionate response from the reader. In all these ways, Byock and Quill succeed. Nevertheless, I want to suggest that Byock offers us the better account of how to think about the theoretical distinctions in this debate in light of patient experiences with death and dying. Following Booth, then, I want to say that my coduction leads me to conclude that we ought to stand with Byock and against Quill in opposing physician-assisted suicide. Here are my reasons.

We can see the strength of Byock's account if we return briefly to consider Quill's core argument against double effect, namely, that it misconstrues physicians' actions when they allow a patient to die. That is the point of Quill's claim that in being given a barbiturate infusion Mr. Kline "was put under the equivalent of general anesthesia and then 'allowed to die' from dehydration." The reason Quill puts the quotes around "allowed to die" in this passage is that he believes that death is the intended consequence for Mr. Kline and so the principle of double effect obscures what is really going on. If we acknowledge the reality of Mr. Kline's death, Quill believes, we will have to admit that killing and letting die come to the same thing in this case.

Now compare what Byock says about a barbiturate infusion. Although Byock admits that sedating a patient with barbiturates is on the border of what is morally acceptable, there is, he says, a meaningful boundary between sedating a patient into unconsciousness to eliminate pain and suffering and suicide or active euthanasia. Why, Byock asks, is it suicide to decline food when one can no longer swallow or when hunger is a distant memory? For Byock, the most important consideration is that the patient is dying. And the consequence is that medical interventions may shift the course of an illness, but they will not halt it. Thus withdrawing a respirator or giving a barbiturate infusion and withdrawing a feeding tube are the same. To continue treatment in either case simply makes it more likely that the patient will die from one disease-related problem rather than another. Giving Michael Merseal sedation, for example, meant that he was more likely to die from dehydration than from seizures. Sedating Mr. Kline increased the likelihood of death by dehydration rather than death by, say, pneumonia. Byock puts the point this way:

> The family of a person who can no longer eat normally or communicate his desires often struggles with decisions about life-prolonging procedures such as surgery to place a tube for formula feeding. In deciding that a loved one will not be allowed to die of malnourishment, a family is making a tacit decision to let the person die of something else. Thus, the declaration by the daughter of an eighty-seven-year-old comatose patient, "I would never let Mom die of starvation," is a decision that Mom must, therefore, succumb to infection or stroke or seizure or blood clot or gastrointestinal hemorrhage. Each complication that is treated merely shifts the physiology of the person's dying, it does not halt it.[25]

Although Byock's discussion of barbiturate infusion does not directly respond to Quill's claim that double effect obscures the reality of the physician's intent in cases like Mr. Kline, it is important in at least reminding us that whatever the physician does is likely to affect the course of death. So the fact that death is inevitable and that the physician will have a hand in the death in one way or another does not mean that the physician killed the patient. But more than this,

Byock's discussion of Michael's case can help us to see that there is a meaningful distinction between foreseeing and intending death.

Recall that before Michael Merseal was given barbiturate sedation, he was placed on round-the-clock Versed and his fluid intake and nutritional supplements were dramatically reduced. As everybody in the case knew, this course of action could well result in Michael's death, but it was undertaken in an attempt to control Michael's nearly back-to-back seizures and the vomiting and choking associated with his tube feeding. Indeed, after Michael's nutritional supplements were entirely eliminated, his family waited for his death. Instead of going into a coma and dying, however, Michael woke up. Byock reports his explanation to Michael's father as follows: "My best guess is that until we started the Versed the seizures had been coming so frequently that he's been in that post-ictal, sort-of-irritable, 'gorked' state almost continuously for weeks. It was like a hibernation. And now that he seems to have stopped seizing, he's woken up."[26] As Byock tells the story, Michael's improvement was dramatic. For several months he was relatively free of seizures; he regained the ability to eat solid food; and he became like a happy six-month-old child.

I want to be clear here. I am not suggesting that it is the possibility of a "miraculous" recovery that distinguishes killing from letting die. I am not, for example, suggesting that the reason to oppose killing in this case is that if Byock had given Michael a lethal injection instead of the Versed, then the family would have been denied the last few months of joy. Instead, my point is that Michael's unexpected, if brief, recovery demonstrates that there is a meaningful distinction between foreseeing and intending death. When Michael's family decided to withdraw nutrition and hydration to eliminate the suffering associated with vomiting and choking, they foresaw that death would occur. But the goal of their action was the elimination of pain and suffering, not Michael's death. If the goal of their action were Michael's death, then Michael's family would not have begun feeding him again when he emerged from his coma-like state. Had Michael died when his tube feedings were stopped, the relief from his suffering would not have come from his death but from the control of his seizures and his choking that the Versed and elimination of tube feedings facilitated. In short, conditions 2 and 3 of the principle of double effect were met in this case in a way that would not have been possible if Byock had given Michael a lethal injection.

Could not the same thing be said about the case of Mr. Kline? Quill's argument, remember, is that giving the barbiturate infusion to Mr. Kline is not meaningfully different from giving him a lethal injection because it cannot be meaningfully said that the physician's intention is anything other than bringing about death. Yet, in light of Michael Merseal's case, this claim seems mistaken. Suppose that the morphine given to Mr. Kline had controlled his pain without causing hallucinations. Surely Quill would not have given the barbiturate sedation. Or suppose that the barbiturate sedation had been temporarily stopped and the hallucinations had not returned. Surely the barbiturate infusion would not have been restarted. If under either scenario no further action would be taken to cause death, then a meaningful distinction can be drawn.

Indeed, Quill himself acknowledges that strictly speaking the principle of double effect can be consistently applied to this case. Although the action of sedating the patient has the bad effect of hastening death as well as the good effect of controlling suffering, it is defensible because the physician need not aim at death. In the traditional language, death is a foreseen but unintended consequence and so the doctor's actions are permissible. Nevertheless, says Quill, "barbiturate sedation and terminal voluntary dehydration stretch our principles to the breaking point."[27]

Toward the start of this chapter I noted H. Richard Niebuhr's call for testing the dramatic truth of experiential narratives and his observation that the test is frequently rooted in a community. I think we can now see that Quill's plea for legalizing assisted suicide on the basis of his experience with dying patients does not fully withstand the sort of critical scrutiny that Niebuhr urges on us. Recall that in his supplemental declaration to the Second Circuit Court, Quill argued that given the distinction between assisting suicide and withdrawing treatment "some dying patients who are in agony that can no longer be relieved . . . have no such options [for relief] under current legal restrictions." We also saw that in *A Midwife Through the Dying Process* Quill argues that the legal prohibition against assisted suicide stands in the way of the physician's threefold promise that the patient will not die alone or in pain and that all struggles will be faced together. We are now in a position to see that neither of these claims is true. Given the possibility of administering barbiturate sedation, patients' agony can be controlled and physicians need not abandon patients as they die.

Moreover, barbiturate sedation is consistent both with the principle of double effect and with the distinction between killing and letting die. As the Supreme Court noted, the distinction between treatment withdrawal and assisted suicide is widely accepted in our community. So Quill is in effect asking us to abandon a long-standing moral consensus on the basis of experiences that do not in fact require such dramatic change.

In arguing that Quill is mistaken in advocating for the legalization of assisted suicide, I do not mean to question either his motives or his integrity. Indeed, if we return in closing to the case of Jane Smith, we can see why Quill is so passionate in his convictions. In Quill's view, he was unable to fulfill his promise to Jane Smith because the law prevented him from giving her a lethal injection. The result, he says, is that he is haunted by the image of Jane's friends holding the plastic bag over her head in a desperate attempt to complete what the barbiturates alone had been unable to finish.

Yet it is precisely this image that must finally give us pause about Quill's position. Although providing barbiturate sedation is admittedly an unusual treatment, it is recognizably a treatment. Michael is suffering from uncontrollable seizures, and the barbiturate sedation ends his suffering. Mr. Kline is suffering from terrifying hallucinations, and the barbiturate sedation ends his suffering. Indeed, if Jane Smith's suffering had become uncontrollable, barbiturate sedation would have been an option in this case. Yet Quill says that only a "highly intellectualized" account could see a difference between terminal sedation and euthanasia. But the difference between putting a plastic bag over a comatose patient's head and waiting for a comatose patient to die is not the least bit intellectual; it is concrete and palpable.

In one of the two passages with which I began this chapter, H. Richard Niebuhr hinted at the need to assess the stories of personal experience differently from, say, a scientific case history. Properly evaluating stories of personal experience requires the use of reason and emotion. As Niebuhr puts it, "the heart must reason"; the self "cannot make a choice between reason and imagination but only between reasoning on the basis of adequate images and thinking with the aid of evil imaginations."[28] For all his extraordinary compassion, his sensitivity, his courage, I fear that Dr. Quill is the victim of his own imagination. Haunted by the ghastly image of his friend, Quill advocates a world in which there will be no more Jane Smiths. Yet, in accepting Dr. Quill's claim that withdrawing treatment is nothing more nor less than assisted suicide, in agreeing with him that there is no difference between passive and active euthanasia, I fear that we would move closer to a world not free of Jane Smiths but filled with them.

PART TWO

THE PRACTICE OF CAREGIVING: CARING FOR CHILDREN

4

"IT'S WHAT PEDIATRICIANS ARE SUPPOSED TO DO"

MARGARET E. MOHRMANN

Thoughtful observers of primary care medicine usually recognize consistent differences between primary and tertiary care practice that have significant implications for the theory, teaching, and practice of medical ethics. Eric Cassell's 1997 book, *Doctoring: The Nature of Primary Care Medicine*,[1] for example, provides practical and theoretical grounding for the claim that primary care medicine is based on conceptions of medical practice and the physician-patient relationship that differ in important ways from those which underlie the methods and direct the attention of a bioethics rooted in hospital-centered medicine.

In their 1986 monograph, *Professional Ethics and Primary Care Medicine,* Smith and Churchill write, "[p]rimary care calls for an expanded medical ethics . . . and a fuller sense of the professional norms which underwrite medicine's activities and give them social sanction." More particularly, they "argue that the goals of primary care bespeak . . . the need for a moral imagination which is informed more fully by patient experiences and social priorities."[2]

The need for that kind of informed moral imagination is perhaps nowhere so evident as in the day-to-day practice of primary care pediatrics. Unlike the primary health care of adults, pediatrics is characterized by an emphasis on well-child care; that is, a significantly greater percentage of patients and families come to the pediatrician for health maintenance, disease prevention, and general advice. Moreover, the general pediatrician is necessarily concerned with the child's growth and development—the processes of physical, emotional, cognitive, and social maturation that require for their fulfillment much more than the absence of disease. In addition to the diagnosis and treatment of the child's illnesses as they arise, these professional concerns must be addressed not only with the child but also, and usually primarily, with the child's parents or guardians, in a distinct and complex variation of the "physician-patient" relationship. Bioethics' traditional concentration on the question of who speaks in the best interests of the child is useful here but may not entirely capture the interplay of roles, responsibilities, and purposes in primary care pediatrics.

This study seeks to learn about the moral imagination at work in primary care pediatrics from its practitioners. Four pediatricians were interviewed over a period of two months, each for a total of approximately four hours. The interviews took place outside their practice venues, at a time of their choosing; only the author/interviewer and the individual physician were present. Prior to the first interview, the participants were given a list of topics on which the discussion would focus and were asked to recall stories of patient encounters that had raised moral questions for them. I transcribed each interview from written notes and asked the participants to read the notes from their interviews to assure that they accurately represented our conversation. This paper is based on the transcribed interviews, as are my analyses and conclusions.

The four participants are in the practice of primary care pediatrics; one of them, Dr. D, specializes in the care of adolescents. Dr. D completed medical school in 1978 in England; the others are graduates of three different United States medical schools: Dr. C in 1986, Dr. B in 1987, and Dr. A in 1991. Dr. A finished law school before attending medical school; Dr. C worked for a few years after college, mostly as a high school teacher and baseball coach. Dr. D's practice is based in a university medical center; the others work in three satellite offices, associated with but not housed in the same medical center. All four, to varying degrees, are involved in teaching medical students and pediatric residents.

The stories these pediatricians chose to bring to our conversations are full of rich detail and consternation. They are tales of complex interactions that challenged the doctors' ability to foster and preserve the physician-patient/parent relationship while discerning and attempting to respond to the needs of the children and families involved. In each story, the language of, and concerns about, relationships and roles predominate; the stories do not sound much like the sorts of dilemmas commonly presented to bioethicists for consideration.

I should acknowledge the peculiar character of my own voice and the effect of my ear on this chapter. I speak as a primary care pediatrician, a medical educator, and a theological ethicist; these facets of my career and scholarly pursuits are inseparably linked. Although I undertook the study and the interviews as an ethicist, I inevitably heard the stories as a pediatrician. It was only at the point of analysis that I recognized my unquestioning acceptance of the participants' identification of difficulties with the physician-patient relationship as the outstanding moral issues in their practices. That is, their stories matched my own clinical experience and convictions so well that I did not pause to press them for clarification and justification of their insistence on the moral significance of the relationship. Consequently, I use their stories to introduce and exemplify my own (and others') understanding of the pivotal role of the relationship[3] in the medical and ethical work of primary care.

THE STORIES

Dr. A

Dr. A talked about the parents, both mildly mentally retarded, of a child who is apparently also handicapped:

> They lost benefits, and I had to write a letter describing the baby in order for the parents to get disability benefits back. My problem was how to get them the benefits without severing my relationship with them by saying it too strongly, how to say it in a way that maintains the relationship. They don't really understand their own limitations or their baby's; the baby seems normal to them. I've spent two years developing the relationship and getting the baby cared for.
>
> The issue is helping them be realistic but maintaining my relationship with them. It's a relationship that allows them to walk in and out of the office at will, because they can't really think ahead about the baby's needs. They need the flexibility to come in when they identify a problem.
>
> My first obligation is to the child. It goes beyond optimal health care to optimal living environment. It requires working with the parents. . . . And he's not an easy baby. He wheezes, and he's had these funny seizures. . . . I have to interpret for them what they're hearing from other specialists. It taxes all the resources the office has.

It has long been observed in medicine that a "good"—that is, open and trusting—relationship between patient and doctor is essential for accurate diagnosis and effective treatment. Trust between a patient or family and their doctor may begin with their faith in the doctor's medical knowledge and skills, but it is sustained by their belief that the doctor also knows and cares about them. The latter belief develops over time, and the relationship is formed and deepened as the physician hears, recalls, and refers to narrative details of the patient's or family's life.

It is in the context of such a relationship that patients grant doctors the information—about their symptoms, their personal and family medical histories, their social situations, and so on—and the intimate contact with their bodies in the physical examination necessary for the formulation of diagnoses and plans likely to address the problem correctly. Patients' willingness to give true and complete personal information depends on their belief that the doctor will use that knowledge well (medically and morally) to serve the patients' interests. Likewise, it is only within the relationship that recommendations for treatment and further evaluation are accepted and carried out. Patients' readiness to follow the doctor's advice depends on their belief that the doctor has heard and understood the problem fully and is acting to relieve the problem in a manner appropriate to their particular needs and desires. Put succinctly, in the absence of a relationship of trust, patients are much less likely either to accept prescribed therapies or to return for recommended follow-up visits designed to monitor progress, reconsider treatment plans, and anticipate further problems.

Thus, a significant part of Dr. A's emphasis on the relationship with her patient's parents has to do with assuring continued trusting interaction so that she can help them take care of their child. In this particular situation, forming and maintaining that relationship require that she work carefully within the parents' understanding of their child's abilities, and that she and her office staff be prepared to assist them with many of the tasks of daily living. She understands these efforts to be moral obligations of her professional practice; therefore, situations that threaten the stability or continuity of the medical relationship are ethical issues.

Dr. B

The physician-patient relationship has undeniable instrumental value for enabling correct diagnosis and treatment. But the management of illness is not the only thing going on in Dr. A's story, nor is it the issue in the tale told by Dr. B. His story is of a young couple who have tried, unsuccessfully, to bear children and are now considering adopting a child from a foreign country. They have come to Dr. B for guidance, both because they would choose him as their pediatrician and because they are friends through church. He puzzles over how best to advise them:

> They're now being asked to accept three siblings from Romania, five and a half, three and a half, and ten months old. They came in to look through the medical records with me, and asked me to help them make a decision. I know them from church; they're life-long Catholics with a very alive faith that's very important to them. I'm trying to help them make a decision that's good for them as a family, not based on guilt.
>
> I know the couple is saying to themselves, "God has presented me

with these children. I asked for children; can I say no to these?" . . .
But then there's the other side: the language difference; we don't
know their past history but it's probably awful; how much rebellion
and anger will there be? . . . How do you express the permanence of
love to a child without English? . . . They asked for and got medical
records, but they're scant—maybe two pages per child, and most of
the lines are blank.

I asked them, "Who's supporting you in this decision? Where do
you go for help? I can give medical advice and be your friend, but not
your spiritual director." . . . I talked with them about the challenges of
their not knowing English with all that means—like how do you warn
them a car is coming? And about the big changes in their lives after
six years of being alone together.

I asked Dr. B to summarize his role in this encounter:

Primarily, to help interpret medical data as accurately as I can, with
lots of qualifiers. Plus, offering them an ear for whatever they want to
talk about; support them; ask the hard questions; suggest they talk
with someone else, too—outside medicine—because I shouldn't be
their only adviser, especially in spiritual matters.

In primary care pediatrics, effective health care has to do not only with management of illness and assessment of growth and development, but also with matters of parenting and the nature of the child's home life. The instrumental value
of the physician-parent relationship extends to providing the context and platform
for teaching, empowering, even changing parenting practices to promote the
child's and the family's best interests. In Dr. A's story, the limited cognitive abilities of the parents bring this task to the forefront. But in Dr. B's narrative as well,
his attentive, knowledgeable, and honest relationship with these potential parents
enables him to help them consider facets of parenting, from their perspective and
that of the children, that are relevant to the decisions they must make. Dr. B
understands his obligations to include not only interpreting medical information
but also listening, supporting, and guiding parents—including guiding them to
other sorts of advisers—as they learn to take on the parental role. In a situation of
limited information and troubling possibilities, this sense of professional obligation makes the question of how best to advise the couple a difficult moral issue
for him.

Dr. C

In their attempts to help assure healthy environments for the children in their
care, pediatricians are sometimes torn between continuing to work with parents

in situations that could threaten the child's welfare and breaking the relationship of trust by asking for legal protection for the child. The next story illustrates this dilemma dramatically.

Before taking on his current position, Dr. C was in a university-based practice in another city, where he provided primary care for a number of children with complex medical problems. He tells the story of a situation that occurred some years before our conversation, but it was still fresh in his mind.

> This was a homeless family, bikers; later I realized they were probably really outlaws. There were five children. The youngest, Anna, was brought in in respiratory failure at about seventeen months. She'd been diagnosed a year before with CP [cerebral palsy]. She was still breast feeding; anytime they tried to feed her anything else, she choked and gagged. . . . She was in the hospital four months. They found out she actually had methylmalonic aciduria [a congenital metabolic disorder] as the cause of her CP. She was ventilator dependent, and had no home to go to. A social agency finally found them a house, but the family was really nomadic and unsafe. . . . But it was clear that they really did love this child.
>
> So, she went home with them and got her [medication], and in twelve months she was off the ventilator and walking. She went from about a two-month developmental level to near age level. But then I started getting reports of abuse. . . . I had to file a [child protective services] report. Then her mother threatened to kill me, and she fired me. [Child protective services] tried to keep Anna at home, but then they found out that the parents had been abusing not only their children, but the home nurses Anna had. The nurses were just too scared to say anything before. . . . But it all came out, and the parents are both in jail now for a long time. The kids are in foster care, in two homes, and they're doing okay. Anna's thriving.
>
> My dilemma was about whether to keep trying to work with them. I knew calling [child protective services] would end my relationship with them. There was just no way I could help this family back to "normalcy." They really scared people. The moral question was about trying to keep the relationship, to help them trust us that we'd be there for them for health care. Maybe I should've called [child protective services] earlier. . . . But I had no direct evidence; they were just very rough with the kids.

I asked him to clarify what he considered to be the ethical issue at stake:

> What's right and just for the child and the family. They're still a family. There was no outright abuse. Does just their being so different

from me entitle us to remove their children? Just because they're so outside society? They kept them very clean; they were very nice kids; they were all in school. I had a hard time every day dealing with my feelings. I didn't want to put forward my own biases if the kids were okay. This is an extreme example of how much power we can have if we use it. It was particularly hard for me to call [child protective services] because I had to think hard about whether I was doing it for the wrong reasons. In cases where there is obvious abuse, I don't have any problem calling them.

At what point, as the evidence of mistreatment unfolds, does the pediatrician's task shift from working within the relationship with the parents in order to promote the welfare of the child to asking legal authorities to protect the child from the parents? Most child abuse statutes require professionals to report even the suspicion of abuse, but doctors' ethical obligations also compel them to consider whether the reporting itself could destroy what may be a family's only sustained connection to social support and "normalcy," to use Dr. C's pointedly ironic word. Add to that conflict the difficulty in defining abuse that does not take the form of discernible fractures, whip marks, or the like (the "outright abuse" to which Dr. C refers), and the moral puzzle intensifies. Whose standards of parenting, of discipline, of health and well-being apply? When does a different "style" become actionable mistreatment? The primary moral obligation to act in the best interests of the patient confronts Dr. C with a genuine ethical dilemma when the interests served by keeping a troubled family intact conflict with the interests served by breaking up a dangerous family.

Dr. D

The previous three stories raise questions of relationship and the physician's role, especially as it extends beyond what is traditionally defined as health care. These questions likewise permeate Dr. D's narration about the Dawson family:

> Lana is twenty years old and retarded; her mental age is probably less than nine years. She has had one child, Barbara, by her mother's boyfriend when she was twelve years old. Her mother [Mary] has custody. [Lana] was sexually abused in the home, and now is sexually provocative and undiscriminating—and states that she wants to and is going to have another baby. The concept of providing care for this family means dropping any preconceived notion of goals. It seriously challenges why I do what I do.
>
> Barbara is being raised by her maternal grandmother, who didn't stop her boyfriend from impregnating her twelve-year-old retarded

daughter. They come to see me primarily to prove [to various social agencies] that they've been. Am I having any impact on these people's lives, to promote health and well-being, to maximize the children's potential for a full adult life? . . . There aren't big medical problems; the issue is social chaos. . . . I just throw up my hands, do what I can, be consistent, and be there for them when they come.

Barbara is up-to-date on immunizations; she's in school; she's relatively clean and well dressed. She's also a whiny, pseudosophisticated eight-year-old who already flirts. . . . She has had zero success in school; she has significant learning disabilities. . . . There are no competent adult role models at home. She gets mixed parenting, if any. She gets into bed with Mary and her boyfriend—Barbara's father, whom she calls Granddaddy—who's supposedly "always wearing boxers." She's learning few appropriate social boundaries and lots of inappropriate ones. I don't know what she learns about, say, stealing or alcohol or drugs.

I suspect this family is not unique, but I know this one. I've been seeing them for ten years or more, and have watched the pieces fall out, not fit together.

This story, while similar in some ways to the one told by Dr. C, has its own particular poignancy, for the doctor as well as the family. Here Dr. D struggles to find a way to help a family with whom she believes she has been unable to form an effective, stable relationship of trust. The professional and ethical helplessness Dr. D expresses, however, is belied by one striking characteristic of the tale: how well she knows the Dawson family. The unabridged version of the story includes even more details about Lana's, Barbara's, and Mary's lives, details that show not only that Dr. D has been paying attention but also that the Dawsons trust her enough to return to her office repeatedly over "ten years or more" and to tell her what is happening in their lives. The relationship may not enable Dr. D to be the kind of physician for the children that she would like to be, but there is reason to think that the connection may be helping this unruly and isolated family in ways that are not measurable by our usual standards. Who can say what the family would be like without their occasional contact with a doctor who has been willing to "be consistent, and be there for them when they come" for so many years?

This speculation highlights another potential value of the physician-patient relationship, demonstrated as well in the other stories related here. The relationship may have a placebo effect; that is, it may be a form of treatment in itself.[4] In each story, the physician's interaction with parents takes the form of a concerned and nurturing involvement that also demonstrates and advocates clear standards of behavior and care. The relationship thus is not only the context for effective management of illness but also an enactment and experience of the kind of human courtesy and attention that characterizes good parenting and healthy home environments.

Given this point, perhaps it is true that, in addition to its instrumental values, there is a first-order good that can be ascribed to a trustworthy physician-patient/ parent relationship. The experience of being part of a relationship of trust, in which one's needs and desires are taken seriously and responded to fittingly, is a good in itself. Especially for some of the parents described here—who may in their other associations be perceived, and who may perceive themselves, as unloved and unlovable—the experience of being invited into and held within an alliance focused on their interests and those of their children may be one good thing in their lives.

It must also be said that the physician-patient relationship may be a first-order good for the doctor. In the midst of the exhaustion and anxiety of medical practice, the experience of being welcomed into a relationship with others who trust your skills and your good heart is richly sustaining and can be a continuing opportunity for growth in trustworthiness and fidelity.

WHERE IS MEDICAL MORALITY LEARNED?

The complex stories recounted above are notably consistent in that the issues identified as moral questions are embedded in the doctors' relationships with the families they see and in the expanded roles the families' needs seem to call for. These pediatricians associate their professional ethics very closely with their ability to form and maintain strong and healing alliances with patients and parents, and with their capacity to recognize, accept, and effectively carry out intricate and unanticipated professional obligations.

Why do they make that association? What has led them to identify medical ethics with the physician-patient relationship? It can be argued that physicians who choose to be primary care pediatricians do so because they wish to find both the challenging and the satisfying aspects of their work within interpersonal connections rather than, say, within the highly technical skills of a microvascular surgeon. But such a claim only pushes the question back one step without answering it. The query remains: Why do they locate medical morality in relationships rather than in dilemmas at critical decision points? What becomes clear in the interviews is that the doctors' lives before and parallel to their careers in medicine, permeated in one way or another by religion and its teachings, crucially determine their perspectives on their work, shaping what they learn from their experiences in practice and in medical training.

Medical School and Residency

The four participants in this study attended medical school before their respective universities instituted required courses in medical ethics. Nevertheless, I asked what they had been taught, even indirectly, about ethics and about the physician-patient relationship. Their answers included Dr. C's blunt response that he was taught nothing about these things and Dr. A's considered estimate that she was taught in medical school "10 percent" of what she needs to know to care for the family in her story. Dr. B recalled a few classes that brought in "a more human touch" but also some unpleasant, even "disgusting," experiences: "They brought in people who were really retarded or had significant neurological abnormalities and just paraded them past us. It was a sideshow atmosphere. We were shocked by what we saw and disturbed by how it was done." He contrasted these unsettling episodes to what he had learned from following his family doctor around when he was in high school and college:

> I used to round with our family doc at home. He's a really good guy; he *cared* for his patients, knew his limitations. So, in med school, when I saw the callousness and detachment of some . . . folks, I knew it was wrong. I could fall into it, but I knew it wasn't good and right. I still held on to the ideal of listening to patients, trying to meet their needs.

Dr. D, the earliest to graduate, was the only one who said that moral principles that continue to influence her practice had been taught or, at least, confirmed in her medical training:

> [In medical school] there was a fair amount about the doctor-patient relationship, about confidentiality and professionalism. Maybe only two lectures, but I took them very seriously. . . . What we were taught was reinforced by clinical teachers, who explicitly modeled especially attention to the patient's privacy; they always included the patients in rounds. [During residency] there was a relatively strong code of conduct, strong sense of loyalty to patients, but we didn't get the modeling from leaders as I did in England. I really missed that and determined to do it myself. The level of integrity is important. I didn't expect it to be taught, but in these places I expected it to be shown to me. And I did find it.

Experience in Medical Practice

In each interview, after exploring their educational backgrounds, I asked the participants what they had learned from patients and whether and how experiences in practice had formed or altered their understanding of ethical medicine. Their answers reveal more about each physician's ethos of medical practice and openness to the influence of patients. Although they all practice primary care pediatrics and see relatively similar patient populations, the doctors take disparate lessons from their experiences, suggesting that the more basic influence on their medical morality lies elsewhere.

Here is Dr. C's answer to the question, "What do you think you've learned from your patients?"

> Everything. They always have a story to tell, and you can never know when you're going to hear it, so you always have to listen. Ninety-nine percent of them really care about their children, and we just have to find ways to help them do that, to help them do it on their own, because they generally know how.

I then asked him how his medical experience had shaped his morality as a physician. Dr. C's answer highlights basic principles that are now generally included in medical school teaching about ethics and professional relationships, but that—for him—carry the conviction of experience and personal discovery:

> Everyone has a base to start with, but you have to think about what the patient needs. Try not to be either overly enmeshed or overly distant. You need to see what they need and want to talk about, not your own agenda. But by doing that you can usually take care of your agenda, too. Honesty is most important: showing you're a person and that they are, too. And you have to be honest enough to disagree if you need to. It sounds trite, but I'd emphasize more the way I'd like to be treated. We hear all the time that doctors don't really listen, and every day I try to do that. It all comes from being honest with myself and, if I am, about what I think and feel about the patient, then it comes across that way.
>
> Parents want to know not the pathophysiology of HUS [hemolytic-uremic syndrome], but why their child yells at them or doesn't do well in school. The day-to-day issues are so much a part of practice. And when a child comes in sick, I can remember something they've told me in the past, and I can ask about how that's going. That's what practice is about. . . . Inherent in practice and in a commitment to practice is the ethical issue of being present for families—in the attention you give, in follow-up.

Dr. A was perhaps the most explicit about the difference between what she had learned about medicine in her training, and what her patients were teaching her about the role of a pediatrician in their lives. She finds, however, that her clinical experience, while reinforcing her prior assumptions about the moral issues characteristic of medical practice, has not significantly shaped her professional ethics:

> I now realize that most of what I do is about social issues, not medical issues. I thought I was going to be treating disease, and you're not. You're treating a lot of things, and disease is just part of that. You have to know how to treat asthma, but you're also dealing with the smoking in the house and whether they can afford the medicines. There's more than disease that impacts on health.
>
> I'd say it's not so much that my idea of my role as a doctor has shifted so much as it has expanded. With the continuity [of patient care] comes more knowledge so maybe you can address the issues with more understanding. It makes you be creative about how to address the issue when there isn't an answer, or not a clear answer, anyway. Each patient wants to be special. It needs to appear each time as if they're the most important person in your practice. . . . Conveying respect and that sense of importance sometimes takes conscious effort, especially when you're busy. They want to be heard, to be taken care of, to have that time with you.
>
> It's accepting people's differences and going forward with them, and sometimes that's the hardest thing in general. . . . My tenets are still there, but with patients you have to be able to realize that they may be following a different path, and you need to go with them to some extent.

In considering what she has learned from her patients, Dr. D. integrates the medical and nonmedical aspects of what she does to portray a more complicated view of health care than she had anticipated at the outset of her career:

> [My patients have taught me] how the disease is wrapped up in an illness. How the complexity, the richness of their lives is behind whatever "complaint" comes in. . . . Patients have taught me to ask the right question, or to think about the right question to ask. I've learned how to hone it to the individual situation.
>
> I didn't realize it would be such fun, so rewarding. It's very rich— the interaction with the children, participating in the love between parents and children. Of course, mixed in there is also what I learned in medical school; this is not glorified social work. Part of what I'm doing in playing with a child is assessing well-being and, with the parents, seeing that the love, the parental interaction is there.
>
> My concept of primary care has changed. I very much now see it as empowering people to take care of themselves, to ask the right

questions, to interpret their own needs, making my patients not dependent on me, getting them to the next level of confidence.

Her reply to the question of how her experience has shaped her morality as a physician adds justice to her previous comments about love, embracing the two primary themes of theological ethics and, perhaps in different terms, of the ethics of medicine:

> My sense of justice: People mess up and how bad that can be, especially when someone is unwittingly involved, a child or a bystander. Life's not fair. Things aren't parceled out equally. Some people lead extremely difficult lives. This leads me to child advocacy, child protection by working for healthy families, providing birth control, being there for the uninsured.

Dr. B had much to say about the difficulty of learning about the broader role of a pediatrician during the years of residency training, because of fatigue and the amount of work to be done:

> The more volume, the less you see the person; you see [the disease], not the kid and the struggling parents. . . . You're trying to preserve yourself, too. You're hungry to learn clinical stuff, but not as hungry to learn how it affects the family. You need to care for the urgent things, and the rest can wait—and others can do it, like social work. It's not my job.

Because the earlier portion of the interview had indicated that he no longer fails to see "the kid and the struggling parents," I asked him what influence, if any, he thought his patients in practice have had on changing the "It's not my job" attitude of residency.

> They helped break down some prejudices. No matter what their background or SES [socioeconomic status], there are people who think society owes them and people who are very appreciative of what others do for them, whether they're from [the country club] or have been stepped on all their lives. They're just different flavors of needy. The sense of entitlement is not related to SES. So, I don't look at people and think I know how they're going to react.

He went on to talk about how he now struggles to be present for his patients during the busiest seasons of the year—trying, that is, not to fall back into the pattern established during residency of being too preoccupied to attend to the rest of the picture. I asked Dr. B how his medical experience as a practitioner has shaped his professional morality.

> It's really more the other way around. My experience elsewhere shapes how I approach medicine. It's more my experience in my home, life, volunteering situations, discussions with other couples about spirituality and life in general . . . these are more prolonged, intense discussions where I learn about morality and how I approach other people. Because most encounters in medicine are rather short and not so intense. . . . If I'm seeing people at a reasonable pace, how well do I get to know my patients? I get to know them fairly well, but I don't think with the vast majority that I get to the level of their changing how I approach the morality of what I do.

The pediatricians' varied answers to questions about education and experience, which help fill out their portraits, fit well with the story each has told. Dr. A's analysis of the physician's expanded role and the basic principles (respect, tolerance) of her duty to her patients echoes the core issues at stake in her dealings with the impaired parents of a developmentally delayed child, and perhaps also reflects her earlier education in law. Dr. B brings to his work a moral perspective largely formed outside his medical career. In an early version, that viewpoint led him to choose his family doctor over competing medical school models as his standard; his "experience elsewhere" now governs his construal of matters in his practice, including his approach to the would-be adoptive parents who seek his counsel. Dr. C's emphasis on honesty and his articulation of the fundamentals of good practice illuminate both his effort to remain loyal to Anna's biker family and his dissatisfaction with his education. The lessons Dr. D has learned from her patients sound as though they all could have been learned from ten years with the Dawson family alone, but they also exemplify her ability to discern what she seeks, whether it be the integrity of her teachers or the love between parent and child. Although Dr. B is most explicit about the extraprofessional determination of his view of the job and its ethical facets, it seems clear that the moral discernment of each of these pediatricians can be attributed less to their education or their medical encounters than to other formative influences they have brought with them to those experiences.

Upbringing: Family and Religion

I asked Dr. D to identify the sources of her concern for integrity in her teachers and colleagues. Her answer: "Family and church." She went on to describe her parents' explicit attention to their moral obligations, with an overt religious grounding:

> I saw my parents making decisions, dealing with issues, discussing things, respecting and taking care of people, no matter who. . . . There were expectations of charity and sharing, of caring for people within the family and others outside. There were Christmas dinners when there would be people—strangers—my parents had met at the train station who had nowhere else to go for dinner. . . . There was a strong sense in my childhood of obligation, responsibility, and loyalty. . . . We went to church [Anglican] every Sunday, and to Sunday School. I was good; I listened and tried to make sense of what I heard. . . . I remember the part about what you do for the least of God's children, you do for me.
>
> The religious stuff is so embedded. . . . [Things I've learned to do as a professional] fit with what I already knew about respecting people where they are. It's an integral part of me. That may explain why I end up doing the kind of work I do; it fits with who I was growing up. The church's teaching constantly informs and backs up what I do.

Dr. A had quickly assessed the contribution of medical school training to be "maybe 10 percent" of what she needed to work with the family she had described. My next question to her was, "So where did you learn it?" Her answer begins with two statements weighted by prior assumptions, the sources of which then become clearer:

> Part of it is just being a pediatrician. It's what pediatricians are supposed to do: taking responsibility for children. . . . And I guess from my upbringing. I'm from a very Brethren, traditional Protestant background of helping others, a supportive community. . . . I don't think I'll ever get away from that. . . . The basic moral tenets are so inbred that I can't imagine giving them up.
>
> Neither of my parents is college educated; there are no models of professionals in my family. What they modeled was work hard and you'll get where you're going. . . . My family is very relationship-oriented. . . . Relationship is just what I'm used to. . . . In large part it's religious, but other things, too.

For Dr. B, concepts of the support and mutuality that characterize relationships come primarily from his wife and their experiences in marriage. When I asked him, in the context of the story he related, how he had learned that it was important to ask patients or families the source of their support, he said, "My wife's a smart woman. . . . It becomes clear in what we do with each other. Where you get your advice and strength, other than your spouse, is important. We're not each other's only source of support. Strong marriages need that outside support." Dr. B and his wife are active laypeople in the Catholic Church and teach pre-Cana classes for couples engaged to be married. He credits his wife with reviving a dormant spirituality that had been present in his childhood experiences but not strongly fostered:

> My father was Lutheran, and my mother and brothers Catholic, so we didn't go to church together. There was no prayer in our home. . . . I was in Catholic school till the seventh grade. . . . We did go to church; I was an altar boy. . . . In college, it was college during the week, church on Sunday. I almost never missed mass, but it wasn't really part of my life. . . . Involvement in the church was for the priest and older people. I wasn't involved until I married [my wife], who's always been involved. She woke me up. . . . I don't want to short-change my spirituality growing up. I remember clearly some important experiences then.
>
> Growing up I had very clear prejudices in the way I thought; part of it related to what was going on in society, racial prejudice. . . . I had no recognition of the difficulty that if you've always lived in such deep poverty, how tough it is to get out of it, and how few people manage to. I had no recognition of the need to address those problems, to try to help.

When I asked what changed him in regard to recognizing issues of race and poverty, his answer was again his wife "and some people in our [pediatrics] department who are more spiritual."

Religion is a more ambivalent, though no less significant, part of Dr. C's background; the family influence has been decisive. His father is a psychiatrist, "very into how we are as people," whose practice ethos and experiences with personal illness and unresponsive doctors during Dr. C's childhood taught Dr. C the basic premise of his work: "I wanted people who come to me to know I'd listen to them." He then told two stories about his family. He prefaced the first by saying, "I want to be like my dad. I look up to him greatly; he's my role model." The story concerned a serious controversy in which his father demonstrated his firm adherence to principles of confidentiality and fidelity to his patients. "So," Dr. C concluded, "he talks it and acts on his beliefs every day."

The second story is about his father's—and subsequently his own—relation to religion. Dr. C's father is the grandson of a Hasidic Jew:

> Both my parents were raised in observant Jewish families, but they decided not to live that way or to raise us that way. My parents are not "religious." I was not raised in the synagogue; I didn't go to Hebrew school. But when I was twelve years old, my father said that

he wanted me to do my bar mitzvah. It was exactly the wrong time to ask me that. He hired a tutor for me. It lasted one month. I said, "I won't do it." I thought it was hypocritical. So I've never had my bar mitzvah. I know both my parents were hurt by that. A couple of times since then, I've tried to go back and do it. Once was near the end of med school; a rabbi tutored me for a while, but I never completed it. It's still unfinished business for me. Maybe I will at some point. It's an important symbol for my dad, that his grandfather's beliefs are being followed. It's like the importance of Passover now. That's the one thing we do observe. It means something to my family; it's spiritual, about freeing the slaves and freedom of the individual. We did it for the first time with [our children] this year; I don't know if we'll keep on doing it. I feel like an outsider in the Jewish world.

I asked whether he thought his father's integrity, so important a model for Dr. C, is related to his Jewish background.

He thinks so. But I have a hard time listening to him about it. He thinks he's very Jewish spiritually and feels like he leads a Jewish life. There are father-son issues here, of course. I really felt the hypocrisy growing up, and I get angry about being left always feeling like an outsider. . . . I do consider myself spiritual; that's important to me. . . . But I miss being part of a group, part of something we can be in as a family.

In one way or another, each of these pediatricians has been shaped by strong religious influences present in childhood and continuing to permeate their thinking as adults. Dr. A's emphasis on duty and right relationships; Dr. B's certain sense of what is good and of the importance of mutual support for negotiating the exigencies of both daily life and professional practice; Dr. C's dedication to honesty and loyalty to his patients, carrying on his father's legacy of professional character; Dr. D's search for integrity and commitment to serving those in need—all reflect not only the basic assumptions and teachings of their families' religious traditions, but also the doctors' adult relation to religion, even in the case of Dr. C's conflicted sadness about his unrealized Jewish heritage. The influence of these spiritual characteristics becomes even clearer when the pediatricians speak of more particular ethical dilemmas that arise in their practices.

SPECIFIC ETHICAL ISSUES IN PRACTICE

In addition but still related to problems of maintaining relationship and taking on expanded roles, the pediatricians identified other ethical conundrums they find particularly difficult to deal with and, in some cases, distressingly frequent. For Dr. B, the issues tend to arise with adolescent patients and illustrate the confusing dilemmas that can accompany attention to principles of confidentiality and truth telling in a pediatric practice. Here he presents not only the dilemma but also how he has worked it out in practice, although without entirely resolving his discomfort:

> More and more, it's meeting the needs of an adolescent and parents, walking that confidentiality line. What should the parents know, have a right to know. How to persuade the adolescent they should share this with the parent, and how to know they won't go home and beat the kid over the head. . . . I try to understand what's my legal obligation to some degree. I use that as the starting point. I lean toward recognizing that the adolescent is the patient; that's who I'm trying to serve, not letting them flounder. I had a fifteen- or sixteen-year-old [patient] a few weeks ago, afraid she's pregnant. We talked about if I do the test here, how to keep it confidential. If I do it here, the bill goes to her dad. Here's your options. But what if it's positive? Can you tell them? How are you going to handle this? . . . I did a few sports physicals recently, talked about their experience with alcohol, marijuana, about dating. "Can you talk to your parents about this?" "NO." We talked about keeping communication open. I talk with parents separately. I don't say what we've talked about, but ask if they feel they can talk with their teens, and encourage them to talk. I try to keep it generic to help them stay available.

Issues of confidentiality in the care of adolescents also trouble Dr. C, who told a story about an eighteen-year-old whose father insisted on being told test results and was astonished to hear from Dr. C that he could not give him any medical information about his daughter without her permission. Adhering to the important principle of confidentiality seems a potential interference with the doctor's relationship with parents:

> I think most parents are trying to give their teens independence, and they accept the confidentiality stuff. In terms of my talking with parents about that, I'm usually comfortable once I've said it, but I often have a hard time getting it out, saying it in a way that's acceptable and understandable to parents. There are issues of my relationship to the parents.

For Dr. A, difficult ethical questions revolve around "the consent and caregiver issue." In her rural practice, she has a significant number of patients who are accompanied by "the grandmother or the uncle or someone who's not a relative. And I have to say, 'Treat or not treat?' " Balancing the moral and professional obligation to care for the child, to give needed immunizations, or to provide specific medical therapy, with the legal and moral obligation to honor parental rights, is not always easy or possible. In her description of the problem, one can hear clearly conflicting requirements of beneficence and respect for autonomy:

> It's like giving a shot to a patient who comes in with the grandmother, who doesn't have custody. Sometimes I do it, although it's compromising parent autonomy. I cringe each time, but you gotta do it because the child needs to be cared for and has a good guardian. I do everything possible to get the caretaker to bring in the permission from the parent, or to get custody, but that doesn't always happen, and you still have to take care of the child.

Considering that Dr. D's specialty is adolescent medicine, it is not surprising that the ethical issues she identifies concern "sexual issues in younger kids who are thrown out into the adult world without knowing how to act there. And giving them birth control doesn't begin to deal with it." She tells what she calls "a generic Teen Health Center story":

> A fourteen-year-old girl wants to have a baby, refuses birth control, comes in frequently for pregnancy tests. My moral head says she's much too young to be a parent; I need to stop her. My realistic self says there's no way you can prevent it, but keep bolstering her with some messages: that she's worth something, that she has a future, that she can let herself be fourteen and wait before tying herself down. So I can only watch and wait—and accept and love her.

The participants also identify ethical issues arising from managed care and the differing expectations imposed by insurance companies, the medical center, and their patients. As Dr. A says, remaining true to her ideal of beneficence, "You end up doing what you think is right. You do what's best for the patient first." But Dr. D finds the systemic, political questions—matters of justice—to be primary ethical problems in her work:

> My biggest moral issues have more to do with the medical system than with my patients. The way we can solicit extra funding for what we do is to come up with programs—something innovative, cute— when we can't even get people to come into the office when they're sick. . . . It's not a matter of people slipping through the net; there's not even a net. . . . It's this whole thing of turning rights into privileges.

Health care should be a right. . . . If you fit whatever special program we formulate, then you get the privilege of care. But it begs the question of comprehensive health care.

Dr. D also worries that the care she gives can be significantly compromised when patients are unable to pay because they are uninsured and not covered by governmental programs for indigent care. She sometimes delays medical evaluations of certain problems because the families cannot afford the charges:

I don't know if I'm jeopardizing care or not. . . . Some people work forty hours a week without getting adequate health insurance. . . . When money is scarce, paying for potential health problems by buying insurance is hard, when there are also present needs to meet. It's a societal issue, making people choose health coverage or not. . . . Not only is the discrepancy between rich and poor greater, but also between savvy and unsavvy, the computer users and not—even getting what you need over a telephone, and not everyone has a telephone. It becomes a much bigger socioeconomic issue. . . . We're not going to have the best health care until we address that.

Reflection on specific ethical questions—of confidentiality and consent, of helping teens too young for pregnancy, of the inequities of the health care system—led each interview further into matters of religion. The doctors spoke both of the ways in which their religious backgrounds and beliefs figure in their recognition of and response to these issues, and of any more overt role that religion may play in their work.

THE ROLE OF RELIGION

Dr. B told me of a patient who had died, a young child with a complex neurological and hormonal disorder. The disease had caused profound developmental delay and repeated episodes of critical illness and allowed no hope for future physical or cognitive growth or maturation.

I sort of suggested letting go. . . . I raised the question [with the parents] of whether it was okay not to use the technology we have, which led us to end-of-life issues. I was very direct about the development issues, the big picture. It's not that developmental problems mean that it's okay to skimp on technology, but it is okay to put it into the equation.

How had Dr. B settled on the particular formulation in that last sentence, since there are many people, including some of his fellow Roman Catholics, who might disagree with one or the other clause? His reply:

From *my* approach to religion. I ask myself, why am I keeping this person from heaven? Death is really a natural part of things; I don't fear that. . . . My approach for end-of-life care has to do with the belief that there is a heaven, there's no pain there, and it's not a bad thing to let someone go there. I don't know where or how I draw my lines. I try to balance it with the belief that we're called to do something here on earth; we all have a purpose, although we may not understand it. I'm here to alleviate suffering, to allow folks to function. And surely folks with handicaps function, but there comes a point where humans are not able to—I don't know the word—teach? Work? I take care of a handicapped child who teaches me and others so many things. But, if someone is reduced to no dignity, all pain, that's where I draw my line.

When I asked him to say more about "*my* approach to religion," he said, "There's one maxim that's been pretty important for me, the one about treat others the way you'd have them treat you. We're all God's children, and I should treat everyone equally and with respect." His answer was a succinct combination of the scriptural law of reciprocity, or the neighbor-love command, and the theological underpinning of the ethical principles of justice and autonomy. These precepts appear to govern the way in which Dr. B resolves both the ethical and the religious conflicts that accompany his care of sexually active teenagers. After he had described the dilemmas of confidentiality and counseling recounted in the previous section, he explained how his religious beliefs affect his approach to these problems.

The hardest one was when I worked with a sixteen-year-old who was pregnant. For me, there's no question that life begins at conception. So for me to talk about "What are your options?" . . . I don't feel comfortable with abortion, but obviously all teens know that's an option. I leave it with saying there are clinics, et cetera, in town where you can explore that option. I can take the easy way out because I don't do them. As a doctor, I can't say, "This is wrong; you're not going to murder your fetus, are you?" But, internally, I want to say that. Why some teens *want* to get pregnant I just can't understand. And giving a child up for adoption is in some ways unnatural and difficult. Keeping the child is a real problem. There are no good options. . . . That's probably the hardest one where my religion comes in.

Some would say, "You had the opportunity to speak out against abortion. Why are you so weak?" It comes down to what are my legal obligations: It's the law; it's constitutional; it's okay. What is my medical obligation, the standard of care in the community? *Then*

what are my beliefs? Maybe it's a weak compromise, but I have to
satisfy the medical/legal obligations. I can mention it as an option,
but not counsel for it.

The problem of compromise also comes up for Dr. A, whose moral beliefs,
strongly grounded in her youth in a Brethren community, may conflict with professional expectations of her as a pediatrician and counselor to adolescents exper-
imenting with new behaviors. Like Dr. B, she balances her beliefs with her medical and legal obligations to her patients, couched in her preferred categories of
beneficence and the importance of relationship:

I have to talk with them about birth control and take a realistic
approach with them, despite the fact that I believe absolutely in abstinence and no smoking or drinking. I have to optimize what's there for
the child and not impose what I believe. I'll talk about abstinence and
not smoking or drinking in terms of optimal health. But sometimes I
come out of a room, after giving birth control pills to a thirteen-year-
old who's smoking and drinking and her parents don't know about it,
and I wonder, what did I just do? I fall back on my medical training
and do what the child needs in order to be as safe as possible. It is a
problem, but the way I work it out is that the child comes first. And
at least I know if I can keep her from getting pregnant and avoiding
abortion and STDs. ... But at least I'm the one who talks about
abstinence and what about talking with your parents and how to do that.
... At least by giving the birth control, we've moved a little closer
together; it's a kind of compromise. Otherwise I'll just push her away.
I value the relationship first. That's what medicine and primary care
are about, the relationship. And, of course, legally I know that she has
a right to birth control and can make that decision. I could pawn it off
on someone else, but I'm there and have the relationship with her.

Both Dr. A and Dr. B seem to regard certain religious injunctions as prima
facie rules, which they take very seriously for themselves but can set aside for
their patients in the service of conflicting or more compelling precepts, like the
neighbor-love command and the duty to obey the laws of the state. Not all physicians strike the same balance.

Dr. C sternly criticized a former colleague who interpreted the relation among
his religious, legal, and medical obligations somewhat differently. Dr. C may
speak more vehemently than Dr. A or Dr. B would, but his ethical pronouncements nevertheless accurately capture the sense of the choices they have made:

I had a colleague ... who [for religious reasons] wouldn't even
advise patients about contraception. He took it to a degree I don't

think was good. It was wrong ethically. He was violating their
options, their choice. The patient should have the knowledge, the
option to decide. If he isn't comfortable, he shouldn't be seeing
adolescents, or at least make it clear up front. He's using his belief system to override their choices. "Paternalism" is too mild a word for
that. . . . The principle is giving patients knowledge of their options.
Medical ethical principles take precedence over the principles of religious beliefs.

Dr. C finds benefit in his own lack of formal religious beliefs. Despite his
expressed discomfort, even anger, at not having been brought up to be knowledgeable about his ancestral faith nor to be at home amid the rituals and community of Judaism, he nevertheless interprets his nonreligious state as helpful for his
work as a physician. That is apparent in his reply to my query about the influence
of his particular religious background, such as it is, on his practice:

Eclectic, open. I'm not so strongly into one area. I'm open to hearing
what people use to help them, whatever it is. I think we see . . . the
emphasis on, say, Christianity among our patients, and how they use
their belief system to help them through tough times. At first, I
thought it was a kind of denial—"God will take care of this"—but I
think it's really a form of support.

Do they have to understand a problem the way I might? No. I'm
probably not an atheist, maybe more agnostic. I think it helps me
understand people from different backgrounds. A good doctor should
see the belief system in patients, and use their religion, respect and
foster it.

Similarly, but for different reasons, Dr. D finds no conflict between her religious beliefs and her professional obligations: "I found my place in medicine that
fits my beliefs." She speaks more of the way in which religion pervades her
approach to patients and her understanding of her role as physician. For her, as
for Dr. B, respect for persons has a distinct religious basis, and the neighbor-love
command affects her understanding of her work:

The concept of ministry is very important to me: seeing, finding God
in everybody, respecting that. Increasingly, I respect my patients'
autonomy; I have ten, twenty, thirty minutes with them and then
they're going to be making the choices. The only person I can be critical of is myself, ultimately. And, if I really work on loving them as I
love myself, I'll be kinder to myself.

Religion is the framework for my whole being, but not consciously

present all the time each time I see a patient. It's there more as a concept. It fits with what I'm trying to do about empowering, respecting.
With a little surprise, I find that ministry is what I'm doing. I developed my own style of practice and find that it speaks to, it informs my
theology. . . . I look for knowledge of God everywhere, including
from my patients.

Most of the discussion about religion with the interviewees concerned the
effects of faith on their practices. However, the three participants who are actively
engaged in a religious tradition also spoke of religion as a personal support in
their work, beyond what it teaches or calls them to be and to do. One of Dr. B's
dominant themes is the necessity of the support he finds in his marriage, family,
and friends, all centered in the Roman Catholic Church. Dr. D spoke of the way
in which her faith grows and upholds her in such difficult work: "It's constantly
sustaining. If I let it happen, God works through me. I can recognize God's love
through my patients. I couldn't have anticipated this, or thought it, twenty years
ago. My 'religious consciousness' is more mature; I'm closer to it." In a similar
way, Dr. A explains why her spirituality is a necessary background for her
approach to medicine: "It's hard to sustain without it, hard to maintain the compassion. I guess some can, but I don't know how. You have to draw on it for your
own support in order to be able to extend support to the people you're caring for."

CONCLUSIONS

Some of what is learned through these interviews comports well with the traditional subject matter of bioethics. We hear the physicians speak, in their own
terms, of respect for persons and the importance of physician beneficence.
Concerns for justice come through clearly in Dr. D's problems with inadequate
health care coverage and Dr. C's attempts to be fair in his judgments about a family whose behavior seems to violate societal norms. However, what is distinct
about the stories told here is the overriding importance to the physicians of forming and maintaining relationships with patients and their parents, and the strong
religious foundations of their ethical principles and approaches. The latter point
appears to be true of Dr. C as well as of the three more traditionally religious participants, given the notable influence on him of the character traits that his father
attributes directly to their ancestral Jewish identity.

These doctors reemphasize the importance of the physician-patient relationship in their identification of confidentiality issues in the care of adolescents as a
major ethical concern in their practices. Adolescent matters are difficult because
the relationship with the parents must shift as the child matures from dependency
to independence, and physicians' must not only make the change in focus them-

selves but also help the parents recognize and accept their new position in relation to their child and to their child's doctors. One of the primary skills of
pediatrics is the ability to work effectively and smoothly within a triangle or
quadrangle composed of patient, parent(s), and physician. This working relationship is usually formed during the child's infancy and then changes gradually as
the child matures. However, the final version—the mature adolescent's independent, private relationship with the doctor—may emerge not gradually, but suddenly, when an issue arises that obligates the pediatrician to regard the child as a
virtual adult, with the right to confidential care. The ethical dilemmas that bedevil
this shifting phase in the relationship are the obvious ones of adolescent con-
sent/assent and of defining the areas for which the law effectively emancipates
teenagers. But the problems are also the more subtle ones of how to preserve the
relationship with parents while significantly altering it in such a way that the
doctor can help them to allow their teens to become healthy, independent adults.

As is clear from the initial stories told here, the matter of preserving physician-
family relationships can be problematic not only during the patient's adolescence
but also at other points in the family's life, when inescapable professional obligations may call the doctor to disagree with or confront the family about difficult
issues that may be open to multiple interpretations. The pediatricians in this study
have little trouble deciding the proper treatment for clear-cut medical illness, but
they find many pitfalls in deciding proper procedures for managing the problems
associated with inadequate or "abnormal" parenting, social chaos, or extreme
poverty that so often come to the physician for advice and relief. The nuances,
intricacies, and central importance of the physician-patient relationship are clear
to those who practice primary care medicine, and those practitioners would benefit from serious ethical attention to the subject.

The relation of religion to these doctors' ethical views of their work suggests
another point of interest for the field of medical ethics. Much of bioethics' interest in religion focuses on the place of theology in the formulation of ethical theory and the place of religious belief in conflicts that arise in medical decision
making. These interviews demonstrate another significant role of religion: the
formation of some doctors' understanding of the nature of medical practice,
approach to their interactions with patients and families, definition of their roles
and tasks, and inclination toward certain forms of practice. Dr. D spoke of "the
religious stuff" being "embedded"; Dr. A considers the moral teachings of her
religious tradition to be "so inbred that I can't imagine giving them up." Dr. B
attributes his becoming aware of the needs of his patients and the relational
aspects of his job to the inseparable combination of his wife and his renewed religious engagement. Dr. C's consistent practice maxim—"I wanted people who
come to me to know I'd listen to them"—was formed by his father's experiences

and exemplary professional life; despite his ambivalence, Dr. C joins his father in recognizing the impact of their Jewish heritage.

There is a parallel between the embedded nature of the religious influence in these doctors' lives and their emphasis on the central moral significance of the physician-patient relationship, within which the professional ethical issues are likewise embedded rather than appearing as occasional, isolated decision points. The religious language of neighbor-love and of seeing others as God's children— words of duty and care—permeates these interviews just as the primacy of rela- tionship permeates their practices. The doctors do not speak of calling on partic- ular religious symbols, rituals, or rules, like the command not to kill, in response to an urgent, defined ethical question, like whether to remove a patient from life support. Instead, we see their professional and personal lives, deeply informed and marked by their religious inheritance, in open and engaged relationship with the lives of their patients and their families, enacting traditional religious injunc- tions to love and to serve others.

For these doctors, the "others" are not the generic neighbor of the scriptural precept, so often lost sight of as theology focuses its attention on the part of the command that insists we be people who love. Their neighbors are individuals with names, with unique stories that are attended to carefully, with specific needs that are respected and responded to. Moreover, a strong sense of duty flows from all these interviews; each physician is capable of saying, "It's what pediatricians are supposed to do." The sense of duty comes not from medical school teaching, residency training experience, or patient demands, but from religiously grounded and experientially reinforced notions of "obligation, responsibility, and loyalty," to quote Dr. D.

It is also clear from the material presented here that, even for the participants with strongly normative religious beliefs, accepted professional obligations take precedence over religious mandates. Drs. C and D identified no areas of conflict between religion and medical practice. Drs. A and B do identify conflicts, but they state clearly and without hesitation, as though they were reciting an obvious moral given, that even though they believe certain things, their obligation as physicians is not to impose their beliefs. Rather, they must present their patients with information and assistance that will allow them to make and carry out their own decisions about their health care and behaviors.

This observation raises particular questions for medical ethics, policy, and per- haps law. The pediatricians interviewed have no question that the medical and legal requirements of their profession override their individual beliefs about cer- tain behavioral choices. They were unable to tell me where or how they had learned to assort their allegiances that way; they took it as an implicitly under- stood consequence of taking on the professional role. Drs. A and B also made clear that their religious beliefs were one reason they did not specialize in gynecology, the field in which they might be called on to perform or recommend abortions. The decisions they make and the counseling they provide as pediatricians may compromise their convictions about such matters as premarital sex and parental rights in ways that trouble them, but these responsibilities are not as difficult to carry out or live with as direct complicity with abortion would be.

Drs. A and B state that they cannot impose their beliefs on their patients; for Drs. C and D, the question of imposition does not arise. However, there are physicians—Dr. C, with disapproval, has given an example of one—who have not accepted the tacit moral premise of medicine that seems so obvious to the subjects of this study, and who instead give unquestioning precedence to their personal religious convictions in matters of conflict. Perhaps such doctors would not speak of "imposing" their beliefs on their patients but rather of a faithful integrity that does not allow them to compromise those beliefs in obedience to any other moral code, or even of an overriding religious obligation to witness to their beliefs at every opportunity, including professional ones. What has the profession of medicine or the discipline of bioethics to say about this matter?

There appear to be at least three ways in which this question could be addressed. First, given state subsidies for medical education and state governance of the privilege of practicing medicine, and given the constitutionally secular nature of the U.S. government and public institutions, perhaps codes of medical ethics should include provisions that obligate practitioners to set aside certain religious mandates when and if they conflict with ethical and legal standards of medical care. That would entail requiring, for example, that persons who will not perform abortions not be certified as gynecologists.

A second possible approach is that the controls should be less absolute and require only that practitioners whose religious beliefs conflict with legally permissible medical practice post some sort of notice in their office waiting rooms declaring, for example, that this physician will not recommend or prescribe contraception for unmarried persons, or will not perform, discuss, or refer patients for abortions. Or, as a third alternative, medicine and bioethics together should recognize that the right of religious expression is too fundamental and important to be overridden by professional obligations (or that religious convictions and motivations are so intrinsic to the morality of many practitioners that to set them aside or diminish their importance might threaten the possibility of ethical medical practice) and leave patients and doctors to negotiate the issues as they arise.

I believe the first option is both justifiable and desirable, based on the state's investment in the medical profession, its interest in assuring equitable health care, and religious warrants for justice and respect for persons. However, I must also acknowledge that it is highly unlikely such a mandate could be successfully enacted. The second option—a "truth-in-packaging" law for physicians—may be more achievable and still approach the goal of fair, complete, and honest care. Given the central importance of the physician-patient relationship to the practice of good medicine, and of honesty to that relationship, it would seem reasonable to require at least that before patients enter into a relationship with a particular doctor, they must be made aware whether the doctor will withhold information about or access to certain forms of medical care.

When asked where she learned to recognize and agreed to take on the expanded physician's role that primary care pediatrics seems to call for, Dr. A said simply, "It's what pediatricians are supposed to do." The moral imperative couched in the phrase "supposed to" is not self-evident; its content and implications need analysis and debate from ethical, clinical, and pedagogical viewpoints. We may all agree that pediatricians are "supposed to" be able to diagnose and treat diseases of children and help ensure healthy growth and development of the children in their practices. The consensus begins to falter, however, when we wonder what pediatricians are "supposed to" do in regard to abusive parents, inadequate community resources, or insufficient funding for child health care. The accord may break down entirely when we ask what pediatricians are "supposed to" do with their religiously based moral convictions in the face of patients or families whose behaviors or needs ask the doctor to compromise or set aside those beliefs. What *are* pediatricians supposed to do?

It is important to hear, through these doctors' voices, how seriously they take that question and how much is packed into their answers by virtue of their own backgrounds and religious traditions. The professional ethics—the moral imaginations—of these four pediatricians is intricately enmeshed with their practices and with their beliefs, "patient experiences and social priorities."[5] Lessons for medical ethics from these articulate, compassionate physician voices include the need for attention to the content and centrality of the physician-patient relationship as an ethical obligation and a moral good, and attention to matters of policy and guidance regarding the interrelation of religious and professional ethics.

5

ETHICS, FAITH, AND HEALING

Jewish Physicians Reflect on Medical Practice

LOUIS E. NEWMAN[1]

Healing has long been associated with divine power and, accordingly, the earliest physicians were frequently individuals in positions of religious authority. Certainly within western religious traditions, the ability to heal has frequently been closely connected with God and/or God's chosen representatives.[2] Moses intercedes with God to heal his sister Miriam's leprosy,[3] Elijah's prayers restore life to a deceased child,[4] and, of course, Jesus' power to heal is confirmation of his divinity.[5] In many native and nonwestern traditions as well, the shaman is both healer and religious leader.[6] Likewise, the opening words of the famous Hippocratic oath reflect an awareness of the close connection between healing and religion: "I swear by Apollo the physician and Aesculapius . . . and all the gods and goddesses. . . ." This long and widespread association between healing and divine power is hardly surprising. If, as Job declares, it is God who gives life and takes it away (Job 1:21), healing is nothing less than a manifestation of this very power channeled through human practitioners. From this perspective, it is no exaggeration to suggest that medicine is the most inherently religious of all professions, for it aspires to preserve and extend that most precious of divine gifts, life itself.

Modern western medicine, grounded as it is in the natural sciences, shares little if anything with this traditional, religious view of healing. Especially in recent decades, as the state of medical technology has advanced dramatically, the scientific character of medical practice has been greatly reinforced. Medical education continues to reflect a strongly scientific, mechanistic perspective; medical students are taught the biochemistry of the human organism, the appropriate pharmacological remedies for various diseases, and the technologies available for diagnosing and treating medical conditions. Even the growing interest in "alter-native medicine" and the movement toward more humanistic training of physi-cians has done little to alter the prevailing scientific orientation toward medical training and practice. Any suggestion that physicians possess special religious power or play a specifically religious role would be dismissed out of hand by most modern practitioners and patients alike.

It is this contrast between the traditional religious and modern scientific con-ceptions of medical practice that frames this study. My goal here is to explore the possibility that remnants of a more religious orientation toward medicine con-tinue to play a role in the lives of some contemporary physicians. Aware that some physicians are, after all, people of religious faith and active in religious communities, I set out to discover how, if at all, their religious commitments intersect with their professional practice. In particular, I was concerned to inves-tigate the ways in which the personal values and religious beliefs of some physi-cians influence their sense of professional responsibility, their relationships with patients, and their understanding of the healing process itself. To this end, I con-ducted extensive interviews over a period of three months with six pediatricians and pediatric specialists, all of whom identify as committed Jews and lead active Jewish lives. In questioning them about their personal backgrounds, religious commitments, and the values that guide their professional lives, I attempted to discern the intersection between religious symbols, values, and experiences, on the one hand, and the moral virtues of medical practice as they see them, on the other. What I discovered was a nexus of connections richer and more subtle than I could possibly have anticipated. As a result, I quickly abandoned any hope of establishing clear, causal connections between specific religious beliefs or prac-tices and specific professional attitudes. In their place, I discovered that each of these physicians is profoundly aware and appreciative of the religious dimensions of his medical practice, even if not all would identify those dimensions in similar ways or even construe them as "religious."

THE PARTICIPANTS

"... a doctor, like a writer, must have a voice of his own, something that conveys the timbre, the rhythm, the diction and the music of his humanity...."[7]

In choosing participants for this project, I attempted to select individuals with significant Jewish commitments who also had an interest in issues of faith and medicine as well as the willingness and inclination to discuss them with me.[8] In the interests of ensuring some commonality of professional experience and pro-viding a basis for comparing their views, I decided to interview only pediatricians and pediatric specialists.[9] I also attempted to achieve some diversity with respect to number of years in practice and to include those with both liberal and conservative religious orientations, in order to minimize the possibility that my responses would be skewed by such factors.[10]

Plainly, the small sample of participants ensured from the start that the results of these interviews would have no statistical significance. I cannot claim that the views these individuals shared with me are representative, even of the small subset of physicians to which they belong. My point is not to generalize in any way from these individuals to others who are engaged in pediatric care, or who are Jews, or who practice in the Midwest; still less am I working toward a comparison of this group of physicians with any other. Instead, my goal has been to explore the moral and religious contours of medical practice as they are experienced by one small—but very thoughtful and articulate—group of practitioners. These results will have significance if their voices resonate with other health care professionals and/or if they prompt scholars of professional ethics to investigate a broader range of issues or examine old issues from a new perspective.

Robert Karasov completed his medical training at the Mayo Medical School and now practices pediatrics in one of the largest medical groups in the Twin Cities. A person of enormous energy, he juggles multiple commitments: chairing his Department of Pediatrics, serving as the president of the board of a newly established Jewish high school, serving as a *mohel* (one who performs Jewish ritual circumcision), and helping his wife raise their five children. Straddling the Conservative and Orthodox Jewish communities, Karasov is very traditional in his religious practice, but generally liberal in his theological perspective. Asked about the personal experiences that have made him the sort of doctor he is, he responded, "Being married for twenty years, and all the natural ups and downs . . . raising five children . . . and the ups and downs you have as a parent—that has made me a much better doctor."

David Lee, born in Minneapolis and trained at the University of Minnesota, has practiced pediatrics for twenty years and speaks with pride about the loyalty of his patients. Studious by nature and clearly drawn to medicine partly for the intellectual challenges it offers (he was a math major in college), he is a shy man who appears somewhat self-conscious as he answers questions in a slow, measured way. Jewish summer camp was among the most formative experiences of his teen years, a tradition that continues with his children. He is now traditional in his Jewish practice and struggles to integrate his Judaism with the other dimensions of his life. Asked what aspects of his practice he is most proud of, he responded, "Being intellectually honest, educating parents and patients, and realizing how to accommodate the idiosyncrasies of my patients."

Mace Goldfarb has been practicing pediatrics for more than thirty years in a small clinic of mostly Jewish physicians. He considered internal medicine, but he was drawn to the resilience of children and the chance to watch them grow up. As he approaches retirement, he reflects on the changes that have taken place in medicine over the course of his career. He and his wife, who is a Jewish educator, have visited Israel several times and have raised their children (all now grown) with a strong sense of Jewish identity. In the late 1970s and early 1980s, he twice volunteered a few months of his time to work in refugee camps in Cambodia and Uganda. When asked how those experiences had affected his perspective on medicine, he answered, "I enjoyed humanity more. I wasn't as disease-oriented, or as scientifically [oriented]. There were things I couldn't explain, and yet you can give people solace. [I realized the importance of] giving comfort and just realizing what people are going through. I appreciated the lives of people."

Daniel Kohen is a behavioral pediatrician with an international reputation for his work on hypnosis. Trained at Wayne State University, he has been practicing for twenty-eight years, including more than five years with the U.S. Health Service on a Navaho reservation. A consummate storyteller with a quick wit, he is outgoing and clearly thrives on the relationships he establishes with patients, often children suffering from chronic pain or exhibiting a range of behavioral problems. He inherited his basic Jewish values from his parents, but his Jewish identity has been formed most decisively by his experiences as an adult. He and his wife now attend services regularly at their Conservative synagogue, although he admits to being less active than he would like. In describing his therapy with patients, he commented, "My best work is when I'm working intuitively." On the wall of his office is a large poster of Einstein with the caption, "Imagination is more important than knowledge."

Stacy Roback is a pediatric surgeon who began his medical training intending to go into academic medicine and certain that surgery was the one specialty he would never choose. A person who values the opportunity to see the results of his efforts promptly, he answers questions about his professional values confidently and without hesitation, reflecting the sort of decisiveness one might expect of a surgeon. The only adopted child of Jewish immigrants who fled Eastern Europe during World War II, his Jewish values were influenced by their Zionism and concern for social issues. He expresses a deep sense of comfort with Jewish ritual, although he is considerably less certain about his faith in God. In response to questions about relationships with patients, he mused, "I guess I was a little bit more of a 'holistic-y' type guy before that word was even on the map. . . . To me it's a lot more of a personal encounter than an event-driven encounter. I just find it not within my frame of reference to drop out of the picture."

Galen Breningstall is a pediatric neurologist who began his career in an academic position at Temple University but then moved into private practice in search of more extended and meaningful relationships with patients. Given the nature of his practice, he frequently finds himself in the position of having to inform parents that their children have life-threatening illnesses. A quiet, pensive person, he answers questions directly and wastes no words. In college he was a student of the humanities who discovered an aptitude for science only late in his career, at about the same time that he grew disillusioned with Eastern Orthodoxy and found his spiritual home in Judaism. He is now a member of an ultra-Orthodox synagogue; he covers his head and wears the traditional fringed garment (*talit katan*) at all times. On his application to medical school, he wrote, "There is a calling which comes from one's needs and I accept and affirm this calling. It leads me in the direction of academics, reading, and study in the humanities and sciences. There is also a calling which comes from one's being needed and I accept and affirm this calling. It leads me in the direction of the directionless, the perplexed and hurt. Medicine is the profession wherein I can listen to both these callings simultaneously." Today he continues to affirm the truth of those early insights.

In a series of extended interviews with each of these doctors,[11] I heard stories of the events that shaped their lives as individuals and as professionals, listened to their reflections on professional responsibility and on the qualities of their relationships with patients. I asked them about the values that inform their medical practice and the religious/spiritual experiences that have shaped their lives as individuals and as professionals. Their answers to these questions gave me some insight into the contours of their professional moral lives and enabled me to understand the sorts of moral choices they must make day by day and the ways in which they think about those choices.[12] In what follows I make no attempt to analyze the views of each physician in his own right. As I quickly discovered, the ways in which their responses coalesced were more instructive than the individual differences among them, important as they might be. In fact, they held a number of significant perspectives in common; in presenting these perspectives I hope to convey some of the moral and religious dimensions of medical practice as they collectively experience it.

THE MORAL DIMENSIONS OF MEDICAL PRACTICE

Physicians have moral responsibilities that move in several directions, toward patients and their families, colleagues, their employers, and society at large. For the purposes of this study, I have restricted my focus to the first of these spheres. As a practical matter, physicians typically spend the greatest proportion of their time with patients, and so that would appear to be the natural context in which to raise questions about their professional ethics. Moreover, whatever the actual distribution of their time, caring for patients arguably is the essence of physicians' professional life, the work for which they are trained. Certainly, it is the locus of the richest interpersonal experiences that physicians have in their professional lives.

As I explored the nature and meaning of patient relationships with these physicians, two dimensions of professional experience emerged as focal points of moral responsibility: experiences of power and of powerlessness. In the remainder of this section, I briefly sketch the ways in which both power and powerlessness figure in the lives of these physicians. In the section that follows, I turn to the moral dimensions of these dialectically related experiences. As I will suggest, the distinctive virtues that these informants identify as central to their professional lives—compassion, humility, and hope—express themselves both in the ways they exercise their (considerable) power and in the ways they experience their own powerlessness. I turn next to a consideration of how these experiences and the virtues that they call forth reflect a religious dimension in the professional lives of these physicians. In the concluding section of the paper, I reflect briefly on the implications of these findings for those who attempt to study the ethics of professionals, as well as for those engaged in medical education and those (especially rabbis) who seek to address the religious needs of Jewish physicians.

Power and Powerlessness

The power that pediatricians and pediatric specialists exercise may be so obvious that no extended discussion of this point is required. First and foremost, their special training and expertise enable them to diagnose and treat illnesses, from relatively trivial respiratory infections and rashes to life-threatening cancers and heart conditions. Quite literally, they hold the health and the very lives of our children in their hands. And, of course, dramatic advances in medical technology have further enhanced this power, especially with respect to the treatment of premature infants and newborns with congenital abnormalities. The pediatricians and pediatric specialists I spoke with were obviously well aware of the ways in which parents—especially first-time parents—rely on their advice and their power to heal. More than once they acknowledged that they liked being trusted; clearly, they derive some professional satisfaction from being able to use their expertise to help others. Karasov and Goldfarb both remarked on the fact that it is "a good feeling" when parents rely on their judgment, a sentiment that the others would very likely share.

Patients encounter the power of physicians in a myriad of other ways. Physicians control access to medication, to tests and special therapies of all sorts, and, in many health plans, to specialists with expertise in the particular area of concern to the patient. As parents have become increasingly well informed and proactive about the health care their children receive, they turn to pediatricians with requests that specific tests be performed or that certain specialists be consulted. In such situations, pediatricians must make decisions about how to exercise their power to give or withhold access to these medical services.

But physicians play powerful roles in the lives of their patients in far more subtle ways. Frequently they are privy to intimate details of a family's situation (e.g., the state of the parents' marriage or the emotional difficulties that an adolescent is experiencing). In these situations and others like them, these physicians must make choices about whether to counsel their patients and, if so, how; whether to be more or less directive; whether to give advice gently or firmly or not at all; whether to provide more information or less (especially in cases where more information might lead to more anxiety); or whether to follow up on a patient's situation more or less aggressively. In cases where there is widespread consensus on the proper course of treatment, some of these decisions are dictated by standard medical practice. But just as often they are matters of discretion, depending in part on the sort of role that the doctor chooses to play—as educator, counselor, family friend, or surrogate parent. Each of these roles is plainly possible, and each brings with it a subtly different kind of power to influence the lives of patients and their families. The opportunity to play any of these roles in the lives of their patients, whether or not doctors choose to embrace it fully, is yet another inescapable dimension of the power that physicians can exercise.

Yet, for all the power they wield, these physicians are acutely aware of their limitations. Their individual knowledge is limited, and each of these doctors spoke of the need not infrequently to consult others for a second opinion, even if only to confirm their own judgments. Some talked of diagnoses they had missed, especially early in their careers, sometimes with disastrous results. These experiences were invariably chastening. Karasov spoke of misdiagnosing a child's acute appendicitis as an experience that "will stick with me for the rest of my life," and Breningstall recalled a missed diagnosis of meningitis that resulted in a child's death as probably "overt error and incompetence." Aware that they cannot be perfect, they also recognize that they cannot allow errors, however serious, to immobilize them. In Roback's words, "You have to cut your losses and move on." However they choose to deal with their mistakes, the very fact that doctors are limited and imperfect practitioners presents a moral challenge: how to minimize the likelihood that they will make errors that compromise the quality of the care they provide and how best to learn from those errors when they do occur.

Moreover, the state of medical knowledge is itself imperfect, a fact that physicians may appreciate more fully and accept more readily than do patients. Goldfarb commented, "So much of what we do in medicine is untested. . . . A lot of what we do is trial and error." That being the case, physicians often face questions about what therapies to employ and especially about when it might be appropriate to recommend alternative, nontraditional therapies to their patients. Some of the doctors I spoke with indicated that parents increasingly are aware of alternative treatments and press them to endorse these nontraditional therapies, or raise pointed questions about why they will not. In responding to these requests, physicians must decide how best to fulfill their duty to care for patients when their own power to provide a cure may be limited or in doubt.

In some situations, the physician's power is not simply limited but entirely absent. When a patient dies—notwithstanding the physician's best efforts and the use of all the resources available to medical science—physicians confront their ultimate powerlessness. Kohen spoke at length about his first confrontation with that reality as an intern: "I remember feeling a combination of helplessness and sadness, and being hit in the face with the reality that doctors really don't save lives, at least not all the time, or don't cheat death, at least not all the time. I learned that very early and I'm glad for that. . . . Sometimes the patient dies and that's the way it is. . . . I learned that the operative word was 'influence' and not 'power' and not 'control.' " At such points, the practitioner is faced with a different moral challenge: What is my responsibility to my patients, or to their families, when I am powerless to heal them?

The foregoing list of experiences and questions by no means exhausts the moral terrain through which pediatricians and pediatric specialists must travel daily in the course of ordinary practice. Yet, as these issues surfaced, it became apparent that the moral texture of their professional lives is multifaceted. With power, in all its forms, comes responsibility, although the best ways of exercising that power and the precise extent of that responsibility are rarely clear-cut. When confronted with the limitations on one's power, or its absence altogether, the moral questions that arise are hardly less profound. For even when they find themselves unable to do successfully what their professional training has prepared them to do, they continue to feel a responsibility to the well-being of those entrusted to their care. In such cases, the challenge is to define and fulfill a kind of responsibility that can no longer be defined or fulfilled strictly within the bounds of professional competence.

As I listened to these physicians discuss these aspects of their moral duties to patients, I was struck by the extent to which certain characteristic virtues repeatedly emerged as central to their professional lives. Indeed, they often used virtually identical language to describe the ways in which they respond to certain sorts of situations, or think about their role as physician and the values that guide their practice. These values and virtues are what might be called the "goods internal to the practice of pediatrics," as these six physicians see them.[13] That is, the moral challenges facing physicians who treat children can be met most successfully when certain characteristic human qualities are cultivated; this particular professional activity appears to necessitate these sorts of moral traits. Three such virtues stand out—compassion, humility, and hope.[14] As I describe the perspectives of these physicians, it will become apparent that in many instances these "goods" are interconnected, and sometimes they are not distinguishable. Still, it will be useful to consider each separately.

Compassion

"I remind them [medical students] that for all its technological power, medicine is not a technological enterprise. The practice of medicine is a special kind of love."[15]

The roots of compassion lie in our ability and willingness to recognize the humanity of others, to see in them creatures like ourselves, and so to exhibit concern for their well-being. Given that physicians devote their lives to caring for others, perhaps it is not surprising that when asked about the qualities that make a good physician, several of these doctors listed compassion and caring above all. And while this perspective may be shared by physicians of all sorts, I sensed that it was particularly important to the ethos of those who care for children. Some stated that they were drawn to pediatrics in particular because children are more vulnerable than adults, less able to care for themselves, and thus more in need of the care that they can provide.

Compassion, as these physicians understand it, is intrinsic to quality medical care, not extraneous or superfluous. As Roback put it, "It was my observation early on that the people who cared were in fact the best doctors. . . . I still think that's probably correct. [There were] people with a great fund of knowledge and/or who were very skilled with their hands, but if they didn't care, somewhere in the patient encounter it became adverse." Goldfarb offered a utilitarian explanation for the fact that compassion is essential to medical care: "You can't give direction or advice to people if they don't think you like them or that you feel they are something special." In short, patients will not take your medical advice to heart if they don't feel that you care about them as human beings. Perhaps that is because, as many have observed, patients don't deal with their medical problems from a comfortable, therapeutic distance; they live with them and know that a medical condition, if serious or long-lasting, affects all aspects of their being.[16] Little wonder, then, that they are better patients if they sense that their caregivers appreciate their human situation, as distinct from caring about their medical condition.

Thus, all these doctors readily affirmed that compassion for patients is all about attending, in the words of the Christian ethicist Paul Ramsey, to "the patient as person."[17] Even as he questioned clichés about treating the "whole person," Lee acknowledged the essential truth of that orientation: "I only treat the part of the patient that's relevant, and often that's more than the part they're complaining about." This view was especially striking coming from Roback, insofar as surgeons are often stereotyped as interested in fixing discrete physical problems rather than attending to the situation more globally and over the long term. Commenting on the importance of dealing with the guilt that parents commonly feel when their children have a serious medical condition, he observed, "You have to deal with those problems. Actually, you don't *have* to deal with them. You could choose to ignore them. But somehow I don't think your obligation stops with your putting a bandage on the kid."

Given this way of thinking about compassion in medical care, it stands to reason that developing strong relationships with patients is central to their practice. Kohen put it most succinctly: "It's the enduring relationships that make a difference to me." But each in his own way talked openly about how showing compassion contributed to the deepening of their relationships with patients. Breningstall, reflecting on the unfortunate case of parents whose two young children were both diagnosed just weeks apart with Krabbe's disease, a degenerative and usually fatal condition, commented, "[T]hose kinds of relationships with patients is really what I find interesting in medical practice. Helping people to deal with bad news. Helping people to find positive aspects of the situations that are frequently devastating and terrible. Being there and hearing the feelings and emotions of the parents of the patients." Karasov, speaking from the perspective of a general pediatrician, reflected, "So much of what we're dealing with is stuff that's going to get better on its own anyway. Really what we're doing as doctors is reassuring people and letting their bodies heal themselves. It's more the emotional comfort that we give them, rather than the physical healing." And Goldfarb noted that treating people is "about giving people a chance to open up, not about the disease but about their lives and what they do, what makes them tick."

Compassion and its correlate, concern for the human situation of the patient, can express themselves in numerous concrete ways. Sometimes it means ordering tests that one knows will produce no new information of medical significance, as a way of relieving the anxiety of parents concerned about their children's health. At other times, it means suggesting to parents that they explore alternative therapies, even if one has little confidence that they will work, again because doing so is important to their emotional well-being. Almost invariably, it necessitates listening attentively for what the patient is saying "between the lines," seizing opportunities to address the emotional and psychological dimensions of a medical condition, as well as the willingness to show through one's gestures and in the tone of one's voice that one appreciates the existential situation of those one treats. However it may be expressed, all of the physicians who participated in this study insisted that compassion must be more than just a *feeling* or *attitude;* it must be *translated into action* in a way that enables the patient to recognize the physician's concern.[18] Indeed, Goldfarb noted at one point that he was not especially adept at this: "It's an area that I don't feel as comfortable with as probably I could. . . . I'm not as emotionally involved as I could be." Yet, at the same time, he acknowledged that he regarded this as a failing: "It's something I would strive for. I think it's important."

Often the caring and compassion demonstrated by these doctors far exceeded what might be necessary to maintain a strong therapeutic relationship. Perhaps the most striking example of this was Roback's response when one of his patients dies, even if that happens years after his surgical intervention. In addition to sending a personalized condolence letter to the parents, he makes an effort to attend the funeral, and he makes a charitable contribution in the patient's memory. He talked matter-of-factly about the father of one patient who died three years ago and who continues to invite him to have lunch each year, just because the father finds it valuable to stay connected. Fully aware that these steps go above and beyond the call of duty as most physicians would define it, he still insists that his actions are part and parcel of his professional responsibility: "I just can't see not doing those things. It just doesn't seem to me to be like putting the ribbon around the box. It seems to me like it completes the circle, whatever that means, for me. Maybe not even for them, but for me." Clearly, such expressions of compassion serve no utilitarian purpose in terms of caring for the patient. Rather, for Roback, they are expressions of human solidarity with those who have experienced a tragedy. He recognizes that for parents in such situations connecting with him is a means of dealing with their grief, and participating in that process is part of what he signed on for when he chose to become a pediatric surgeon.

For each of these doctors, then, compassion entails a willingness to extend the scope of their involvement in patients' lives, to demonstrate not merely professional concern for the aspects of their condition that they have been trained to treat but human concern for their condition as a whole. In some measure, as we have seen, they view this level of concern as integral to providing medical care in the narrower sense. And yet it is equally evident that compassion often expresses itself in ways that are quite extrinsic to the therapeutic encounter. In the final analysis, it involves reenvisioning one's professional role in the lives of those one serves and with it the very purpose of the professional encounter. Kohen put it most dramatically: "Though I'm not sure that I've ever written it down on the syllabus, or in the objectives for my rotation, what I want to teach residents is how to nurture the souls of their patients." In whatever individual ways each of these doctors might state this, it is their awareness that their patients have souls—and that proper medical care must reflect that fact—that underlies their manifold expressions of compassion.

Humility

For these physicians, the need for humility arises in a number of contexts. First and foremost, awareness of their own limitations necessitates a certain humility. Most noted that this awareness developed slowly over time, as their store of experience increased. In Lee's words, "after being in practice for a while, you learn never to be absolute unless you're 100 percent sure." In his case, this awareness often expresses itself in the qualified way he speaks to patients: "It looks normal to me, but just in case, we're going to have this reviewed." Karasov pointed out that this experience can be both positive and negative and that both sorts of experience engender humility. "You start out in practice and you learn *the way* to do things. . . . This is the way you were taught. . . . Over the years you have experiences. . . . You get kicked in the teeth a few times, you have patients complain, you learn what works, what doesn't work. . . . Suddenly, what you had learned was fact . . . things that you were so cocky about, you learn aren't true. So you get more mellow and more humble."

Of course, this attitude is especially reinforced when these physicians reflect on mistakes that they have made. Speaking of one case in which he missed a diagnosis with tragic results, Goldfarb reflected, "You hope you learn from it. It keeps your humility up. That's why they call it the practice of medicine, because you're constantly practicing. You really don't have all the answers." Potential mistakes, as well as actual ones, led some to reflect on this need for humility. Karasov put it starkly: "Every patient who walks through the door is a potential save or a potential screwup. So it keeps you humble." For Karasov, recognizing the power that he wields—to cure or to destroy lives—reminds him to be exceedingly cautious. In short, knowing what they don't know, and knowing how serious their own mistakes can be (and sometimes have been), these physicians affirm the importance of cultivating humility. While none reflected directly on the question of what would happen to their professional practice if they failed to acquire this virtue, it is not hard to infer the answer from the stories they related. Somewhat paradoxically, then, the very power they have over the lives of their pediatric patients reinforces a certain humility, for that is what helps ensure that they will wield that power responsibly.

But humility is rooted as well in the awareness that medical science is limited. Goldfarb put this most succinctly in quoting Maimonides, the great medieval Jewish philosopher and physician: "The art of healing is vast and the mind of man is puny." Most often, these physicians articulated the importance of humility in the context of their awareness that the results of what they do are so often unpredictable. Patients get well who they expected would not, and vice versa. Reflecting on this fact, Karasov commented, "It's made me a lot more humble.

Not being too dogmatic about what the outcomes are going to be. . . . There is just a lot you can't predict about how kids are going to turn out." Speaking as a specialist, Breningstall echoed much the same sentiment: "On a given day if I understand 10 percent of what I see, it's a good day. . . . There are a lot of enigmatic things that come my way. After having done the conventional thing, following the standard scientific route, you are left with saying that I really don't know what's going on here. I know vaguely this kind of thing, but it's not a satisfying explanation that you are really looking for." In short, medical science, for all its advances, remains a long way from being able to explain all that physicians encounter in their everyday practice. Humility, then, reflects a sense of awe at the complexity and mystery of life, a point to which we will return later.

Finally, Kohen noted that his work with patients is inherently collaborative, so, even when successes occur, he can take at best only partial credit. His understanding of what it means to be a physician is deeply informed by that reality: "I'm a facilitator and a teacher. As such I can be called a healer, but not in the traditional sense of the word, where people come in here with a problem and come out without it. It doesn't work that way. This is a partnership, but mostly what I do is help people unlock doors. They've got to walk through the door. They've got to do whatever they need to do in that room. I can help them manage that along the way. . . . I don't want to claim credit."

Quite apart from mistakes he may have made, or the state of medical knowledge in general, Kohen's sense of humility comes from an awareness of how healing takes place. The healing process requires the active cooperation of the patient, without which all the physician's expertise will not produce the desired results. Lee echoed the same sentiment when he said, "If someone gets better, I don't consider that I healed them. They say that doctors think they're God, but I know I'm not God. So I don't think doctors should credit themselves when their patients get better, other than that they made the right diagnosis." The same point is expressed metaphorically by Rachel Naomi Remen, a pediatrician whose work with cancer patients has earned her national recognition: "Seeing the life force in human beings brings medicine closer to gardening than to carpentry. I don't fix a rosebush. A rosebush is a living process, and as a student of that process, I can learn to prune, to nurture and cooperate with it in ways that allow it best to 'happen,' to maximize the life force in it even in the presence of disease."[19]

Hope

In the course of treating patients, these physicians often recognize that their well-being, and sometimes the specific outcome of their treatment, may depend on the patients' own attitude. Accordingly, several of them expressed the value of being hopeful and communicating a strong, positive message to patients. Lee was most explicit about this point, and it came up repeatedly in the course of our conversations: "It's important to be hopeful, to offer a positive approach"; "I have very positive expectations. I'm a very strong optimist. I think that may make a difference"; and "I think positive expectations are helpful. Just think what the opposite does." Although Lee acknowledged that he had never conducted a study to show that positive messages actually shorten the course of an illness, it was apparent that he believed that children in particular, given their impressionability, do respond to direct positive messages. Goldfarb seemed to assume that as well: "When you have a parent that's positive, thinking about getting better and working towards it, you've got a kid who gets better much quicker too." For both these doctors, then, giving patients and their families hope that a painful illness or even a chronic condition will get better is an important, if not essential, element in the healing process.

Kohen, who specializes in treatment that relies on the mind-body connection, confirmed the essential role that hope plays in treating patients: "What do expectations have to do with outcomes? I think they have everything to do with outcomes. If someone expects to be ill . . . that's going to contribute to them staying ill. Whereas the converse is also true." For that reason, he will sometimes test a patient's psychological readiness to let go of the physical condition that's troubling him or her: "Would it be okay with you if these headaches went away, even if we couldn't explain how that happened?" Recognizing that expectations affect outcomes means that providing patients with positive expectations is part of the physician's responsibility; to fail in this regard would be (at least potentially) to adversely affect the healing process.

Breningstall focused on the value of hope for the parents of children with difficult conditions. "Both the notion of conveying to parents that they have a certain competence, that there is an expectation that they will be able to surmount whatever situation they are dealing with at the moment, trying to give them confidence, things can improve—that's a very important part of things. Giving people that feeling that they can make choices, and that those can be good choices, is an important part of what we do." Here providing hope is less about affecting the result than it is about helping parents cope with the difficulties of a seriously ill child. For Breningstall, and I suspect for others as well, providing hope is closely related to compassion as it was described above. Insofar as one cares about the human situation of the patient (and in pediatrics that must include the patient's family), one's responsibility is to give them the confidence and resources necessary to cope with that situation.

When I discussed hope as an element of medical care with Sheldon Berkowitz, a pediatrician who was not a subject in this study, he explained the issue in relation to one aspect of the physician's power. Doctors plainly have the power to shatter the parents' world when they deliver bad news about the health of their child. That being the case, compassion requires that one attempt to "soften the blow" by offering some hope; without it, you simply leave them hanging with no support to help them process the information you have given them. In this physician's words, "hope is essential."[20] Hope, then, is an essential, indispensable virtue in medical practice, both because it sometimes promotes healing itself (a phenomenon that some doctors in this study linked to the placebo effect) and because, like compassion, it is intrinsic to physicians' duty to respond to patients' and their families' human condition. Hope, in short, has both instrumental and intrinsic value, as it both contributes to healing and represents one expression of compassion, which is a value in its own right.

Given the striking uniformity of these doctors' responses about the major virtues necessary to medical practice, it was surprising that they pointed to a great many different ways in which they came to recognize them. Some pointed to the values that they learned in their family of origin. For Kohen, Lee, and Roback, the values of compassion and caring for those less fortunate were major components of their upbringing. These values, they recognize, express themselves now in their medical practice but would almost certainly have been evident no matter what career path they had chosen. Breningstall, Goldfarb, and Karasov also noted that their sense of compassion, and in some cases of humility, had been instilled in the course of their medical training itself. Each pointed to specific role models (some positive, some negative) whose example taught a valuable lesson about the qualities essential to medical practice. For many, personal experience has played a role as well. Breningstall noted that he lost a son to Sudden Infant Death Syndrome (SIDS) and that, in his words, "that was a very powerful factor in forming [his] approach to individuals with devastating problems. . . . Unfortunately, having personal tragedy helps make you a better doctor." Kohen was acutely aware that his work with the Navaho opened his perspective dramatically, giving him an appreciation for the fact that "we're all on this planet together" and "we all need to help one another."

Interspersed with these reflections on the ethics of medical practice and the virtues of compassion, humility, and hope, these physicians spoke extensively about their religious perspectives, on life in general, and on the practice of medicine in particular.[21] Their responses to questions about their belief in God and about "sacred" moments in their practice provide important evidence about the way they understand their responsibilities as professionals and their mission as physicians. We turn next to these religious dimensions of medical practice.

THE RELIGIOUS DIMENSIONS OF MEDICAL PRACTICE

Religious ways of understanding the world and one's place within it were strongly in evidence in these doctors' comments about their professional lives. Four distinctly religious dimensions of medical practice emerged from these interviews: God's role in the healing process (and the corresponding value of prayer), awareness of the miracle of human life, the physician's role as pastor attending to the spiritual needs of patients, and medicine as a "calling." After looking at each of these dimensions, we will consider how these religious attitudes are related to the virtues of medical practice discussed in the previous section.

Each of these physicians spoke eloquently about the mystery inherent in the healing process and the way in which supernatural powers beyond his control affect the outcomes of medical interventions. Lee stated this most succinctly: "I've had experiences that I can't explain in any other way, other than that there are some forces at work beyond the realm of natural laws as we understand them." Others likewise recognize the existence of supernatural forces that they cannot explain scientifically and struggle with whether those forces conform to belief in the God of traditional theism. As Karasov put it, "I know there are mysteries of the universe. . . . I don't try to figure it out too much. I just know that there are mysteries and forces that affect healing and whether you want to label that as 'God'—I suppose God is as good a label as anything else." Kohen, too, struggles to figure out what to make of those forces in the world: "I not uncommonly have experiences with patients that are not easily explained. I can choose to understand that from a . . . 'that's about God' perspective. Sometimes I feel like I know that and other times I feel like it doesn't matter. . . . There's a lot of stuff that happens in our daily life that I'm very clear that I don't understand. And I'm very clear that it's real and that it has something to do with powers that abound. Most of the time I'm very content to say, 'That's about God in our lives.' I don't understand it other than that."

The striking fact here is not that these physicians struggle to make sense of their religious intuitions about the world in relation to their scientific outlook, but that all of them appeared very comfortable with the uncertainty inherent in acknowledging a mysterious, unknowable element in their lives. Even Roback, who was least certain about belief in God, did not find it threatening: "I'm not uncomfortable with belief in God. I'm comfortable in saying, 'I hope there is.'" This awareness of the a-rational component of experience, and a corresponding openness to the possibility that some divine force is at work in the world, was a frequent refrain in our conversations.

Beyond acknowledging the possibility of God's existence, these doctors often expressed a sense that their professional work was complementary to God's.

Breningstall expressed the strongest views: "God rules the world and really is the ultimate achiever. . . . [I subscribe to] the whole notion that the world doesn't operate by miracles. Everybody has to play their role and do their job. . . . [All our] strengths, talents, and accomplishments are God-given, so that when you reduce it to the ultimate, you're doing your job, but the real credit for what is accomplished is a credit that goes to God."

Goldfarb and Karasov similarly acknowledged a key role for God in the healing process: "I do believe in God. . . . God plays a big role in healing. What we do isn't quite as important as God's role." "You can't wait for a miracle or for God to do the cure, so you do everything you can on the medical side and hope you get some help from the other side. . . . You're God's partner." Others endorsed a similar perspective in less explicitly theological terms: Kohen—"I'm happy to be a partner with whatever power is responsible [for healing]." Roback—"I take it as far as I can and whatever forces come into play from that point on, I'll take all the help I can get." Each of these physicians, then, approaches his work with a sense that his professional success (as measured by his ability to heal patients) depends partly (some would say, ultimately) on forces beyond his control, forces that most of them are comfortable calling "God."

Given that fact, it is hardly surprising that most of these doctors report occasions on which they have consciously called on that divine force to assist them or their patients. Goldfarb recalled times in his practice when he has been faced with a situation in which he was not sure what to do: "I didn't know where I was going, and all of a sudden, I had a realization that this is what I should be doing. . . . It was almost like it was infused into me somehow; [there was a] guiding hand, in other words, saying that this is the right way to do it." On those occasions, he has felt a distinct sense that God was aiding him in reaching the right decision, something that he has consciously prayed for at other times. Breningstall likewise has sought divine assistance at difficult moments in his practice: "I think there are lots of times when you pause and ask for help as you're going into a situation, [such as] 'I really need some support and strength to meet with these parents, or to do this or that, I feel pretty helpless and inept right now. Please give me the strength to deal with this in an adequate way.' "

Lee and Roback were explicit about the fact that they sometimes invoke this power to help patients deal with their illnesses. Lee affirmed, "I do believe in prayer, in the power of prayer. But there has to be an appropriate intention [i.e., not a prayer for the physically impossible]. . . . I think positive thoughts help. I probably have encouraged people to pray . . . though I certainly haven't prayed with them." Roback, again in a less explicitly religious vein, commented, "You sort of feel like any positive vibes that you can throw at a situation certainly aren't going to hurt. I don't think I ever go through the verbal recitations that make it sound in a conventional sense like a prayer. But I suspect it's probably pretty much the same thing. . . . The sentiment and the agony and the time investment and the spontaneity of it are pretty much the same." So, even if these doctors feel uneasy about engaging in prayer with their patients—something they suggested would feel awkward and even inappropriate to their role as physicians—they openly acknowledged that they themselves pray. The divine power that they see at work in the world is something they rely on and seek to invoke in the course of their professional work. Whether expressed in formal prayer or in a less God-oriented language, these physicians sometimes feel the need or desire to ask for help from a power greater than themselves. Judging from their testimony, these prayers are expressed both on behalf of their patients and, perhaps just as often, on their own behalf, as a way to give them strength or comfort as they face difficult professional challenges.

A second, closely related religious dimension of medical practice is a sense of awe at the nature of human life, especially its intricacies and the resilience of the human spirit. When given a quotation from Rachel Naomi Remen to the effect that physicians have a "front row seat on the mystery of life" and asked to say what they have learned from their own front row seat, Roback responded,

> The thing that I've learned is that it's very dependent upon literally an infinite number of things happening in concert at the same moment in time, and if they are not, it's over in less than the blink of an eye. It's very, very, very fragile. If there is anything that is the most convincing argument for me about the concept of a supreme being, it's that the orchestration of this whole thing really does qualify as a miracle. . . . Even in a biologic sense, it's a miracle. And we don't even know yet how big a miracle it is, though it seems to me that every day and every week, the idea of how incredible the whole thing is comes to the fore. . . . It's a biological concert, but if the third string violinist is not hitting a note that's exactly right, and I was sitting in the auditorium and listening, I probably couldn't tell, but in a biologic model, it's a fatal flaw. That, to me, is fairly extraordinary. We're all sort of standing on a rug that could be jerked out literally at any moment. It's pretty amazing what goes on. And we're only at the periphery of it.

Both the fragility and the complexity of human life impress Roback and plainly evoke a sense of awe. For his part, Karasov was clear that this sense of awe grows with one's years in practice. He noted that, after a certain amount of experience, you learn that you cannot learn everything and that the goal is not the mastery of all there is to know. At that point it becomes possible "to appreciate what you don't know instead of just being scared by it."

Other physicians expressed a similar sense of religious wonder but focused on the power of the human spirit that they frequently encounter in their practice. Kohen noted, "I'm in awe of how parents of handicapped kids do their lives. . . . I think that that's got to be power that comes from God. I don't know where else it comes from." In reflecting on his experiences with terribly impoverished families in Thailand, Goldfarb noted, "[Y]et there's a real humanity there, a real love of life. I think that's God's flame." Goldfarb went on to comment on mothers who are drug addicts and similar heart-wrenching situations: "Every person that I see has some sort of spirit, a wonderful spirit. Sometimes it's a question of arousing that spirit, because it's been dampened a lot." Similarly, Breningstall spoke about a sense of wonder and amazement that he feels repeatedly when he observes the power of the parent-child bond, particularly in cases of severely impaired children. It comes as no surprise that physicians have occasion to witness a good deal of human suffering, as well as to observe the power of individuals to cope with their trials and to rise above the obstacles that life puts in their way. The striking point is that these doctors use explicitly religious language to describe these situations. While most were not prepared to attribute human suffering to God, they readily do so for human resilience.

But the religious dimension of medical practice emerges not only in the physicians' perspective on healing and the mystery of human life; it affects the very way in which they understand their role as physicians. Several of the doctors I spoke with acknowledged that they are sometimes called on to play a "pastoral" role with patients. When asked if he had had anything that he would call a "sacred moment" in his medical practice, Roback recalled dealing with parents after they have lost a child in surgery: "Sacred moments are those difficult times when it's you and the family and you've got those critical few moments when people are grabbing on to the meaning of what you're saying and [trying] to have something come out of it that is somehow comforting or spiritual . . . for me personally they tend to be fairly, almost like religious experiences." He spoke at length about the special connection that develops in such situations between the parents and the surgeon, precisely because he is the last person who had contact with their child during his or her life. "To the extent that you can answer all the questions, and relieve the burden and lessen the guilt, ease the transition . . . there isn't anybody else that can do that." As he put it, in those moments, "[Y]ou're more pastor than doctor." Clearly, Roback is comfortable in this pastoral role and understands it as part and parcel of his responsibility as a physician to offer spiritual comfort in whatever ways he is able.

Other physicians, dealing with less dramatic situations, also noted that attending to the spiritual concerns of patients and their families is integral to their practice, or should be. Noting that there is definitely a "pastoral component" to a doctor's work, Goldfarb talked about how grateful bereaved parents are when he visits them. Both Kohen and Karasov acknowledged that they don't explore the spiritual dimensions of the patient's life as fully as they should, given how valuable this exploration can be. Karasov observed, "[T]he whole other part of this alternative approach [to medicine] is spirituality, asking people where they get their spiritual strength. . . . [I]t's clearly documented that that stuff helps; it's not quackery. . . . Periodically I'll make little attempts to ask some questions, but not well at all. That's an area that I'd like to get better at. . . . It takes some skills that I don't have yet." Kohen, for his part, simply noted that these questions should properly be as routine as "Where do you go to school?" though he recognizes that he tends to be passive in this regard, waiting for patients to raise spiritual concerns. Still, he regards it as his responsibility to respond to those spiritual concerns when they do arise.

All of the physicians acknowledged that this pastoral dimension of their work was something for which their medical training had not in the least prepared them. Yet in the course of their work they had come to recognize the importance of these matters and even to relish the opportunity to have an impact on their patients' lives in this more profound way. One could speculate that, as years of experience made the ordinary practice of medicine more routine, they naturally became more attuned to new challenges and new opportunities to care for their patients. In any event, judging from their testimony, spiritual care is a significant dimension of their medical practice, even if it happens on relatively rare occasions and even if (as for Karasov and Kohen) they still struggle to integrate it fully into their practice.

Finally, some of the doctors in this study clearly regard medical practice as a "calling," that is, as a kind of religious responsibility. Kohen was explicit in this regard: "I think it [medicine] is holy work. I don't have any doubt about that." He related this to the Jewish concept of *tikkun olam,* "repairing the world," a commitment that he has come to appreciate increasingly as he has grown older. Goldfarb echoed the same sentiments, though it was less clear how frequently or explicitly this guides his sense of what it means to be a doctor. Breningstall, for his part, reflected at some length about the role that God wanted him to play, the work that he was put on earth to do. "The one question that does inspire, time and time again . . . is, okay, what do You [i.e., God] want from me now, what am I supposed to be doing? Am I doing what I'm supposed to be doing? . . . Clearly, in this very complicated world there was some reason why I was supposed to have acquired a medical education and was supposed to have acquired competence in pediatric neurology. Given that that's the case, am I doing what I'm supposed to be doing?" Breningstall's questions betray a deeply religious conception of his profession and, so too, of the duties that it entails.

The religious components of these doctor's lives—as evidenced by their sense of awe, in their roles as partner with God and pastor to patients and their sense that practicing medicine is holy work—raise a number of questions. Are these religious ways of understanding life and medical practice related to the moral virtues that these physicians identified and, if so, how? How did they come to understand their professional responsibilities in this way? What can their reflections teach us about professional ethics and the ethics of physicians in particular? While this very limited study has yielded rich reflections on the role of the physicians, their moral responsibilities to patients, and their religious perspectives on life, these interpretive questions have yet to be faced. I want now to suggest that what we can learn from this material is both extremely suggestive and, in certain respects, quite inconclusive.

AT THE CROSSROADS: MORALITY
AND RELIGION IN PROFESSIONAL LIFE

The ethnography of the physician's care lags far behind the phenomenological description of the experience of illness. . . . We do not possess an adequate scientific language to capture the essence of the doctor's experience. What the doctor feels is most at stake—what is most relevant to practice—slips through our crude analytical grids. [22]

The preceding sections capture two dimensions of these physicians' reflections on professional life—its moral contours and the distinctive virtues of medical practice, on the one hand, and its religious components, on the other. The interpretive question that must be faced at the conclusion of this investigation is whether these two sets of reflections are interrelated and, if so, how. Having set out to investigate the ways in which religion shapes the moral lives of these physicians, I confront the problem of looking for connections between the religious and moral lives of these professionals that they themselves did not make explicitly. Two quite different ways of interpreting this material suggest themselves.

On the one hand, it is tempting to conclude that the religious attitudes of these physicians do indeed shape their professional ethics in a number of ways. In the first place, the virtues that they identify as central to their professional lives—compassion, humility, and hope—have religious overtones, as they describe them. Caring for children as people (in addition to caring for them as patients) correlates with their sensitivity to the spiritual dimensions of their patients' lives and their conviction that these matters require their attention as physicians. Their sense of humility appears to flow not only from the awareness of their human fallibility but also (and perhaps primarily) from their sense that they do their professional work in the context of God's work, that they are at best partners with those powerful, mysterious forces that bring about healing. Finally, their commitment to providing hope seems closely related to the pastoral role they are sometimes called on to play, whether by bolstering the spirits of their patients when they cannot heal their bodies or (less dramatically) by encouraging their spirits to aid in the healing process itself. Each of the virtues of medical practice, then, appears to correlate with the religious perspectives that these doctors bring to their work.

Moreover, there is evidence here that they understand their work as a whole in a religious context. At least for some of the doctors I interviewed, the practice of medicine is holy work, religiously as well as professionally satisfying. That does not mean that these physicians necessarily practice medicine differently because they are religious. Indeed, it is entirely possible (perhaps likely) that their patients would not recognize them as religious people and, at least most of the time, would not notice that they performed any of their professional duties any differently than do nonreligious physicians. Yet, from the physician's side, the entire meaning of a professional encounter is altered if one sees it as a kind of holy work, an opportunity to "repair the world," or as an occasion for marveling at the mystery and wonder of human life. Quite apart from shaping the particular choices they make or the ways in which they understand professional virtues, religion might transform the experience of practicing medicine, the significance that it holds in the life of the provider. The evidence of those who see medicine as a calling, a "profession" in the truest sense, suggests that they interpret the significance of their work lives in a more expansive way.

In short, one possible conclusion from the evidence assembled here is that religion profoundly shapes the professional lives of these physicians, even if in general they have not consciously thought of themselves in these terms. If, as they attest, providing compassion and hope are as essential to medical care as providing penicillin and regular physicals, it could be partly because they understand healing as something they provide with God's help and with profound respect for the divine spark present in all human life. To those who study religion, it would come as no surprise that one's religious perspective on life could tutor one's sense of professional responsibility—from the way physicians talk to patients and parents about difficult issues to the way they think about routine questions of prescribing drugs and choosing between alternative courses of treatment. In short, it could well be that these physicians practice medicine as they do because they are the sort of people they are, people shaped in part by their religious commitments or, absent firm commitments, by their openness to religious experiences of the world.

Yet this conclusion, however plausible, must not be accepted uncritically, for there is another way to interpret the evidence, a way that does not assume a causal connection between their religious views and their professional ethics. To see that this is so, we need only ask the following question: How shall we interpret any of the hundreds of decisions that these doctors regularly make—to order a particular test, to refer a patient to a specialist, to write a condolence letter to the parents of a deceased patient? Quite clearly, the way these physicians make these choices reflects the way they think about their responsibility and the best way to discharge it. But that, in turn, is shaped by numerous factors, not all of which may be conscious, much less consciously religious. As they related in our conversations, they have been influenced by the sort of medical training they received, the mentors who guided them (especially in the early years of practice), their parents and family members, a host of personal experiences of all sorts, and, perhaps most of all, thousands of patient encounters. The sources of their moral experience are multifaceted, a complex web of influences that have led them to their current views of what it means to be a physician and what sorts of moral responsibilities this profession entails. As they face the moral challenges of exercising their power and confronting their powerlessness, they do so as individuals whose moral character has been developed both within and outside their professional practice.

Moreover, the evidence suggests that their sense of professional responsibility is far from static. They have developed a sense of what they are called on to be and to do in response to their ongoing experience—to the fatal mistake they made (or almost made), to the parent who responds badly to their comments or questions, to the child who responds positively to their optimism and compassionate gesture. Their sense of professional duty is very much a "work in progress," for it is nurtured in the context of their work itself. They have learned about the virtues of medical practice through practice itself, by being present with parents in the face of tragedy and discovering what one can offer them, by being with children in an examining room and learning how to listen attentively. That, after all, is what we meant earlier by referring to compassion, humility, and hope as goods "internal to the practice" of medicine; the practice itself calls forth these moral traits. On this interpretation, their religious sensibilities are but one element, and not necessarily the most important one, in a complex mix of influences that shape their attitudes and choices.

Perhaps that accounts for the difficulty virtually every one of these physicians had in answering questions about how they acquired their sense of moral responsibility. While they could all point to various factors, they were strikingly vague about the source of their professional ethics. I suspect that this vagueness reflects not lack of self-awareness but genuine uncertainty about their own moral development as physicians. So many experiences, professional and otherwise, have come into play that they can hardly be expected to identify which have been decisive.[23]

While we can choose to interpret the data before us as evidence of the influence of religion on professional life, the converse is equally plausible. That is, medical practice itself may have tutored their sense of religiosity. The work of healing, and the experiences of power and powerlessness that that work entails, may have instilled a sense of what the Jewish theologian Abraham Joshua Heschel called "radical amazement" and identified as the most fundamental of religious experiences.[24] In this sense, medical practice is a religious calling for these doctors, not because they bring a religious mission to their work, but because their work calls forth in them heightened religious sensitivity. Perhaps, too, this accounts for the difficulty they had in relating their Jewish practice—ritual observance, synagogue attendance, etc.—to their professional lives. The latter has become an independent locus of spiritual meaning, a place where their awareness of the religious dimensions of life is nurtured as much as (for some, even more than) through the explicitly religious activities they perform.

While these interviews are suggestive, they are decidedly inconclusive. The role of religious belief in the professional lives of these physicians is extremely difficult to sort out with precision. We have ample evidence here that their sense of professional responsibility extends far beyond the matters they address within the limited scope of their professional expertise. Their sense that it is their moral duty as professionals to be compassionate, humble, and hopeful—as well as the particular ways in which these virtues manifest themselves—suggests that they do not rely solely on their particular professional expertise as physicians. But whether this more expansive sense of moral responsibility can be attributed to their religious views is far from certain.

If the causal connections between the religious and moral dimensions of medical practice cannot be drawn with certainty, other conclusions can be. Plainly, these physicians do think of their professional work in a religious context. The religious sensitivities that they express cannot be denied, and this fact in itself has important implications that point in a number of directions.

First, studies of professional ethics have largely overlooked certain dimensions of medical practice, insofar as they have defined the scope of professional ethics as the minimal standards of behavior that must be maintained in order to uphold the moral integrity of the profession. In the case of physicians, such standards include the duty of confidentiality, the duty to provide the best quality of professional service possible, and the duty to protect public health, among others. Failure to fulfill any of these duties would constitute "unprofessional" behavior and, in severe cases, might warrant disciplinary action by appropriate authorities. Yet, as these interviews amply attest, there is a great deal more to the moral life of professionals than merely remaining within the bounds of professional conduct.

Each patient encounter potentially provides opportunities to practice the virtues of compassion, humility, and hope. Because each professional encounter is also a human encounter, physicians always have the option of bringing to it the full depth of their humanity. That will entail stepping outside the bounds imposed by their role, taking into consideration factors that lie outside the scope of their medical expertise, including the psychological and spiritual needs of the patient and family. In doing so, they will transform the moral significance of this encounter, for it will no longer be a strictly professional interaction between a "doctor" and a "patient" but an opportunity to help the "patient as person" and, in some measure, to be "physician as person." Indeed, one of the striking commonalities among the physicians interviewed here is their refusal in varying degrees to acknowledge a sharp distinction between the professional and the personal. Accordingly, their moral duties as professionals and their moral duties as human beings concerned about others cannot be sharply differentiated. To be a morally sensitive physician and a morally insensitive person is, for them, an oxymoron. Although, as we observed above, we cannot attribute this perspective definitively to their religious values, we can note that, religious or not, this way of thinking about the moral life of the physician is almost wholly lacking in the standard literature on professional ethics.[25]

Similarly, among works on professional ethics one finds very few discussions of the intersection between religion and the life of the professional, for most of this work has adopted the vocabulary of secular, philosophical ethics.[26] The possibility that professionals might bring their own religious values to bear on their work, much less that they might regard their professional work as fulfilling a religious purpose, is not mentioned. Judging from the conversations undertaken in this study, that represents a significant lacuna in the literature on professional ethics. Certainly the participants in this study would have difficulty recognizing the moral lives they lead from the theoretical discussions found in most standard textbooks on professional ethics.[27] One can only wonder how differently those books would read if they attended to the richly textured moral experience of the doctors whose reflections are presented here.

A second set of implications follows for those engaged in medical education. Each of the participants in this study acknowledged that he did not acquire this more expansive, holistic sense of his moral responsibilities as physician during his medical training. Moreover, each seemed to feel that it would have been advantageous had that been otherwise. Even now, while the numbers of ethics courses taught in medical schools has increased substantially, the potential role of religion in the moral life of the medical professional seems to have been avoided. Partly, no doubt, this neglect reflects the fact that medical training is largely scientific in character and is assumed to be quite separate from (and perhaps even in tension with) religious life. Despite the long association between religion and healing noted at the outset of this essay, contemporary physicians receive little or no preparation to think about the religious questions that might arise for them or their patients in the course of their medical practice. Were this preparation to become a routine part of the training of physicians, they would be better able to understand what ails their patients, apart from the physiological conditions that they attend to. In the process, they would very likely become better, more effective healers. Though the evidence here again is inconclusive, they might even become more attuned to the subtler moral dimensions of medical practice.

Finally, this study may have some implications that pertain to the Jewishness of the participants and that flow from certain things they failed to say. In identifying the factors that nurtured their sense of professional ethics, these physicians listed a wide range of influences—family, mentors, and personal experience, among others. Strikingly, they had great difficulty pointing to specific ways in which their Jewishness influenced their medical practice, despite the fact that all of these individuals are strongly committed to Jewish tradition and practice and active in their respective Jewish communities. None drew connections between the most significant Jewish experiences of his life and his choice to enter the medical profession. None indicated that Jewish worship or ritual practice directly affected the way he practices medicine or thinks about healing, or that Judaism helped him answer questions about why innocent children suffer. None spoke of a time when a rabbi's teachings illuminated the moral aspects of his professional life. At most, they noted that compassion and caring for others were Jewish values and that Jewish rituals lend their lives a certain meaning and direction. Even Breningstall, by far the most traditionally religious member of this group, spoke in rather general terms about the enormous value that Judaism places on human life.[28]

Certainly, this silence can be interpreted in more than one way. Perhaps these physicians have difficulty connecting their Jewish lives to their professional lives because they do not experience a deep connection. What happens in the synagogue or in their own homes as they perform Jewish rituals and recite ancient prayers simply does not spill over into their work as physicians. Perhaps quite the opposite is the case—that the connection between their Jewish experience and their experience as physicians is so natural, so unconscious, that they have a hard time articulating it. Or perhaps those connections are felt strongly but understood only vaguely, so that they simply lack the vocabulary to identify the ways in which these related dimensions of their lives intersect.[29]

However one reads the evidence here, I suggest that this disjunct represents a failure, or at least a missed opportunity, for the rabbis and the synagogue communities to which these physicians belong. After all, Judaism has a great deal to say about God's role in healing, the power of prayer, and the duty to offer healing and comfort to the sick, to name but a few of the salient topics from our conversations. For their part, these physicians certainly have a well-developed sense of the religious meaning of their work. Yet they may need help making or articulating the connections between their religious tradition and their own moral/religious experience as physicians. In any event, listening to them speak so eloquently about the moral and religious dimensions of medical practice, one cannot help but conclude that their Jewish and professional lives could be more fully integrated.[30] If rabbis were attentive to this possibility, they might help their physician congregants enhance their connection to Jewish tradition, and, in the process, they might discover new ways to do the same for other groups of professionals.

This study ends inconclusively, and necessarily so. Just as these results are not statistically significant, and the causal connections between religious identity and moral sensibility cannot be clearly drawn, so too the implications I have drawn are rather sketchy and open-ended. It is in the nature of ethnographic investigations such as this one that they bring into view a bewildering complexity and richness of experience that does not readily yield to logical analysis or neat categorization. Ethnography, like fiction, attends to the stories of people's lives and reveals the moral depth and complexity of their experience. Indeed, that is its primary virtue and the way in which it serves as a corrective to both abstract philosophical as well as statistical and sociological research into professional life. But there is a price to be paid for unearthing the moral ecology of professional life in this way. The stories that are at the heart of any account of human, including professional, experience are always messy and idiosyncratic precisely because they are richly textured and personal. They provide a window into the hearts and minds of individuals who have much to teach us, but they do not offer us a road map for navigating the world that they open up to us. In all, they offer us no firm conclusions about the relationship between religion and ethics in the lives of professionals, not even in the lives of the handful of individuals studied. Instead, their stories help us to see the religious/moral lives of these physicians more fully and, in the light of that vision, to challenge accepted ways of thinking about professional ethics and to raise new questions about the lessons we can draw from their experience.

PART THREE

COINCIDENCE/CONFLICT BETWEEN
COMMITMENTS: TRANSPLANTATION

6

ORGAN TRANSPLANTS

Death, Dis-organ-ization, and the Need for Religious Ritual

ALLEN D. VERHEY

" 'Brain-dead,' said the doctor." It's the first line in Richard Selzer's story of Hannah in "Whither Thou Goest."[1] It's the first line, but it is hardly the last word.

Hannah and Sam, her husband, had celebrated his thirty-third birthday by spending a weekend at the beach together. On the trip home Sam had stopped their pickup to help a stranded motorist change a tire. Good Samaritan Sam was himself assaulted, shot in the head, and left in the road with a halo of blood. Three weeks later, as preface to his request that Hannah donate her husband's organs for transplantation, the doctor announced that Sam was brain-dead. It seemed reasonable enough, supported by an electroencephalograph that the doctor unrolled to display a tidy flat line. In an effort to reassure Hannah, however, the doctor added, "The only thing keeping him alive is the respirator." That remark, hard on the heels of the doctor's confident announcement that Sam was brain-dead, confused Hannah—and revealed a messy ambiguity that no flat line on a graph could hide.

"Let him go," the doctor said, evidently unable to comprehend the implication of his own diagnosis that he was already gone. The doctor pressed on toward the request. "We would like your permission to harvest Sam's organs for transplantation," he said. And, as if to make it easier for Hannah, he added, "That way your husband will live on. He will not really have died. . . ."[2] This statement confused Hannah still more, and in an effort to restore some sense to this conversation she responded, "Dead is dead."

In spite of her confusion—or perhaps because of it—Hannah allowed the hospital to "harvest" Sam's organs. A week later she received a thank-you letter from the doctor. It informed her that, thanks to her generous gift (and "to the miracle of modern science"), Sam's organs were benefiting seven people. There was a little list of organs and recipients, including information that Sam's heart had been given to "a man just your husband's age in a little town near Arkansas."[3] This information, too, confused Hannah. She was baffled by this situation. She found getting on with her life difficult. " 'Dead is dead,' she had told that doctor. But now . . . she wasn't so sure."[4] "Maybe, she thought, it was a matter of percentage—if more than 50 percent of your husband was dead, you were a widow."[5] She even stopped going to the Evangelical Baptist Church cemetery to visit Sam's grave. "It wasn't Sam in that cemetery, not by a long shot. It was only parts of Sam, the parts that nobody needed. The rest of him was scattered all over Texas. And, unless she had been misinformed, very much alive."[6]

Along with the doubts came resentment. She resented the doctors for covering up their dismembering of people by "soft words of husbandry and the soil" like "harvest" and "transplant." Worse than that, she began to resent Samuel, who "was participating in not one but seven lives, none of which had anything to do with her."[7] And she resented the radio preacher's talk about resurrection of the flesh. "It's a big lie," she said to her born-again cousin Ivy Lou. "There is no such thing. . . . What about Samuel Owens on your resurrection day? . . . They going to put him back together again when the day comes, or is it that to the recipients belong the spoils? Tell me that."[8]

Hannah remembered a story Sam had told her of his own bewilderment with loss. Sam's father had died suddenly of a heart attack when Sam was twelve years old. For a long time afterward, he would think that he had seen his father on the street and would run after the man, calling out, "Daddy." When he caught up with the man, of course, he always discovered that he had been mistaken. His behavior got him into some trouble with strangers and with his mother. When it finally stopped happening, Sam had said, he had felt a mixture of relief and disappointment. Hannah remembered how she had wept for the little boy "who couldn't let go of his father" when Sam had told her that story.[9]

In her own bewilderment Hannah decided to seek out the man with Sam's heart in that little town near Arkansas and to plead with him to permit her to listen to Sam's heart for a little while. Then "she would be healed," she was confident.[10] After she succeeded in identifying the man, she wrote to him, requesting permission to listen to Sam's heart. After the man replied with a polite refusal, she wrote again. After the man reported that his doctor doesn't think it would be a good idea, she wrote to tell him that doctors "haven't the least idea about the human heart except to move it from place to place."[11] The man still refused, but he admitted that he felt bad about it, "like ungrateful or something."[12] Hannah's next letters reminded him of the gift, assured him that she doesn't want it back, and promised that, if he would permit her to listen to Sam's heart, "you will have repaid me in full."[13]

The man's replies grew increasingly impatient and attempted to put an end to the correspondence. In what she promised would be her last letter Hannah asked the man for the gift of a photograph of him. When he sent a picture in reply, Hannah was sure that "that heart is working," and wrote to thank him.[14] The thank-you note evidently succeeded where the request for repayment had failed, for a little while later, the man sent Hannah an invitation to come to that little town near the Arkansas border and to listen to Sam's heart for an hour.

She accepted the invitation. The preliminaries were a little awkward, and when she finally lowered her ear to his left nipple, she could feel the man wince. But she could hear the heart plainly. "Oh, it was Sam's heart, all right. She knew the minute she heard it. She could have picked it out of a thousand."[15] After an hour of listening and remembering, there was a change in both the man and Hannah. He was tender and gentle, even wondering whether Hannah would want to come to listen again. But Hannah said, "There will be no need," confident that her life had been retrieved from the shadows and grateful for the man whose chest, it seemed to her, "was a field of golden wheat in which, for this time, it had been given to her to go gleaning."[16] She was ready to get on with her life, and she was glad for the gift she gave and for the gift she was given.

It is an outrageous story in a way, but it artfully displays certain ambiguities in transplantation procedures. First is the ambiguity that attends the determination of death; the tidy and reasonable criteria for determining that a person is "brain-dead" do not eliminate (and cannot hide) this ambiguity. There is an ambiguity in the responsibilities of care; the needs of the grieving may conflict with the needs of a prospective recipient. These ambiguities can conspire to undercut confidence in physicians. The gift relationship between donor and recipient is itself ambiguous. And religious traditions have had an ambiguous relationship with transplantation. The experience (and the language) of both caregivers and survivors is frequently messy. The task undertaken here is not to eliminate the messiness but to understand it, to appreciate why it cannot be altogether eliminated, and to suggest the potential of religious ritual for pointing a way through the mess in ways that honor both the dead and their gifts.

" 'Brain-dead,' said the doctor." Consider first the development of tidy and reasonable criteria for the determination of death. It was, of course, the ambiguities that attended the first heart transplant that made it important and necessary to develop some tidy and reasonable criteria for the determination of death. The criteria for the determination of brain death, however, as necessary as they may be, do not eliminate the ambiguities.

I am old enough to remember billboards urging motorists to drive safely by joining a picture of Dr. Christiaan Barnard in scrubs to the message, "Slow down! Dr. Barnard wants your heart!" When I saw that billboard (sometime close to

1968, I presume), I slowed down a little and, muttering something about the fact that I was still using mine, I wondered how Dr. Barnard could take a living heart from a person without killing that person. One wanted to assume, of course, that the person from whom the heart was taken was already dead, but how can you know that someone with a beating heart is dead? The question was unavoidable, and the first moral challenge for heart transplantation procedures was to answer that unavoidable question.

The challenge was met with the development of a remarkable consensus that one could determine death by the irreversible cessation of whole brain function, which could be made independently on either cardiac or respiratory arrest. Already in 1968, a Harvard ad hoc committee recommended criteria by which such a determination of death could be made. In 1972, an influential study group from the Hastings Center endorsed these criteria, and in 1981 the President's Commission gave their approval and drafted a Uniform Determination of Death Act. That model law was endorsed by both the American Medical Association and the American Bar Association and eventually adopted by all fifty states.

The unavoidable question had an answer. There is a way to determine that someone with a beating heart is dead, a way to determine that a person is dead independently of heart and lung function, which can be mechanically supported. The answer, the consensus that supports it, and the legislation that gives it effect are of obvious importance to transplantation procedures; indeed, they are morally necessary to certain transplantation procedures. Even so, Hannah's story reminds us that the reasonable and tidy criteria meet the challenge only in part. They do not eliminate the messiness of the situation, or the ambiguity of death, or the kind of confusion that Hannah experienced.

Her confusion is not difficult to understand. The "neomort" appears very much alive, and every reasonable effort is made to "keep it alive" for the sake of the transplant. Brain-dead and ready for surgery, the cadaver is warm, has a good color, and continues to digest and eliminate. Moreover, monitoring continues, along with interventions designed to preserve the cadaver's "health." Even our language almost inevitably expresses this confusing situation. A "healthy cadaver" is an oxymoron. But for the sake of it, we have "brain-dead" bodies on "life-support" systems. After the transplant, the "brain dead" are removed from the ventilator and "allowed to die" or "allowed to die all the way" or "really die." The point is not to call into question the rightness of the criteria, but to suggest why they are insufficient.

The criteria are tidy, but the experience is confusing and sometimes disconcerting even for those who are practiced in it. The doctors and nurses who work in transplantation are no strangers to this confusion. In a fascinating study of nearly two hundred physicians and nurses likely to be involved in organ procurement, Stuart Youngner and his colleagues demonstrated the dissonance between the intellectual understanding of criteria for the determination of brain death and the experience of those who care for brain-dead organ donors. In one part of the study, the doctors and nurses were presented with two cases and asked both whether the patients were legally dead and whether, aside from legalities, they themselves regarded the patients as really dead and why. Only about a third of the total number of respondents and about two-thirds of the physicians were able to identify the criteria for determining death correctly, and "the personal concepts of death varied widely."[17] The "conceptual disarray" that Youngner and his colleagues demonstrated did not suggest that death was being misdiagnosed or that patients were being prematurely declared dead and their organs removed. But the study did conclude that "[t]hough clinicians can tell which patients have permanent loss of all brain function there is no consensus over whether, and especially why, this means they have died."[18] If the professionals find this experience confusing and sometimes disconcerting, then one can imagine how much more difficult it must be for families. For families, of course, the "neomort" is not just a cadaver, but Mom or Son or Sam.

Even without the complicating factor of organ transplantation, the tidy criteria are insufficient. Joseph Fins tells the story of a seventy-seven-year-old Chinese woman who was assessed for brain death. The patient, a widow with a history of poorly controlled hypertension, had come to New York to visit her youngest son and his wife. The daughter-in-law, who had been trained as a physician in China, had urged the patient to see a physician, but the patient had refused. Then she suffered a severe anoxic brain injury after a large intracranial hemorrhage and subsequent cardiac arrest. The son and daughter-in-law were distraught, of course, and when they were informed that the patient would be assessed for brain death, they objected. (Under New York law clinicians are required to make "reasonable accommodation" for religious and moral objections to brain-death criteria.) The daughter-in-law was feeling guilty that she had not been able to convince the woman to have her blood pressure monitored, and she worried that the family in China might blame them for the woman's death. The son felt "marooned between life and loss."

Because his mother was "alive," he could not bring himself to grieve. The tidy criteria for brain death were not what this family needed to clarify their situation and to recognize the death of their mother. The doctors withheld their determination of death while the daughter-in-law and son went through rituals appropriate to dying in their culture.

The daughter-in-law read a large Chinese placard to the patient. With tears in her eyes, she read plaintively rocking back and forth in a trance-like state as she held the bed rail for support. The message, dictated by relatives back home, was one of wishes and blessing, "saying goodbye and asking for forgiveness."

The assessment for brain death was done after the rituals were complete and the family had left the room. The neurologist who performed the test dismissed the concerns of the family about the application of the brain-death criteria by saying, "You are your brain." Others in the room, Fins reported, "were not so sure" anymore.

> After the patient did not breathe on her own, the endotracheal tube was removed. She looked quite peaceful. Her coloring remained good. She remained in a normal sinus rhythm on the monitor. After about eight minutes, she flexed her arms and brought them to the midline in what appeared to be a purposeful movement, only to let them fall slowly to her side. . . . After this, she became dusky. Though it was almost certainly a physiologic response, the change struck me as a profound moment of transition. One resident in the room commented that the patient now "looked dead." One colleague later described it as the patient's true passage. And that certainly was the intuitive sense that many of us had in spite of our training in biomedical science. Even as the neurologist reassured us that what we had witnessed was just a cervical reflex often described as a "Lazarus sign," the intensivist quickly reached for his stethoscope to listen to the patient's heart and lungs. Reflexively, he had to confirm that the patient was truly dead by conventional means, notwithstanding the declaration of brain death that had been made moments earlier. At that moment, science only took us so far.[19]

The story not only displays the insufficiency of the tidy brain-death criteria to eliminate the confusion about the determination of death; it also identifies why the criteria are insufficient: "science only took us so far." Death is a human event. It may not simply be reduced to simple scientific criteria. When the criteria are not acknowledged as insufficient, we risk the sort of reductionism to which the neurologist gave voice. Human rituals are as important to the recognition of death as the scientific criteria that are used to determine brain death. We will return to the importance of ritual, but first it will be useful to summarize the ambiguity surrounding brain death and to attend to certain other ambiguities in transplant.

There may be no better way to summarize the problem than to remember one of the initial challenges to the brain-death criteria. In spite of the developing consensus in 1974, Hans Jonas wrote an essay, "Against the Stream." The worries and suspicions he voiced in that essay did not stem the stream, but they seem remarkably prescient after twenty-five years. Jonas criticized the position of the Harvard ad hoc committee for its effort to provide a sharp line between life and death when, in fact, according to Jonas, life often shades imperceptibly into death. "Giving intrinsic vagueness its due is not being vague," he said. "Aristotle observed that it is the mark of a well-educated man not to insist on greater precision in knowledge than the subject admits. . . . Reality of certain kinds—of which the life-death spectrum is perhaps one—may be imprecise in itself, or the knowledge obtainable of it may be. To acknowledge such a state of affairs is more adequate to it than a precise definition, which does violence to it."[20]

Even if we admit the necessity of some precise criteria, Jonas reminds us of the inevitable ambiguity and warns us against pretending that any tidy criteria can eliminate that ambiguity. Such pretense violates the human experience of both caregivers and survivors.

In addition to this claim about the intrinsic vagueness of the borderline between life and death, Jonas also complained about the consequences and about the sources of the tidy new definition. Concerning the consequences, he worried that the new definition would substitute a diagnostic question for the axiological one and that the body would be commodified: "[T]he question is not: has the patient died? but: how should he—still a patient—be dealt with? Now this question must be settled, surely not by a definition of death, but by a definition of man and of what life is human. That is to say, the question cannot be answered by decreeing that death has already occurred and the body is therefore in the domain of things. . . ."[21]

Jonas may have been wrong when he attempted simply to set aside the question, "Has the patient died?" That question, I think, is morally unavoidable. He was right, however, in insisting that a definition of death not be allowed to substitute for the question "How should he—still a patient—be dealt with?" Both questions are morally important. The danger comes when we assume that we resolve the moral ambiguities surrounding the death of a patient when we can answer the first question. Then we risk thinking that the situation can be adequately handled "by decreeing that death has already occurred and the body is therefore in the domain of things."

Concerning the sources of the new definition, Jonas identified them as "the ruling pragmatism of our time" and "the old body-soul dualism." And he was suspicious of both. It was pragmatism, he said, that motivated a definition of death that served the interests of the expanding powers of transplantation. His suspicion of pragmatism is captured in his characterization of it as "the relentless expanding of the realm of sheer thinghood and unrestricted utility."[22] And it was body-soul dualism, he said, even if in its "new apparition" as "the dualism of brain and body," that allowed us to hold "that the true human person rests in the brain, of which the rest of the body is a mere subservient tool."[23] Against such dualism he insisted, "My identity is the identity of the whole organism, even if the higher functions of personhood are seated in the brain. How else could a man love a woman and not merely her brains?"[24] Hannah would have understood. The neurologist in Fins's story evidently did not.

"They haven't the least idea about the human heart except to move it from place to place." Perhaps it is inevitable that Hannah would be suspicious of doctors like the neurologist in Fins's story. It is not that Hannah, or people like her, sees the doctor as a villain, although, of course, there is the old suspicion of greed. Rather, I think, they see the doctor as a hero but as a tragic hero, as a hero with a tragic flaw of character, as a hero so committed to a certain good end that he ignores the evil, the injustice, or the indignity of certain means to accomplish it. They see those skilled in transplant surgery as crusaders, as powerful do-gooders who are prepared to overlook (or undercut) the vulnerable in order to achieve the good they can do and long to do for other patients.[25]

The public polls concerning transplantation suggest such a view of physicians. On the one hand, the public supports transplantation and celebrates the good it can sometimes do. According to the 1985 Gallup poll commissioned by the American Council on Transplantation, three-quarters of those polled approved of organ donation.[26] And in a 1993 Gallup survey, 85 percent of those polled approved of organ donation.[27] People are evidently glad that we are not quite so helpless and so hopeless in the face of diseased and damaged organs; they are grateful that the powers of medicine can intervene in these sad stories and sometimes give them a happy ending after all, and they are ready to regard the doctors as heroes.

On the other hand, the same polls testify to the public's suspicions. Even those who approve of transplantation are evidently reticent to donate their organs. According to that 1985 Gallup poll, although three-quarters of those polled approved of organ donation, only one-quarter said they would be "very likely" to donate their own organs at death, and only 17 percent said they had completed donor cards.[28] And in the 1993 survey, although 85 percent approved of organ donation, only 37 percent said they would be "very likely" to donate their organs, and only 28 percent reported that they had granted permission for organ donation on a driver's license or donor card.[29] The reasons for this reticence, however, are more interesting than the statistics. In that 1985 Gallup poll those who said they would not donate their own organs gave a variety of reasons: "They might do something to me before I'm really dead." "Doctors might hasten my death." "I don't like to think about dying." "I don't like someone cutting me up after I die." "I never thought about it." "I want my body intact for the afterlife." "My family might object." "It's against my religion." "It's complicated to give permission."[30] Only some of these reasons testify to the public suspicion of doctors, of course. Nevertheless, it is noteworthy that in 1985, some years after the consensus on the criteria for brain death had been formed, 23 percent of the people polled by Gallup said, "They might do something to me before I die," and 21 percent said, "Doctors might hasten my death." (Moreover, those numbers were up significantly from a 1983 poll by Gallup.)

The explanation is not, I think, simply that the public was unaware of the developing consensus concerning brain death. Rather, they were suspicious of it because, as we have already observed, there is evidently some distance between the acceptance of tidy, scientific, and eminently reasonable criteria for the determination of death and the messy, human, and emotional reality of a "neomort." But they also were suspicious of those who sponsored the developing consensus; they were suspicious that it was the work of crusaders.

It is not hard to understand the public's suspicion of the new criteria. When the Harvard ad hoc committee issued its landmark report in 1968, it reported that one reason for updating the definition of death was to make it easier to obtain organs for transplant. That was unfortunate, and it was more unfortunate that that justification for the new criteria was frequently repeated in public discussion of the developing consensus. People got the idea that the reason for the new definition of death was to make organ transplantation possible. The consensus sounded, frankly, opportunistic. Those who did not want doctors to hasten their deaths for the sake of their organs also did not want doctors calling them dead prematurely for the sake of their organs. The public may have regarded doctors as heroes, but they also suspected that they were flawed by their very commitment to care for their patients, ready to hasten the moment at which other patients would be regarded as dead in order to obtain their organs.

That particular suspicion may have been unjustified. The consensus concerning whole brain death may not have been formed in quite so opportunistic a fashion. Indeed, many of those who urged the acceptance of the new criteria, including the influential Hastings Center task force, quite deliberately rejected the need for organs as a reason to adopt the criteria. The need for organs was part of the occasion for the reconsideration of the determination of death, along with the development of life-support technology, but it was not regarded as a justification of the new criteria.[31] Rather, the consensus was formed in the recognition that traditionally death meant not the death of the whole organism but the death of the organism as a whole. It was (and is) an essentially conservative concept of death, even if the criteria for determining the death of the organism as a whole now involved technical assessment of brainstem activity.

If the public was (unfairly) suspicious of the new consensus, that suspicion hints at the public's suspicion of the medical profession itself, and especially of transplant physicians, as tragic heroes equipped with powers to do good but flawed by their hubris. That suspicion of transplantation medicine was shared and expressed in the book by medical anthropologists Renee Fox and Judith Swazey, *Spare Parts: Organ Replacement in American Society.* Their decision to "leave the field" after thirty years of work was a public complaint, not only of inequities but also of the hubris of the transplantation industry. Their complaint about hubris is a description of crusaders who, in their desire to cure organ failure, are unmindful of the evil they sometimes do, ready to trample the embodied integrity of their patients and to neglect their suffering. Such hubris can be traced to a mechanistic dualism that reduces the body either to the battlefield where the war against disease and death is waged or to "spare parts." Hannah's complaint, "They haven't the least idea about the human heart except to move it from place to place," found an echo in the work of these medical anthropologists.

If the public suspicion of the new criteria for brain death was unfair, it is less clear that suspicion of the doctors who supported it was unfair. Indeed, that suspicion has been reinforced by other behaviors. For example, if the transplantation community looked a little like crusaders when they advocated whole-brain-death criteria on the grounds that such criteria would increase the supply of organs for transplant, it reinforced that image when suggestions were made to utilize anencephalic babies for the sake of the great good of making infant organs available. The effort to redefine death or to create a special category of the "brain absent" in order to increase the supply of badly needed organs was understandable enough, but it was troubling. Gilbert Meilaender made the moral point eloquently. "Our obligation," he said, "is not to achieve all the good we can, as if our responsibilities were godlike. It is, rather, to effect all the good that we can within the limits morality places upon us. Not only what we accomplish but what we do counts."[32] Alexander Capron said clearly that what we must not do is kill the living, even if—or especially if—they are among the most vulnerable of the living (or the dying). And he warned the transplant community that to yield to this crusader temptation would lead to the sort of public suspicion and distrust that would, in the long run, be counterproductive to the supply of organs.[33]

To be sure, the public continues to celebrate the good that medicine does and can do, but it regards physicians as ambiguous heroes, tempted by their power. Consequently, the relationship of physician and patient has become increasingly distrustful.

"Hannah . . . cried for the young boy who couldn't let go of his father." The tidy and eminently reasonable criteria for the determination of death do not quite fit with the messy and not altogether manageable experience of death. Death brings a sense of loss and grief. And when transplantation takes place in the context of death, it takes place also in the context of a grief that finds no remedy in tidy criteria. To be sure, those invited to consider donating a loved one's organs need information. They need to be told about the criteria for brain death and why these criteria justify treating a patient not only as dying but also as dead. And they need procedures to protect their rights. But because we are dealing with death, it should not surprise us that they need more than tidy criteria and rational moral principles. Death involves us and repels us more deeply than that. It is not so

easily managed and domesticated. Death requires more than just rational criteria and the impartial calculation of self-interested individuals. It is always a religious event; it invokes consideration of—and attention to—the powers that bear down on us and sustain us (or do not). And it is always a communal event; it involves the dis-member-ment of some community, the dis-organ-ization of our relationships. When death is the context for transplantation, it is little wonder that the "soft words of husbandry and the soil"[34] seem deceptive. The event of death is a dis-member-ment, and transplantation in the context of death can seem the epitome of this dis-member-ment. In this light, one can understand why even those who support the idea of transplantation in the context of health sometimes find consent difficult in the context of death. If, for example, the potential donor is a suicide, the family will be understandably anxious about any action toward the mortal remains that could be interpreted as mistreatment of the person. If the potential donor is an accident victim, the family will desperately hold to the continuity between mortal remains and the person they have lost. And if the efforts to save a person's life had justified treating him or her like manipulable nature, like an object, then it is not surprising if the family insists that the person's death ought to put an end to such treatment, not justify continuing it.

The old body-soul dualism of which Jonas complained is surely operative in the reduction of the body to "spare parts." Surely doctors must sometimes "objectify" the body in an effort to heal a person; surely sometimes they must treat the body as manipulable; but the risks are both familiar and great. Human beings are not to be reduced to their bodies, but neither are their bodies to be consigned to the realm of mere things. We are not in our bodies the way Descartes's ghost was presumably in the machine. We are embodied selves, and communal selves as embodied. People do not live or die or suffer as ghostly minds nor as mere bodies but as embodied and communal selves.

To be sure, because persons may not be reduced to their bodies, there is a discontinuity between persons and their mortal remains. But because persons may not be reduced to minds or ghosts or disembodied souls, there is also continuity between persons and their mortal remains. The continuity helps us to understand why some who refuse to make organ donations give as their reason "I don't want someone cutting me up after I die." It helps us to understand why the first experience of medical students in the gross anatomy lab is frequently replusive to them[35] and why some family members are reticent to consider the dis-member-ing of their beloved son or daughter or parent. The discontinuity helps us to understand how medical students can settle down to the tasks of learning anatomical parts, their places, their relations, and their functions, and also how family and friends experience in the presence of mortal remains that the one they loved is somehow gone.

What the grieving need is not simply a tidy definition of death or procedures that protect their individual autonomy. They need to acknowledge the reality and the sadness of death. They need people to stand with them in acknowledging the loss, the disorganization of their communal selves. They need people who will discipline the human tendencies to deny death and to flee from it, who will stand with the grieving, attentive to the mortal remains, once—and still—identified with the person who has died, once—and still—the medium by which family and friends displayed the affection and loyalty of various relationships. They need people who will respect not only their autonomy but their communal integrity, who will respect both the continuing connections of the mortal remains with the person and the community and the hard reality of the discontinuity that death inevitably brings. They need, that is, something like a funeral ritual.[36] The person is dead; relationships are broken; communities are dismembered. Family and friends need to surrender the person and the mortal remains; they need to "let go." But neither they nor doctors can by decree or fiat reduce the body to "spare parts." It is appropriate to remind those sickened medical students of the discontinuity. However, students who treat their cadavers cavalierly need to be reminded of the continuity, need to be reminded that the cadavers remain the mortal remains of someone who experienced the sights and sounds and smells of the world in it, someone who loved and blushed in it. Similarly, it is appropriate to remind those who refuse to consider organ donation of the discontinuity. And it is necessary to remind all that reduce the newly dead to "manipulable nature" or to exchangeable parts of the continuity. While the discontinuity makes dissection morally possible, the continuity requires that the retrieval of organs be undertaken with all due respect not only for the recently deceased but also for those who are dis-membered by the loss and need to grieve.

"[Y]ou will have repaid me in full." If the first challenge for transplant surgery was the proper diagnosis of death, the second surely was—and remains—appropriate consideration for the recently dead and for the grieving. And if there are possibilities for being mistaken for a crusader in response to the first challenge, the second challenge contains even more such possibilities.

One part of the solution here was provided by the language of "gift." Transplantation has been described from the very beginning as a "gift of life." The Uniform Anatomical Gift Act was an effort to make such gifts easy and routine. The language and the legislation recognized that although Dr. Barnard might want my heart, it was not his to take; it could only be given—and only by those with the authority to make such a gift, that is to say, by the person whose body it is while alive and/or by the family whose responsibility it is to dispose of the body appropriately when the person dies.

The recognition of organ transfer as "gift" is to be affirmed and commended, and the gift relationship is to be protected from the crusaders who would simply take. However, the language of "gift" meets this challenge only in part. Relationships established by "gift" are themselves more ambiguous than we sometimes think. And, in spite of the best efforts of those who would encourage voluntary gifts, death—and thus a gift in the midst of death—can hardly be made routine.

First, then, let it be affirmed that the intuitions that accompanied the Uniform Anatomical Gift Act were sound. Organ donation is gift, and organ recipients receive a gift. The donative aspects of transplantation should not be ignored, and it is perilous to deny them. And to deny them for the sake of increasing the supply of organs looks like the work of a crusader. The continuity of the mortal remains with the person whose body it was (and is) requires that we respect the dead person by treating his or her corpse in ways that reflect the reality of the union between persons and their bodies. It is impossible altogether to separate the way we treat a person and the way we treat that person's body. Indeed, the way we treat a corpse is often the final display of respect or contempt. To requisition the body or its parts would discredit the dignity that should be accorded to the person while alive. It would treat the person, and not just the corpse, with negligible dignity. The gift character of organ exchange protects against the indignity.

The Uniform Anatomical Gift Act affirmed that organs for transplant were gifts; indeed, it capitalized on the characterization of donation as a "gift of life." Although it wanted to make such gifts in the context of death routine, however, neither death nor donation has been routinized.

The transplant community reminds us that donation, or what Arthur Caplan has called the policy of "encouraged voluntarism," has not kept up with the demand for organs. It is appropriate to be reminded of the sad story that many patients "die waiting" for organs. And the response to that sad story must, of course, be compassion and sympathy and an effort to increase the supply of organs for transplant. Compassion, however, needs to be joined not only with artifice, with technology, but also with wisdom and piety. It ought to be a motive not just to "do something," which can mean anything, but to act in ways that are fitting to human experience and appropriate to the human condition. Otherwise, compassion can be the motive of crusaders.

Caplan has effectively advocated an alternative to the policy of "encouraged voluntarism": the policy of "required request." The latter attempts to increase the supply of organs while continuing to acknowledge the normative significance of donation and consent. The idea is simply to ensure that the families of potential donors will be informed of the transplantation option and asked to make a donation. It was quickly drafted into law and adopted by most state legislatures and mandated for all institutions that receive Medicare or Medicaid funds.

Caplan's own telephone survey of ten states where the legislation had been in effect for at least six months revealed two trends. First, there were some small gains in the number of organs available for transplant, but second, there was quite a remarkable rate of noncompliance with the new legislation among doctors and nurses involved in organ procurement, more than 50 percent in many states. Before one joins Caplan in attributing this noncompliance to "professional arrogance,"[37] one might consider the following: the emotional investment in the "neomort" in spite of reasonable (and accepted) criteria for the legal determination of death; the clinical difficulty of attending to a patient both as a patient and as a potential organ donor; or the professional difficulty of both supporting the family in their grief and being the advocate of unknown potential recipients of the organs of their recently dead relative. One might consider, in short, whether the "discretion and sensitivity" the law itself commands are not exercised in at least some noncompliance.[38] What Caplan celebrates as the "routinization of requests"[39] does not make death or grief routine. To be sure, potential donors must be identified and inquiries must be made, but to refuse to allow a physician's "discretion and sensitivity" to override the requirement of a request looks like the decision of a crusader. Death and gifts in the context of death cannot be made routine.

The other proposals to increase the number of organs available for transplant include "presumed consent" and creating a market for organs. A policy of "presumed consent" would allow the routine harvesting of needed organs from any potential donor. It is called "presumed consent" because of the important qualification that a donor or a family would have the option of opting out. That qualification acknowledges that organ donation remains—and must remain—a gift. Moreover, since procrastination and aversion presumably would continue to play a role in these decisions (or in avoiding them), donors and their families would need to be informed of the practice of routinely harvesting organs and of their right to opt out. And presumably a physician's "discretion and sensitivity" would still sometimes override providing that information and making that request (now whether they want to opt out). That is to say, in spite of the policy differences between "required request" and "presumed consent," the practices might not be so different.

James Childress, however, has expressed concern that in some of the places where this policy is in force donors and their families have not been informed of the policy or of their right to opt out.[40] Other critics find it hard to understand on what basis in an individualistic society consent could be presumed and organs taken. Although such a policy favors the language of voluntary gifts and consent even while it licenses the routine salvaging of organs, it acknowledges the importance of the gift relationship too much the way a lie acknowledges that the truth ought to be told. It looks suspiciously like "taking" organs rather than receiving them as gifts. To conscript donors unless they apply for the status of conscientious objectors risks violating the communal integrity of those who are "members one of another" before they are members of the state as well as the embodied integrity of persons by reducing their bodies to "parts" for social use. Transplantation does involve gifts, however much crusaders would prefer it if they could reduce organs to waste to be retrieved to serve a human good.

What "presumed consent" puts at risk, creating a market in organs simply violates. The commercialization of transplantation, the selling and buying of organs as commodities, alienates us both from our communities and from our bodies, rendering us individual choice makers tied to others only by the contracts of a marketplace and rendering our bodies (our selves) commodities. Such a marketplace policy was advanced in 1983 by Dr. H. Barry Jacobs, of International Kidney Exchange, Incorporated. He wrote to thousands of hospitals to inquire whether they would be interested in his plan to purchase kidneys from persons living in poverty here and abroad as cheaply as possible and sell them to sick Americans who could afford to buy them. The reaction was appropriately outrage both in Congress and among transplant surgeons. In 1984, the National Organ Transplantation Act expressly outlawed commercial markets in organ procurement and distribution, and in 1985 The Transplantation Society adopted a special resolution: "No transplant surgeon/team shall be involved directly or indirectly in the buying or selling of organs/tissues or in any transplant activity aimed at commercial gain to himself/herself or an associated hospital or institute," and made violation a cause for expulsion from the society.

Preserving the gift relationship offers donors and their families the best protection against exploitation by a crusader and against the mechanistic dualism that would reduce the body and its members to spare parts. Moreover, gifts are wonderful tokens of a way of life that religious thinkers have regularly commended. It is good to give of ourselves to others, to be generous with others in ways that surpass any claim they may have on us, and graciously to include strangers as well as friends and family in the range of our generosity. Gifts establish or cement relationships. And, to be sure, both donor and recipient celebrate "the gift of life." A bond may be created between donors, recipients, and their families because a part of the donor remains and functions within the recipient, and that bond is often experienced as an enriching and ennobling thing.

The act of giving is a glorious thing, but let it also be recognized that the glorious act of giving can be ambiguous. That point was made eloquently by Renee Fox and Judith Swazey. They point out the ambiguity just below the surface in the mechanisms to protect relatives whose psychological tests suggest that they are not appropriate donors by telling them that they are not compatible.[41] They point out the recognition of ambiguity in the policy of anonymity surrounding cadaver organs, whereas formerly transplant teams were disposed to reveal not only identities but also details about the lives of donors, recipients, and their families. But the ambiguities surface most visibly in what Fox and Swazey call "the tyranny of the gift," the psychic and social effects of being bound to another by a gift that it is impossible adequately to repay, of being trapped either as benefactor or recipient into a creditor-debtor relationship. That ambiguity surfaced in Hannah's effort to manipulate the consent of the man with her husband's heart by reminding him of the gift and of his obligation somehow to repay it. Ironically, it seems not to have been the tyranny of the gift that wins Hannah an audience with Sam's heart but her own gratitude for a simple act of kindness that the donor had shown.

To insist that organs are gifts is not wrong, but it is insufficient. It does not, and cannot, remove the ambiguities surrounding transplantation.

"What about Sam Owens on your resurrection day?" Religious convictions and communities do not provide an easy transcendence over the ambiguities in transplantation. The story of Hannah, for example, reminds us that transplantation has sometimes been seen as inconsistent with Christian conviction about resurrection. Hannah resented the radio preacher's talk of the resurrection of the flesh. "It's a big lie," she said, and used Sam Owens's flesh, now part of the flesh of seven others, as her evidence.[42] Others, convinced of the truth of resurrection, have resented the request that they should be donors. On their "great getting-up morning," they figure, they will need their organs. Cheryl Sanders reports that this conviction (along with distrust of physicians and fears that donors will be declared dead prematurely) contributes to the reluctance of African Americans to donate organs. But she also reports that the effort of certain members of the transplantation community to respond to this conviction by dismissing it as "superstitious," mythological, and nonscientific looks like the act of the crusader. Sanders calls for theological inquiry and conversation, not dismissive ridicule.[43]

Theological inquiry and instruction are obviously important when religious communities confront issues like transplantation. Theological conversations could be instructive both to those who could donate their organs and to those who would harvest them. Theological inquiry, however, should be conducted in the service of particular religious communities, tested by the wisdom of their respective traditions, not conducted in the service of the transplantation community or tested by whether it increases the number of organ donors.

The Christian conviction concerning the resurrection of the body, for example, does not make resurrection depend on the intact condition of the body when it is buried. Rather, resurrection depends on the power of God to make "all things new." The conviction of the resurrection, therefore, is not inconsistent with the donation of organs. At the same time, however, by reminding Christians of the significance of embodiment, the conviction of resurrection of the body should challenge the old dualism of body and soul (and its "new apparition" in "the dualism of brain and body") that renders us immortal souls in a disposable body. And by reminding Christians that the victory over death is finally a divine victory rather than a technological one, it should challenge the hubris of crusaders.

Most religious people are ready to celebrate the good that transplantation sometimes does. Because developments in transplant surgery enable a more effective human response to the sad stories of diseased and damaged organs and the premature deaths they sometimes cause, religious people give thanks to God and celebrate human service to the cause of God. And modest celebration is certainly appropriate. Many religious groups have adopted resolutions approving and encouraging organ donation. Moreover, many religious groups have overcome initial reservations about whole brain death and have explicitly accepted such criteria for the determination of death. (See Appendix.)

Such resolutions may provide a significant reply to some religious persons who refuse to consider organ donations because "It's against my religion." They may contribute to alleviating suspicion of the new consensus concerning brain death. They do not, however, provide a remedy for the ambiguities of transplantation. Moreover, the merely formal acceptance of brain-death criteria in the context of affirming the good transplantation can achieve will probably be seen as insufficient and might be regarded as suspiciously like an ecclesiastical blessing on the crusaders, which has happened before, of course.

Religious communities have provided theological position papers, resolutions encouraging organ donation, and official acceptance of brain-death criteria. Communities that have advocated organ donation as a worthy response in death to the giver of life have an opportunity and a responsibility to develop religious rituals for transplantation, which would acknowledge the reality and the sadness of the deaths of potential organ donors and would honor their gifts. More than once in the course of this paper's account of the ambiguities of transplant we have encountered something of the need for ritual. Ritual actions do not eliminate ambiguities, but they can acknowledge them and provide a way to cope with them. They can recognize tragedy and help the grieving find their way through it. They can provide order in the context of the dis-organ-ization wrought by death. They can nurture community in the context of the dis-member-ment death brings. They can recognize and deal with the human experience of continuity and discontinuity with mortal remains. Death and a gift in the midst of death can hardly be made routine, but they can be made a matter of ritual and liturgy.

In her fine book on ritual, Catherine Bell defines "ritualization" as a way of acting that is designed and orchestrated to distinguish and privilege what is being done in comparison to other, usually more quotidian, activities. As such, ritualization is a matter of various culturally specific strategies for setting some activities off from others, for creating and privileging a qualitative distinction between the "sacred" and the "profane," and for ascribing such distinctions to realities thought to transcend the powers of human actors.[44]

Stuart Youngner, whose study of "conceptual disarray" among transplant teams was cited earlier, has also called for the "ritualization" of transplant procedures. He has suggested that new nursing rituals should be developed for transplantation as a way of meeting the challenge of ambiguity against which the tidy definition of death seems powerless. Such rituals, he said, should "symbolically distinguish caring for the cadaver donor from that of patients and . . . infuse the macabre nature of what is involved with 'gift of life' meaning."[45] There is wisdom there. "Specific strategies for setting some activities off from others" would be helpful to distinguish care for the newly dead from patients in critical condition and to remind all parties that the "life support system" is not supporting a life. These strategies could involve little things, perhaps drapes that look more like shrouds than sheets, perhaps black sheets. Little things ritually performed can powerfully reinforce the fact of death and the professional commitment to honor both patients' mortal remains and their gifts. Even so, to give control over the rituals surrounding transplantation to medical professionals would be to surrender control over the appropriate way to act to the medical community. Patients and their families should be able to draw on their own religious and cultural traditions to deal with death and with the questions of giving organs in the context of death. No "generic" ritual will do, and no purely private ritual will do. To avoid the suspicion that "ritualization," too, can be the work of crusaders, the ritual must privilege death as a human event that inevitably invokes attention to God and to community, and not just as an opportunity for transplant. Religious traditions that have issued resolutions in approval of transplant bear some responsibility for the construction of rituals for such occasions. All traditions have rituals for death;[46] all of them recognize and deal with the human experience of continuity and discontinuity; and many of them have elements that could be used in the context of transplantation. The Park Ridge Center has begun a project investigating ritual as a resource for responding to the needs of patients, families, and caregivers.[47]

There is liturgical work, as well as theological work, to be done. Only so will the horror of death be acknowledged and our aversion to death be disciplined by commitments to a continuing community and to some transcendent cause. The Christian tradition offers resources for that liturgical work. It might be as simple as selecting parts of the funeral liturgy for use in the hospital when organs are to be harvested from deceased members of the Christian community. Other resources include the dirge and the psalms of lament in scripture.

The most complete and powerful dirge in scripture is David's dirge at the death of Saul and Jonathan (2 Sam. 1:19–27). It is a remarkable song. God is not addressed or even mentioned. The dead are eulogized, but the decisive feature of this and every dirge is the contrast between past glories and present misery. In its refrain and conclusion, "How the mighty have fallen," there is a sharp and total contrast to the remembered glories of Saul and Jonathan. Once they were "beloved and lovely"; once "they were swifter than eagles, . . . stronger than lions"; now "how the mighty have fallen." The contrast so important to the form of the dirge has been called "the tragic reversal." It acknowledges the reality and horror of death and gives the grieving voice.

Grief also finds voice in the psalms of lament, but now a voice addressed to God. They are not funeral liturgies, but Hermann Gunkel has identified the individual psalms of lament as "the place where the religion of the psalms comes into conflict with death." The laments reverse the tragic reversal. By their attention to God they move from distress to renewal, from powerlessness to confidence, from anger to assurance, from grief to gift. The invocation of God allows the pattern of the dirge to change, but it does not disallow the sorrow. Laments acknowledge the real experiences of life and the honest emotional reactions that those experiences evoke. There is no pretense, no denial, and no withdrawal to some otherworldly realities. There is no romantic effort to reduce the hurt to some domesticated account of nature, and no technical effort to accomplish a surrogate immortality. Lament calls the faithful to deal with real life and real death. Lament gives the suffering voice, but it also holds them to a meaning and a covenant that promises that the tragic reversal is not the last word. Lament gives form and limits to the venting of emotions and thus helps to give direction to the sufferer, helps to encompass the hurt within a faithful identity. In the psalms of confidence (for example, Ps. 22), the lament reaches past the certainty of a hearing to the gifts of thanksgiving. The psalmist pledges a gift as a token of gratitude; it is gift answering to gift. Resources are available here for ritualizing both death and gift, for the construction of a liturgical acknowledgment of the horror of death and a liturgical pledging of the gift of organs. In the very presence of death, such gifts can be celebrated as a response to the one who gives mortal life and rules even death so that we can rise above our fear and horror in order to serve God's cause and some other's good.

A ritual could signify and express both the continuity and the discontinuity between persons and their mortal remains. The liturgies would not create the simultaneous continuity and discontinuity, but they could help us and force us to acknowledge it. Rituals will not make suicide or accident or any death less sad, but they may provide a way to acknowledge the sadness and to honor the gift, to free families both for grief and for generosity.

Religious rituals could also be helpful in minimizing the "tyranny of the gift," for the gift would be seen as response to God, as response to the one before whom we are all recipients and debtors, as gift answering to gift. Then organ donors and organ recipients are not trapped as benefactors or recipients into a creditor-debtor relationship; they are both recipients, bound together by their common indebtedness to God, and giving and sharing are mere tokens of community. If, for example, some lustration or sprinkling with water were a part of a Christian ritual for such occasions, participants could remember the baptism of the person whose corpse they attend, could acknowledge that baptism and this death as sharing in the death of Christ, and could celebrate both the gift of grace and the gift of this person's life. And in response to the gift of grace and in anticipation of the resurrection, they could not only surrender this member of their body to death but also surrender in death the members, the organs, of this member of their body in the service of others. Such a ritual would also serve, I think, to lower the rhetoric of a surrogate immortality.

In baptism Christians are instructed that "if we have died with Christ, we . . . will also live with him" (Rom. 6:8). The hope is not that our Sams will continue to survive in the breast of another, but that God's cosmic sovereignty will be unchallenged. The hope is not in technology, but in the power of God that makes things new, the same power that raised Jesus and will raise Sam from the dead. Death cannot be made routine, but it can be an occasion for liturgy. Part of preparation for this liturgy could be the request for donation. We would have the functional equivalent of "required request" within particular communities. Indeed, the point could be made more strongly than that. In the Christian tradition, for example, the preparation for this liturgy could remind Christians that, while they recognize life and health as good gifts of God, they also recognize that faithfulness to God does not permit them to make their own ease and survival the law of their being. They may expect physicians to be committed to their ease and survival, but they recognize more important obligations for themselves. And among those obligations are duties to help a neighbor in need, duties to answer the primordial giver with little tokens of their gratitude and generosity. This legitimate expectation of consent would still require "discretion and sensitivity." As death cannot be made routine, neither can gifts in the context of death. Rituals will not eliminate the ambiguities of death and grief and gift in transplantation, but they can help us to acknowledge those ambiguities and to journey through them in ways that nurture both respect for the one now recently dead and the readiness to give the organs that others may live.

Oh, one thing more: Drive carefully!

APPENDIX: STATEMENTS WITHIN RELIGIOUS TRADITIONS

Jewish

Definition of death: The Chief Rabbinate of Israel, on November 3, 1986, accepted "verification" of death by means of "proving that the brain, including the brainstem . . . , has been totally and irreversibly functionally destroyed." A Halakically acceptable variation of "whole brain death" has been found in the concept of "physiological decapitation." Contempoary rabbis continue to express dissenting opinions.[48]

Transplantation: "The following issues are of Halakic concern: the prohibition of desecrating or mutilating the dead, the prohibition of deriving benefit from the dead, the prohibition of delaying the burial of the dead, and the positive commandment of burying the dead. All these concerns and prohibitions are set aside if necessary in order to eliminate a danger to the life of a human being."[49]

Roman Catholic

Definition of death: "wide agreement among Catholic bishops, physicians and theologians that whole brain death . . . is sufficient to constitute death, and that there are available clinical tests which . . . show when this state of affairs obtains."[50]

From "Holy Living and Holy Dying—A United Methodist/Roman Catholic Common Statement," 1989: "The gift of life in organ donation allows survivors to experience positive meaning in the midst of their grief and is an important expression of love in community. [Transplantation is supported] . . . as long as death is not hastened and is determined by reliable criteria."[51]

Anglican/Episcopalian

According to Resolution A-097, adopted by the 1991 General Convention of the Episcopal Church in the U.S.A., the church "recommends and urges" members to consider the opportunity to donate organs after death so that others may live.[52]

Latter-day Saints

There is no official policy encouraging or discouraging donation; the decision to "will" organs for transplant is left to individual consciences. Reports of counsel not to will organs because of doctrine of literal resurrection of physical body are counterbalanced by enthusiastic endorsement of transplantation by individual Mormons (Sen. Jake Garn, Barney Clark, William DeVries). Strong encouragement to donate organs was given in an article by Cecil Samuelson in *Ensign,* the official LDS monthly periodical.[53]

Lutheran

In 1984, the Lutheran Church in America adopted a resolution that observed that "the donation of renewable tissue and live organs can be an expression of sacrificial love for a neighbor in need," encouraged the use of donor cards, and urged those wishing to donate to communicate such wishes to families, physicians, pastors, and hospitals. It urged pastors and church agencies to facilitate donation and governments to encourage voluntary donation, to discourage "coercive donation," to disallow a market in organs, and to assure equitable distribution of organs. The Lutheran Church Missouri Synod adopted a resolution in 1981 that called the church to implement programs to promote donation.[54]

Methodist

A 1988 United Methodist resolution, observing that "selfless consideration for the health and welfare of others is at the heart of the Christian ethic," affirmed organ donation as "life-giving" and a source of comfort to surviving loved ones, and urged members to become organ and tissue donors by signing donor cards.[55]

Eastern Orthodox

Evangelos Mantzouneas, "Organ Donations in the Orthodox Church in Greece," concludes that organ donations "do not violate" a Greek Orthodox account of Christian ethics but "every form of payment is prohibited." Organ donation has been approved by the Holy Synod of the Church of Greece. Serapheim, Archbishop of Athens, stated in 1985 that "to put words into practice" he had willed his kidneys and eyes for donation at his death.[56]

Islamic

Definition of death: A 1989 study sponsored by the Islamic Organization for Medical Sciences, after a thorough discussion, recommended that the diagnosis of brainstem death should be regarded as a sufficient indication of death.

Transplantation: The Islamic Code of Medical Ethics (endorsed by the First International Conference on Islamic Medicine, 1981) reads in part: "If the living are able to donate, then the dead are even more so, and no harm will afflict the cadaver if heart, kidneys, eyes or arteries are taken to be put to good use in a living person. This is indeed a charity . . . and directly fulfills God's words: 'And whosoever saves a human life it is as though he has saved all mankind.' A word of caution, however, is necessary. Donation should be voluntary. . . . In the society of the faithful, donation should be in generous supply and should be the fruit of faith and love of God and His subjects."[57]

Buddhist

It is possible to interpret Buddhist ideals to support the donation of organs, since one ought to help people who are in need. But Buddhist ideals require that the recipient not desire the donor's death "nor desire to prolong his own life." Moreover, "[b]rain death, in contrast to organ transplantation, seems unequivocally opposed to Buddhist ideals."[58]

7

GIVING IN GRIEF

Perspectives of Hospital Chaplains on Organ Donation

ANN MONGOVEN

INTRODUCTION

This project began with a knot in the stomach. As a participant in a conference aimed at increasing organ donation, I was reviewing pages of data on organ donation patterns. The data included graphs tabulating the number of people who had been "approached" to consider donating the organs of a suddenly deceased family member, compared to the number who chose to do so. These data were then analyzed by numerous variables to suggest which factors influence decisions to donate. I realized that each data point in these aggregates represented a family at the worst moment of their lives. While I knew both organ donors and organ recipients, I had never been present when someone actually had to make a decision regarding donation. I began to wonder about the stories underlying these graphs. Suddenly I felt queasy proceeding with the statistical analyses. What is it really like for families to consider organ donation in moments of unspeakable grief and duress? What is it really like for those who are called to be present with people facing that sort of decision?

This investigation was designed to give voice to one group "called to be present" with people in such situations: hospital chaplains. It explores their experience as pastoral care counselors to families facing the difficult choice of whether to donate organs. Chaplains offer firsthand views of the intense, complex processes of family decision making. Their collective experiences highlight questions about organ donation policy that may not be adequately addressed in contemporary public policy forums.

BACKGROUND: ORGAN DONATION/TRANSPLANTATION PRACTICE IN THE UNITED STATES

Some general background on organ donation is necessary to explain how I came to explore the experience of chaplains as a unique prism that might shed light on a spectrum of issues related to organ donation/transplantation.

Once considered heroic harbingers of futuristic medicine, organ transplants are becoming increasingly common forms of treatment for end-stage organ disease in the United States. Currently about 21,000 transplants a year are performed, of which about 17,000 are made possible by cadaveric organ donations.[1] Both the frequency of transplantation and the success rates of transplantation vary by organ. For example, kidney transplants are both more common and more successful than lung transplants. Approximately 12,000 kidney transplants are now performed each year, 75 percent of those using cadaveric organs, with one-year survival rates of about 95 percent. In comparison, approximately 850 patients receive lung transplants, and their one-year survival rate is about 75 percent.[2] Regardless of the odds of success, transplantation represents the last and best possible chance for life for many potential recipients.

Organ transplants remain among the most expensive medical procedures routinely performed; thus, issues of access to care and insurance coverage for transplants have generated considerable public attention. But for many patients awaiting transplant, the biggest barrier is organ availability. Cadaveric organ donations have not kept pace with the demand. Thus, more than 4,000 patients on waiting lists die each year without receiving transplants. Political disputes over how to allocate scarce organs have become heated, with related controversies attracting increased press coverage and governmental attention during the last several years.[3] In light of these facts, ameliorating the "organ shortage" has become a primary goal of various governmental and nonprofit organizations.[4]

A nonprofit private contractor of the federal government, United Network of Organ Sharing (UNOS), currently maintains organ waiting lists that prioritize potential recipients on the basis of medical criteria, severity of illness, length of time on waiting list, and, for some organs, locality of residence. Regional nonprofit organ procurement organizations (OPOs) are charged with promoting donations, securing organs, and transporting them to appropriate matches. Organ recipients directly reimburse the costs of organ "retrieval."

This chapter will employ certain technical terminology adopted from OPO practice. An "approach" is an intervention with the family of a potential donor. In the approach encounter, the family is informed that donation is a possibility and is asked to make a considered decision about whether to donate. The "primary approacher" is the person who takes a lead role in informing the family of the donation option. Primary approachers may be physicians, nurses, OPO staff, chaplains, social workers, or caseworkers. Next-of-kin are said to "accept" approach if they consent to donation. "Acceptance" or "consent" rates indicate the percentage of families specifically asked to consider donation who actually decide to donate.

Approach practices are changing. The trend is toward decreasing involvement in approach by physicians and increasing involvement by OPO staff and pastoral or social work staff. The use of certain designated nurses, as opposed to nurses generally, is also increasing.

Regulatory measures also affect approach practices. Over the past five years, increased regulation has aimed at ensuring that all potential donors are approached, and most states now have "required request" laws mandating approach of all potential donors. The 1998 revisions of criteria for hospital Medicare and Medicaid eligibility dictate that all hospital deaths be reported to OPOs and charge OPO staff with screening deaths that are medically appropriate for organ donation in order to ensure approach.

New federal regulations specifically governing approach procedures are currently being implemented. The law mandating these procedures took effect in August 1998, and OPOs were given until August 1999 to comply. According to the new regulations, which were devised explicitly to increase organ donation, primary approachers must either be OPO staff or have completed a training program sponsored by the OPO. Obviously these regulations may affect chaplain involvement in as yet undetermined ways.

WHY FOCUS ON HOSPITAL CHAPLAINS?

During the last several years, I participated in two forums on issues related to organ donation sponsored by the U.S. Department of Health and Human Services. I came to those forums as an ethicist trained in religious studies but as a "laywoman" on transplant issues. One forum was an open federal hearing in which all parties were invited to air their views on allocation of transplant livers and efforts to increase donation. The other was an internal DHHS conference aimed at evaluating the efficacy of various public efforts to increase organ donation. At both forums, staff from various regional OPOs played prominent roles.

Two emphases of the OPO representatives led me to seek the voices of hospital chaplains. First, several OPO personnel testified at the federal hearings that involving hospital chaplains in approaches tended to increase acceptance rates. They attributed this phenomenon to the chaplains' sensitivity and communicative skills. These witnesses implicitly encouraged OPOs to foster chaplain involvement in donation approach *because it increases acceptance rates*. However, no chaplains or representatives of chaplains' professional organizations testified. In fact, strikingly, no representatives of organized religion testified, although the hearings were open to the public.

Second, at the public hearings and even more clearly at the internal conference (which was primarily attended by "transplant professionals"), OPO representatives' testimony presumed that a "successful" approach is one in which families consent to donation. That is not surprising, given that OPOs' professional mission is to procure organs for transplant. Others involved with a family facing a tragic death might have different reasons for that involvement, however, and thus might define a "successful" encounter by different criteria. The hospital chaplain's charge to provide pastoral care to the patient and family is a broad and open-ended vocation. It is a mission that extends beyond issues of organ donation, although it might include addressing such issues. Chaplains employed by hospitals, as are all those interviewed in this study, face challenges intrinsic to their professional institutionalization—challenges that extend beyond issues of organ donation. Hospital chaplains are employed to be patient/family advocates regarding spiritual and social issues, and advocacy may entail questioning explicit policies or implicit practices of the institutions that employ them. How, then, do chaplains see their role as it pertains to organ donation? How do they integrate their approach to discussions of organ donation with other aspects of pastoral care? What do they consider the goals of their encounters with families facing donation decisions? Are these goals generally consistent with social goals of organ donation policy, or do institutional and community pressures to increase organ donation pose potential conflicts of interest for chaplains?

DESIGN OF THE STUDY

In order to investigate these questions, I conducted telephone interviews with nine chaplains who have extensive experience providing pastoral care to families facing a donation decision. These chaplains reside in several different OPO regions in various areas of the country, and some have worked in different OPO regions in the course of their careers. They also work in various kinds of hospitals—state university hospitals, private for-profit hospitals, not-for-profit hospitals with religious charters, and community hospitals. The majority work at hospitals with transplant units, a fact that many raised and discussed spontaneously in interviews.

The chaplains are all Christian. While each is trained to and does minister to people of various religious and nonreligious backgrounds, their own denominations include Roman Catholic, Lutheran, United Church of Christ, Disciples of

Christ, and Baptist. Both male and female chaplains were included in the interviews. While race/ethnicity was not an intentional criterion for chaplain selection, at least one chaplain was African American and another had special interest in outreach to minority communities.

All the chaplains interviewed personally approved of organ donation. In fact, they all demonstrated some consideration of organ donation as morally praiseworthy. However, their relative optimism or pessimism about transplant and their degree of commitment to transplantation as a social good clearly varied.

In the interviews, the chaplains were invited to share narratives of their experiences, respond to questions, and raise their own questions. Different interviews included different emphases, depending on the experience and focus of the chaplain. However, certain issues were addressed in all interviews: chaplains were invited to share best- or worst-case stories related to donation requests; to describe common issues raised by family members wrestling with a donation decision; to address whether they preferred to be the "primary approach" person or whether they preferred an alternative role; to note any issues of particular concern to pastoral care; to comment on their experience working with OPO staff, medical staff, other hospital employees, or other clergy in cases of potential donation; to suggest institutional or process considerations that they felt contribute to particularly sensitive or insensitive approach; and, in light of the previous inquiries, to articulate what they saw as the goal of their encounters with families facing donation decisions.

ORGANIZING MOTIFS IN THE INTERVIEW RESPONSES

The interviews revealed many differences among the chaplains regarding their experiences and their preferred form of participation in organ donation decision making. The chaplains disagreed about which institutional formats and which kinds of chaplain involvement promote appropriate goals while avoiding dangers in the donation process. Yet they uniformly agreed on what those goals and potential dangers are.

Two notable consistencies in the interviews provide an infrastructure, which helpfully organizes the spectrum of differences. First, all of the chaplains interviewed located their perceived role in organ donation within a broader context of grief support. Second, all articulated tensions that they perceived as inherent in their role as pastoral caregivers to distraught families facing donation decisions.

The emphasis on grief support was universal. One chaplain began his interview by stating, "We consider organ donation in the context of comprehensive grief support" (first sentence). Another repeatedly said, "You've got to be sensitive [to] the grieving process; that's the most important thing." In all of the interviews, they discussed the connection between pastoral support and a conception of grieving as a process.

Chaplains also consistently noted potential tensions between their role as pastoral support counselors and the interest they might have in obtaining organs for donation, stressing the priority of the former over the latter. Their discussion of these tensions was usually self-initiated, and several chaplains explicitly identified the recognition of these tensions as part of their professional challenge.

These two recurrent themes—the location of organ-donation consulting within the context of overall grief support and the explicit recognition of professional tensions—pervaded the discussion of more specific issues. Significantly, they helpfully framed the most intense disagreement exhibited among the chaplains, disagreement on process considerations and particularly on the question of whether the chaplain should be a primary approacher. These two axes of shared concern also define some notable contrasts between chaplains' ways of addressing organ donation with the approach of OPOs and public policy makers. Those contrasts, which will be explored in the conclusion of the chapter, challenge certain public policies to promote organ donation that are rarely questioned.

CHAPLAINS' RESPONSES TO FAMILY MEMBERS' CONCERNS

The chaplains' discussion of family concerns demonstrated their tendency to locate organ-donation decision making within a broad construct of grief support. They considered how various aspects of organ donation affect the family's ability to accept the finality of death, to honor the deceased, to maintain family harmony and strength in the midst of tragedy, and to begin or continue a productive grieving process. Conversely, their impression of family concerns guided their own deliberations about how to provide grief support and how to negotiate tensions inherent in their professional role.

All of the chaplains stressed that every family faced with a tragic choice regarding organ donation reacts differently to the traumas and decision making involved. All also noted that the progression of events leading toward a pronouncement of death makes a significant difference to the experience of family members. Cases in which the patient is ascertained to be dead before the family is on the scene, cases in which an assessment over several days is needed to confirm brain death, or cases in which the patient may be slowly moving toward brain death (with diminishing brain activity over an extended period of time) pose different psychological challenges both to the families and to chaplains supporting them in pastoral care. Nonetheless, when asked whether any family concerns tended to come up repeatedly, several commonalities in experience emerged. General concerns include difficulties in understanding brain death, the psychological challenge of "processing" the death, and the desire to make a decision the deceased would approve. In addition to concerns about whether the family's religious tradition supports or questions organ donation, broadly religious concerns arise about demonstrating respect for the body and about appropriate ritualization of death, loss, grief, and tribute.

"Decoupling" vs. "Psychological Decoupling"

Most potential organ donors are pronounced brain-dead while on life support, a scenario that raises particularly difficult emotional issues for family members. Their family member is "dead," but the body is warm and the chest is rising and falling. The medical profession, OPOs, and public policy forums have long supported the "decoupling" of information regarding death and potential organ donation, which means that the family should be informed of death by medical staff prior to and separately from an approach regarding organ donation. Decoupling generally reduces family confusion about whether the person is "completely" dead and alleviates family concerns about whether desire for organs might decrease incentives to do everything possible for the person. Taken together, the chaplains' comments underscore the importance of decoupling. Two respondents explicitly used that language. When asked about process considerations, one respondent's first response was to emphasize "decoupling is very important!" Others appealed to decoupling to articulate one reason for their reservations about physician approach, which was prevalent among the interview pool. They suggested that physicians should not be primary approachers because that would tend to confuse decoupling; the doctor's role is to confirm death.[5]

Perhaps more interestingly, though, the chaplains' various comments explicated the difficulty of truly decoupling the process of informing the family of death from approaching the family about organ donation. They implicitly considered decoupling from the point of view of the family attempting to process psychologically what had occurred, rather than from the standpoint of information providers.

All of the chaplains noted that confusion about brain death sometimes occurs among families facing a donation decision. Chaplains might view this confusion as de facto evidence of a problem in information flow or as an inevitable aspect of the "letting go" process, depending on the respondent and on the particular narratives from which he or she drew. Several chaplains gave examples of families' questions that indicate a lack of conceptual understanding of brain death, particularly a failure to grasp that brain death equals death. The chaplains viewed those questions as evidence of a communication problem between medical staff and family. For example, one chaplain described a case in which a family asked her whether the (brain-dead) family member would die before or after the organs were removed. She noted that when such a question arose, she felt it was her job to "slow down the process" and ask medical staff to reconvene and address technical questions about brain death with the family.

Most chaplains emphasized the difficulty of "psychological decoupling" (my term) even when informational decoupling had occurred, and even when family members had an accurate intellectual conception of brain death. Several noted that knowing and accepting are different stages in any grief process, regardless of brain-death or organ donation questions: "It's always one thing to be told a loved one is dead, and another to truly accept that he is dead."

Others emphasized that the specific circumstances in cases most likely to result in the possibility of organ donation—circumstances entailing artificial life support—make acceptance of death particularly difficult. One chaplain sarcastically questioned how a family can be expected to neatly separate issues of the finality of death from questions about organ donation, when the only reason the individual is maintained on life support after confirmed brain death *is* the possibility of organ donation. In context, the chaplain was not questioning the practice of maintaining life support. Rather, he seemed to be noting that in the most *physical* sense, the hospital itself does not (and could not, consistent with enabling donation as a possibility) "decouple" death and organ donation. Expanding on a point also raised by several others, this respondent explained that when the patient's initial brain activity status was not clear, families could be particularly confused as they attempted to process events. In such cases medical staff often actively encourage the family to touch and talk to the person, perhaps for several days, while brain activity is assessed, in case the person is actually comatose and capable of receiving some communication. After brain death is confirmed, the family is suddenly told the person—whose appearance has not changed at all—is dead. As a rhetorical "exclamation point," this chaplain described one case in which the family had been encouraged to communicate with the ventilator-dependent patient for five days; at that point, brain death was finally confirmed, and he was pronounced dead.

In response to the challenge of "psychological decoupling," many chaplains stressed the importance of language, including sensitive transformations of vocabulary. Several noted that after a family had digested the concept of brain death, the chaplain stopped using that term and simply referred to the person as "dead." Others noted a critical point where they stopped talking about the person and his or her life in the present tense and began using the past tense. One chaplain stressed the comprehensiveness of his efforts in this regard. In his response to families, he consciously moved from talking about "brain death" to talking about "death"; from talking about the person in the present tense to talking about the person's life; and from talking about "life support" to talking about "artificial˙ life support." Of course, perceptive challenges abound. For example, in the case in which a person was ventilator-dependent for several days while brain waves steadily decreased toward zero, the chaplain began using the term "artificial life support" when it became clear there was no hope; this change occurred before it was appropriate to begin talking about the person as "dead."

In addition to such perceptive challenges, there are challenges of consistency. Many chaplains noted either their efforts to encourage consistent vocabulary among the range of medical and service staff interacting with the family, or exasperation at their lack of influence on others' speech. It can confuse families, for example, if some staff members describe their loved one as "dead," while others continue to use the technical term "brain-dead."

One chaplain described a case in which the family had found the concept of brain death particularly hard to digest but was moving toward a psychological acceptance that death had occurred. The chaplain had been particularly attentive to the vocabulary used to describe the situation and had encouraged the same awareness among the nurses. But when the nursing shift changed, a nurse started talking to the family about what would happen when "the life support is turned off." According to the chaplain, "that just threw them through a loop!" After all, they had been told repeatedly that there was no "life."

All of the chaplains defined their role as facilitators of the complex processes of psychological acceptance entailed by a shocking death and located their contribution to organ donation decision making within that larger facilitating role. Thus, they emphasized the need for "time," questions of "timing," and "sensitivity to the process" in their comments; many respondents dramatically repeated these words. The chaplains shared a concern that institutional stresses in the hospital and the logistics of organ donation could unduly pressure families with respect to time. One respondent repeatedly characterized her primary role as "slowing things down for the family."

In order to support the family in the process of acceptance, all of the chaplains stressed the importance of taking care of what one respondent tagged "little things, which are somehow always big things." Repeatedly mentioned "big little things" included a quiet, private place for the family, moments when they were left alone, and the provision of phone access and Kleenex. One chaplain repeated the claim that "we just take care of everything for them at that time [while a family is processing a sudden death]." Asked to elaborate, he noted that he routinely takes care of parking, including the payment of any tickets, for the family—who probably dashed to the hospital in an emergency.

The repeated stress on "timing" and "process" crosscut the chaplains' perception of family concerns and linked their perception of family concerns to their perception of their own appropriate goals, roles, and measures of success.

What Would Johnny Want?

In addition to the challenges of "processing" the death, family members often face questions about the deceased's preferences regarding the organ donation decision. One chaplain said the first question of a good approach, no matter who conducts it, should be to ask whether the family has any indication of the person's wishes.

All of the chaplains said the decision for or against donation was generally easier for families who did have such an indication, either from a written source or from conversation. (By law, the next-of-kin has the authority to make the decision regarding donation, regardless of the expressed wishes of the deceased.) Without such indications, several chaplains perceived themselves to have a facilitating role, encouraging the family to discuss the general values of the deceased, and whether or not donation seems to accord with those values. Several chaplains linked consideration of the decedent's wishes to their notion of a successful approach. One specifically claimed that, regardless of donation or refusal to donate, the approach was successful if the family did—and knew that they had done—what the deceased would have wanted. Linking the issue of the decedent's values more indirectly to "success," several respondents noted that families who felt confident they had honored the decedent's wishes were more likely to be happy with their own decision, and thus more likely to have that decision contribute positively to their grieving process. Again, the chaplains shared the tendency to locate consideration of organ donation within the context of the family's long-term grieving process.

Innovative Ritualization

Most chaplains suggested that both the issue of "processing death" and testifying to the decedent's values play a role in ritual considerations for families. Families also raise concerns regarding general respect for the body as a symbol of respect for the decedent's life. Several respondents noted questions commonly asked by families: whether everyone closest to the deceased will have "a chance to say good-bye" (an issue of particular importance if close relatives are coming from out of town); whether organ donation will mutilate the body in a way that precludes an open-casket wake (it does not); whether the people retrieving the organs will treat the body respectfully. Interestingly, several chaplains noted being asked whether they had witnessed an organ retrieval (they had) or being asked to attend their family member's retrieval; one had even been asked by a family if they could attend.

One chaplain's worst case involved lack of respect. A father asked if his son, whose organs were being retrieved, was in the operating suite. An attendant curtly replied, "Only a corpse is in there."

Some concerns for proper ritual were related to specific religious traditions. For example, one chaplain facilitated the ritual bathing of the dead for a Jewish family who wished to donate; members of the community came to the hospital and performed the bathing while the brain-dead person was still on a ventilator.

Ritualization provocatively connected to the chaplains' concerns for the acute challenges of "processing" death in these situations, particularly, but not exclusively, when decisions were made for donation. In such cases, families have to take leave of a warm, artificially respirated corpse, a scenario that can render closure difficult. However, several chaplains explicitly emphasized the similarity of ritual challenges among cases involving cessation of artificial life support, regardless of the donation decision. Most of the chaplains presumed that providing appropriate rituals was part of their ministry to families facing technologically mediated final farewells. Some echoed the language of the families in speaking of "giving everyone a chance to say good-bye." When I pursued what that meant, it generally referred to some simple bedside ritual, such as the whole family touching the person and each other, or saying prayers around the bedside. In addition, it might mean arranging for individual family members to have brief private solitary moments with the deceased. One respondent particularly worried about people who wanted an individual good-bye but "no one hears them," presumably in part because of time pressures for organ retrieval. One chaplain who stressed her role as a facilitator of ritual could not respond when I followed up by asking what concerns about ritualization families had expressed. She laughed at "drawing a blank" and suggested that she "didn't give them a chance" to have concerns because she "immediately encouraged" them to think of ritualizing what was happening to the person and to their relationship with the person.

Ritualization can symbolically include the deceased in a decision to donate whether or not the explicit wishes of the deceased were known. Many respondents described discussing organ donation as consistent with the decedent's values during bedside "good-bye" ceremonies that they facilitated. Through the ritual, the organ donation indeed became the "gift of life" of the deceased, rather than a mere accident of his or her death.

Even the exception to common themes on ritual proved the rule of its presumed importance. After one chaplain failed to raise ritual considerations throughout the interview, I specifically asked him if families expressed any concerns about appropriate ritualization. He sighed and replied, "I'm afraid we don't pay as much attention to ritual considerations as we should. . . . Of course, I generally pray with the family around the bedside before retrieval begins." These rituals interestingly defy traditional conceptual or theoretical groundings: The patient is actually dead and thus past "good-byes" or healing rituals; at the same time, these are not funeral rituals. Yet experientially rituals seem to help families process the acutely felt liminality associated with situations of artificial life support. The chaplains suggest that making room and time for ritual may be an important part of sensitive organ donation approaches, regardless of the family's ultimate decision on donation.

Other Religious Issues

In addition to issues surrounding ritualization, several other religious issues were raised by families served by the chaplains. Families often want to know whether their particular religious tradition or denomination condones, allows, or disapproves of donation. One chaplain noted that this topic could generate exceptions to his general caution against initiating theological conversation or questioning disinclination to donate. When people immediately claim, "My religious tradition won't allow donation," which in many cases "is just not true," he asks them to identify their religious tradition/denomination and presents any information he has on that tradition's position on donation.

Some families want to discuss images or stories from their tradition related to donation, but several chaplains noted these families were a minority. As one said, "Most families worry more about whether they can get in touch with Relative X in time for consultation than about what the Bible says about donation."

For those who do pursue theological inquiries, several motifs were mentioned as relevant. Working with a Catholic family, one chaplain analogized organ donation to "communion." Another cited the good Samaritan story as a parallel to organ donation. He stressed that, as in the biblical parable, the "neighbor" awaiting transplant could be anybody, defined by need and by the mercy shown. Again, the chaplains stressed perceptive challenges. They considered it important to have a sense of where families "were at" before embarking on such explorations. Several stated that they would discuss religious motifs only if the family initiated that discussion. Discussions of imagery deemed supportive of donation might be comforting to families leaning toward donation but coercive to families leaning against or struggling with ambivalence.

Many of the chaplains stressed that religious imagery could weigh against donation. For example, several pointed out that some Christians have very bodily notions of their hoped-for "resurrection," deriving from the Gospel stories of Jesus' resurrection. These Christians might have a special reluctance to "mutilate" the body. One chaplain explicitly noted that while he did not personally agree with that theology, he "could not say it was wrong" [outside the Christian tradition]. "Which stories or images should I pick out?" asked another chaplain, implying that his reluctance to initiate discussions of religious imagery was related to his effort to refrain from any subtle pressuring of the family. The one chaplain involved in promoting organ donation among church communities explicitly articulated a theological stance that seemed to be presumed by most of the others—a conviction that the overall biblical message presses toward donation. Yet he suggested that the appropriate place to discuss religious imagery as it pertains to donation was at routine church worship and fellowship, rather than in moments of crisis.

The religious beliefs and practices of cultural minorities can raise special concerns, including concerns that Christian chaplains may be particularly unlikely to anticipate before encountering a specific case. One chaplain had been involved in cases in which linguistic and cultural interpreters had been called in to assist discussion with Muslim and Hindu families. Another described a case in which a Native American refused donation because his tribal tradition emphasized being buried "whole" so that one's organs could be transferred to one's next life in animal form.

The chaplains repeated acknowledgment that some religious imagery, including imagery within culturally prevalent religious traditions, may be in tension with organ donation—a striking observation in light of current policy initiatives. Literature and presentations on organ donation by the Department of Health and Human Services and regional OPOs consistently but oversimplistically claim that "all major faith traditions" support organ donation.

The religiosity/nonreligiosity of the chaplain and family raised issues. All of the chaplains welcomed family clergy as primary pastoral support when available—"I get out of the way then"; "I play second fiddle then"). One nevertheless described this relationship as trying. He had seen cases in which he felt the clergy pressured the family against donation without being well informed on the religious tradition's understanding of the issue, "but I just had to bear it." Some who worked at tertiary care centers mentioned that family clergy were often unable to be present because of distance. One noted with some irony that because he did encourage family clergy involvement, he personally tended to have much more active roles with nonreligious families facing donation decisions. Several chaplains felt families with weak or no religious affinities demonstrated as much need and desire for "pastoral support" as strongly religious families.

Special Issues

In addition to common concerns that tended to be raised by many families facing donation, chaplains reported concerns that are particular to specific groups. Almost all the chaplains mentioned that in their experience African American and Hispanic families were less likely to donate and attributed this reluctance to their greater "distrust of the system." One chaplain stated that he considered this mistrust historically justified. He had been involved in outreach to African American Christian churches in his area to promote organ donation.

Several chaplains noted that the general experience of families in the hospital significantly affected their stance toward donation. Families who perceived that they had received callous treatment by the medical establishment might project their anger onto the approacher. One chaplain described a case in which a woman refused donation explicitly because the doctor (who was uninvolved in the approach) had mistakenly told her sister that her aneurysm could wait a week for treatment, and she blamed that doctor for the death. On a more positive note, the same chaplain attributed her hospital's general "good record" on donation in part to its overall reputation as a patient- and family-centered hospital. It is a not-for-profit Catholic hospital with an orientation to patient/family support "right in the mission statement."

Other chaplains who raised similar issues stressed the panicked sense of loss of control that comes with any tragic death. One emphasized that anyone facing such loss of control might refuse donation simply to exercise control but proposed that this tendency could be exacerbated if the family had not been treated sensitively by medical staff.

Another respondent connected the issue of control to a class of particularly frustrating cases in which he had participated. These were cases in which the next-of-kin claimed, "I know I should donate" or "I know Johnny would have wanted me to donate," but "I cannot." The chaplain found this situation, which he had faced repeatedly, particularly challenging. ("Half of me wants to push, but the other half knows I need to support.") At the same time, he expressed understanding for the seeming paradox expressed by such family members: "The family may think, 'I had no control [over this disaster]; now I do. I can say no. But I know that's not right.' " In such cases, simply "waiting out the internal tug of war with them" might be key to helping the family make a more logically consistent decision. All of the many chaplains who raised cases in which venting, projection, or control may have influenced decision making particularly worried about those cases because they feared the families might regret the decision later.

CHAPLAINS' PERCEPTIONS OF GOALS AND STANDARDS OF SUCCESS

More than any other factor, shared concern for the family's grieving process influenced the chaplains' articulation of their goals. Organ donation approach and resulting decisions were evaluated by how they promoted or impeded the acceptance of death, how they impacted family dynamics, and how the family might look back on them over time. The shared commitment to facilitating constructive grieving processes led the chaplains to two common focuses. They all explicitly stated that they view the needs of the family as more important than the need for organs. Accordingly, they all stressed a commitment to act as a facilitator to family discussions, aimed at promoting consensus in the family.

Facilitating Family Unity and Healing Amidst Grief

The consensus that their pastoral support role clearly prioritized needs of families over needs for organs was striking not only because of its unanimity but because the "process" orientation entailed contrasts with the "outcome" orientation of OPOs who are specifically charged with obtaining organs and increasing donation. Many chaplains defined their process focus in terms of future comfort level. The majority wondered aloud how the family would think about the decision "six months from now," "one year from now," and suggested that if the family would make the same decision—whether for or against donation—that was a "successful" case. Several others considered a case successful "if it helped the family work through the grief process."

Examples of "best" and "worst" cases confirmed the chaplains' emphasis on the grieving process. Worst cases often were defined by real or potential family regret. After discussing concerns that the family might feel pressure to donate, one chaplain noted there was a "flip side." He then lamented cases in which families of potential donors were not approached—perhaps because medical staff thought it would be "too hard on them"—but might realize belatedly that the deceased person could have been a donor. (He noted that this problem was decreasing because of required request protocols.) Another chaplain described one of his "worst" cases as one in which a furious woman came back to the hospital months after her daughter had died. She belatedly learned her daughter might have been an organ donor, but no one had asked her at the time of death. The concerns expressed by these chaplains dovetail with stresses of OPO staff, who portray one aspect of their mission as ensuring that no one "misses the chance" to donate.

Most respondents described "bad" scenarios in which family decision making might generate later regret. More than half mentioned cases in which they believed people had been approached before emotionally accepting that death had occurred. They felt that those people refused donation because they were still refusing death and that they might regret the decision later. They emphasized that it was the family's potential regret, not the loss of the organs, that they considered "a nightmare." They distinguished between this scenario and appropriately considered refusal to donate. "I would not lose any sleep [if the family refused donation after appropriate consideration]." (It was striking how many respondents discussed their ability or lack of ability to sleep as it raised issues about the cases.) The common perception that cases of improper timing occur "all too often" may explain why every respondent believed that appropriate approach per se would increase the donation rate.[6] Thus the shared emphasis on attention to timing: "being sensitive to timing"; "realizing it takes time"; "slowing things down for the family"; "making sure the family has accepted death, not just been told about it, before approach."

Just as worst-case scenarios indicated disrupted or dysfunctional grieving processes, best-case scenarios conversely emphasized constructive contribution to family grieving and family relationships. Family consensus was viewed as critical, and all the chaplains considered their role in facilitating family discussions as central to pastoral care. Interestingly, no respondent distinguished the family member with legal authority to make the donation decision from the whole family. The family as a relational web was clearly their locus of concern. This perspective may contrast with that of OPO staff, who, consistent with their mission and their legal obligations, may focus special attention on the legal next-of-kin.[7] The best cases described by the chaplains involved "the whole family being happy about the decision six months down the road" or the belief that "the decision helps the family through the grieving process." One chaplain highlighted issues raised by many when she discussed a particularly troubling case with a successful resolution. The case involved a seven-year-old Little Leaguer who, with parents cheering in the stands, slid into a base and ended up on a respirator pronounced brain-dead. The parents' initial reactions were radically different, one strongly in favor of donation and one opposed. The chaplain said, "[I] was so worked up over this case" and considered it "so important that they come together, that I help them come together." In the end, they came to agree to donation and felt good about the decision. The chaplain said, "I was so happy. It wasn't because they donated. I would have been happy if they reached consensus the other way, too. I just wanted them to come together so they could go through this together."

Within the process-oriented focus on the family grieving process, donation seemed to be viewed as an added plus, though not the standard of "success." Almost all of the chaplains expressed satisfaction at seeing willing donor families "feel like they made something good come of something bad." Yet only two chaplains expressly included donation in their definition of a positive outcome, and they qualified that heavily. They considered the "very best" outcome to be "donation *and* feeling good about the decision" but stressed that "feeling good about it" was "the most important thing." The respondent who was most restrained about chaplain involvement in organ donation pressed this rationale beyond the individual case. He explicitly stated that he would rather see his hospital "err on the side of losing organs rather than on the side of putting pressure on families."

Articulation of Tensions

Paradoxically, the chaplains perceived their roles to be both clear and fraught with tension. In conjunction with the focus on family grieving processes, all formulated a vocational obligation to prioritize the grieving family's needs over society's need for organs. In addition, all discussed a mission to facilitate family discussion and consensus. Yet, strikingly, all of the chaplains explicitly noted tensions they perceived as inherent in their roles. In short, because they considered pastoral support to entail a "process" focus on the family, they worried about bringing "outcome" pressures to their encounters. They all wished to distinguish their role from organ procurement; virtually all joined the refrain, "It's not my job to get organs." They used language of "bracketing," "putting aside," or "leaving behind" their knowledge of what good the organs might do in order to put the spiritual and psychological welfare of the family first. That could mean "bracketing" general commitments to organ donation, specific commitments to transplant patients, or both.

The majority of the respondents not only had firsthand contact with transplant recipients and those on waiting lists for organs but also had provided pastoral care to such patients. Many spontaneously raised related challenges: "It's hard. I know what it's like on the other side"; "It's hard. I'm working with these folks in trauma on the third floor. Up on the fifth floor I've got patients waiting for organs"; "It's hard. I used to be on the transplant ward." Interestingly while all the chaplains thought that conflicting commitments demanded "bracketing" when they counseled potential donors, none of the chaplains thought their work entailed an impossible conflict of interest.

In fact, most identified their exposure to "the other side" as positive for their interaction with donor families. Several felt it important that they had a "realistic" knowledge of transplantation. Because they had witnessed many outcomes—both bad and good—in transplant cases, they could more easily accept refusals to donate. (This repeated theme sharply contrasts with the lack of attention to negative outcomes in public education drives on organ donation, which portray all donations as "gifts of life.") In addition, several chaplains had been asked by people considering donation whether they knew what it was like for people "on the other side," and they thought it had been helpful to the family to be able to talk about that.

In addition to those who discussed looking "at the other side," two respondents mentioned looking at the "big picture." Like all the chaplains, they supported donation, and, significantly, one was among the only two to include donation in his definition of "best outcome." Yet these chaplains were the most questioning of the stress on transplantation compared to other health or social goods that may compete for financial and political support—particularly increased insurance access and preventive medicine. One respondent explicitly worried whether, in the aggregate, we had passed an overall transplantation level that was defensible given trade-offs with other goods.

Both felt that considering the "big picture" of health care access in our society helped them to focus on process rather than outcome, and to avoid undue investment in the outcome of particular donation decisions. Again this explicitness is striking in the light of public campaigns to increase organ donation, campaigns that fail to ask "instead of what?" questions raised by transplantation. In general, their contact with many kinds of patients and medical tragedies seemed to encourage chaplains to consider organ donation and transplantation in a broad context rather than as a specialized area of concern.

For some chaplains, while it might "not be my job to get organs" when counseling a potential donor family, that might in fact be their perceived job in other professional capacities. One noted that his experience with low acceptance rates among African Americans led him to become involved in outreach to African American churches specifically aimed at increasing support for organ donation. Another paused while stressing that he had to "put aside" the desire for donation when working with grieving families. He laughed and said, "but we [chaplains] do wear many hats. I am also on the board of [my regional] OPO." Interestingly, the other respondent who was particularly associated with her OPO—she had gone through an OPO training specifically designed to increase acceptance rates—never identified that close association as a potential conflict of interest. She was one of only two respondents to include donation in her description of best outcome, but she also explicitly identified facilitation of the grieving process as the defining goal of her involvement with any particular family.

Chaplains, then, tended not only to identify perceived sources of tension but also to embrace the challenge of negotiating such tensions as an intrinsic challenge of their profession rather than view role tensions as something that could or should be structurally avoided.

THE CHAPLAIN'S ROLE
IN THE APPROACH PROCESS

A critical question in the interviews was whether chaplains preferred to be primary approachers or to be available as a consultant to the family while someone else made the primary approach. This question proved critical because the answers were strikingly different, while the rationales for different answers proved strikingly similar. Again, they expressed two overriding concerns: to prioritize the needs of the grieving family over the social need for organs, consistent with pastoral care commitments, and to enable the chaplain to play a facilitator role with the family.

All of the respondents had clear feelings about serving as primary approachers. They also seemed impelled to explain their positions; this question generated the longest responses and the most impromptu referrals to actual cases and perceived parallels. This question also may have generated the greatest ambivalence among the chaplains; while all provided clear answers, it was the only question that prompted repeated inquiries about what other respondents were saying. Basically half the respondents preferred to be primary approachers, and half considered that role inappropriate. Of the latter, one expressed "mixed emotions." He generally preferred not to be the primary approacher but noted it might be best for him to do so in certain cases, particularly cases where he had been with the family throughout an extended crisis. One chaplain, voicing a view unique among the respondents, did not feel he should be routinely present or involved in consultations about organ donation. He felt he should be involved only if the family specifically requested pastoral support. The others all seemed to prefer to be offered as a resource to deliberating families in some overt way, although they differed on the question of primary approach.

Those who rejected a role in primary approach thought that they could best accomplish the "bracketing" of outcome pressures and play a facilitating role if someone else did the primary approach. They were particularly concerned that the family might inevitably see the primary approacher's main goal as obtaining organs, and they wanted to dissociate themselves from that goal: "I don't want them to think I am a vulture swooping down for the organs"; "It's important that I not be seen as just part of the system"; "I want the family to know I am there for them regardless of their decision on organ donation."

Significantly, the conflict of interest was not perceived as simply a matter of appearances. Several specifically linked a rejection of primary approach to caution about competing pulls on themselves. They implicitly suggested that avoiding participation in primary approach was a form of "procedural bracketing" (my term) that reinforced the necessary psychological bracketing of outcome desires. However, they were concerned about being symbolically present to families throughout the process. Two specifically mentioned that they would like to be physically present at the time of primary approach while somehow being clearly delineated from the primary approacher. In addition to desiring "procedural bracketing," several who preferred a secondary role claimed it was easier for them to maintain a facilitating role with the family if they were not the one to raise the issue.

The respondent who rejected routine involvement shared many of these con-

cerns but felt that even a secondary role in approach, without the family requesting pastoral support, placed the chaplain in a conflict of interest: "I don't want us
seen as being an administrative representative for different initiatives in the hospital." His restrained view of the chaplain's legitimate role was provocative
because it corresponded with acute questioning of institutional incentives and
social presumptions. He was the only respondent to raise issues of financial
incentives ("Hospitals make a lot of money on organ retrievals"). While considering donation "good," he questioned social emphases on transplantation compared to other health issues, noting high negative outcome rates and huge relative
expenditures. He questioned whether heavy emphasis on transplantation might
reflect the social prevalence of vitalism, the belief that "life is always the most
important thing"—a view he felt professional religious ought to contest with a
"broader view of reality." He was the only chaplain to suggest that the chaplain's
job might be to take a "prophetic stand" against the hospital administration if the
chaplain perceived hospital or outside staff to be pressuring potential donors (a
situation he suspected at a nearby hospital, while his own was "pretty passive" on
organ donation).

Differences among respondents in the extent to which they saw institutional
co-optation as a danger highlight some complexities of organ donation. The hospital is the locus of most institutional pressures on chaplains, but organ donation
is institutionally diffuse. Hospitals don't obtain control over organs they retrieve,
and OPOs manage much of the retrieval and transfer. Thus while the "prophetic"
responder stressed hospital-related pressures (both financial and nonfinancial),
another respondent said organ donation "was way down on his list" in terms of
issues that might put him at odds with hospital administration. Others seemed to
consider "the system" as all the administrative layers that a family might
encounter, the lumping OPOs, hospital administration, even general social pressures for organ donation as "the system" from which their pastoral care commitments demanded some insulation.

Significantly, the chaplains who generally or sometimes favored making the
primary approach shared conceptions of goals and dangers with their colleagues
who did not, but they felt that primary approach better enabled them to prioritize
family needs over the need for organs and to play a facilitating role. They liked
the control over the process offered by primary approach because they felt it
allowed them to focus on the family's needs in their particular grieving process:
"I know better than an outsider where they are at in the grieving process, especially if I have been through the whole crisis with them"; "I can slow things down
if the whole thing is going too fast for them"; "I like for us (chaplaincy staff) to
do the primary approach because I like the way we treat families." Part of the
power they attained in acting as primary approach was explicitly described as a
power to protect the family from undue pressure for the sake of obtaining organs:

"I can make sure no one is putting pressure on them if I control the approach." Like those who rejected primary approach, these chaplains explicitly sought to distinguish their role from organ procurement and to make sure the family correctly perceived that it is not their role. As one said, "I have to make it very clear in how I present the information that I don't think there is any right answer other than what is right for them."

Like the others, they spoke of their need to set aside commitments they might feel to potential recipients. However, they seemed more concerned about what might be called the "compared to what?" question. They feared that someone else doing the primary approach might be less likely than themselves to have a commitment to the grieving family that was both noninstrumental and clearly informed. Such a commitment could be conveyed to the family by the chaplain's presence throughout the crisis; the chaplain was not there just *because* the person might be an organ donor. One chaplain who strongly preferred primary approach also emphasized that whenever possible, he wanted to be called in before the person died because "it is easier to minister at death if I was there before." All the respondents favoring primary approach felt their contact with the family was critical and feared isolation if someone else did the approach. As one chaplain put it, "If it's not me, and the OPO person comes in, and maybe the nurses' shift has just changed, they could be there with a stranger; they could be facing this with all strangers!"

In some ways, the chaplains who preferred primary approach had the most narrow vision for the OPOs' ideal role. These chaplains noted that when things worked well with their primary approach, they simply called the OPO representative when the decision was "a done deal," either to report a refusal of consent or to request the OPO staff to walk the family through the administrative procedures of donation consent. Two specifically noted that they liked to introduce the OPO staff to families who had decided to donate, apparently to provide symbolic continuity between decision making and administrative enactment.

While these chaplains viewed the role of OPOs most narrowly in one sense, in another sense they were the chaplains most closely associated with their OPOs. One noted a particularly fruitful long-standing working relationship with an OPO staffer. Another had participated in a special OPO training initiative; she participates on a special hospital team that cooperates with the OPO to ensure sensitive approach and to increase acceptance rates. She apparently considers the OPO to have a primary role in training and organizing medical, pastoral, and social work staff, who are then empowered to play a primary role in approach themselves.

Discussing their preference for primary or secondary role in approach, all of the chaplains wanted to distinguish their role from organ procurement. Yet, significantly, they all had generally positive views about OPO staff. Most had regular contact with OPO staff on cases involving potential for transplant. Several commented unsolicited that they considered these staff professional, efficient, and sensitive. As noted, one had voluntarily attended training with her local OPO in an initiative explicitly designed to increase consent rates. Another said the OPO "does a good job." Several mentioned having close and friendly working relationships with particular OPO staff. Two noted they had had different experiences in two OPO regions, with one OPO more involved in primary approaches and secondary consulting than the other.

Of course, the new federal legislation may transform approach practices in ways that directly affect chaplains. Fewer than half the respondents were aware of new federal legislation, passed while the interviews were in progress, that requires primary approachers to be either OPO staff or OPO-trained. Two respondents were concerned that their role in organ donation counseling might be diminished as a result of the legislation; they feared their OPO might respond to the legislation by taking over all primary approach. Another chaplain assumed his OPO would respond to the law by increased OPO training of volunteers rather than by exclusive use of OPO staff in primary approach. He considered the legislation "a good thing" because "the OPOs generally do a good job [with the training]." One respondent who worked in a community hospital geographically distant from his OPO office feared the legislation might actually reduce donation rates from hospitals such as his own. He was concerned that OPO staff were less likely to come there in person and that opportunities for donation might be lost because the most appropriate staff available for approach were not legally permitted to be approachers.

The coupling of a generally positive assessment of OPO staff with the chaplains' careful distinction between their role and organ procurement is suggestive. It indicates that their concerns about appropriate interaction with family and OPO in the approach process are not concerns about personnel but rather concerns about appropriate professional roles.

CONCLUSION: RAISING DONATION CONSENT RATES AS GOAL, OR AS EXPECTED BUT UNINTENDED EFFECT?

A generation ago, as organ transplantation was being pioneered, Paul Ramsey considered policies on defining death by examining the relationship between intent, public policy, and organ donation.[8] At the time, given the increasing use of life-support technology, the whole brain definition of death was being advanced as a legal substitute for the traditional "heart-lung" definition, which was untenable for patients on respirators. Ramsey was troubled that the demand for organs was explicitly offered as one argument for accepting the whole brain definition of death. He carefully distinguished between two possibilities: defining death *so as to* promote organ donation vs. defining death in a way that has the *expected but unintended* effect of promoting donation. Ramsey's acceptance of whole brain death depended on the rationale. He accepted the defense of whole brain death as a way to verify death within new technological contexts, in ways consistent with long-standing understandings of death and commitment to patients. He acknowledged that the newly recognized definition of death would have the foreseeable consequence of promoting organ donation (by allowing organ retrieval from brain-dead patients on respirators, rather than requiring respirator withdrawal first, which results in deterioration of the organs). However, he expressed grave reservations when the whole brain definition was defended *because* it would promote organ donation. From his point of view, defining death *so as to* promote donation would mark a dangerous instrumentalization of the patient.[9]

Ramsey's distinction—between designing policy *so as to* promote donation vs. designing policy that has the foreseeable but unintended consequence of promoting donation—illuminates contrasts between the chaplains' perspectives and those demonstrated by OPOs and policy makers. The distinction is both descriptively clarifying and normatively provocative. OPO representatives consistently speak of structuring approach processes *so that* donation rates increase. (Recall that one impetus to this project was hearing several OPO representatives encourage use of chaplains in approach *so that* acceptance rates increase. OPOs have also endorsed hospital sponsorship of comprehensive grief-support programs because acceptance rates are higher in hospitals that have them.) Most recently, the "*so that*" has been ensconced in new federal legislation governing organ donation approach, the stated purpose of which is to increase donation. On the other hand, chaplains consistently speak of increased donation rates as the expected but unintended effect of sensitive pastoral care to grieving families. This basic difference underlies a series of other contrasts between language and attitudes of chaplains and of the OPO community, a family of differences that beg normative questions.

The language used by OPO staff and that used by chaplains to describe encounters with family radically differ in ways that underscore this basic distinction. In fact, the language of "approach" comes from the OPO community. Usually one approaches somebody *for* something. Significantly, none of the chaplains interviewed spontaneously used the language of "approach" to describe the task of informing family members about donation options. While they were all familiar with that language and adopted it when specifically asked if they preferred primary approach or other roles, their self-initiated descriptions of their role emphasized pastoral care and grief support.

Clearly the distinction between intended effects and foreseeable but unintended effects parallels the different definitions of success presumed by OPOs and chaplains. If the intended effect of careful approach is to obtain organs, approach acceptance (consent) rates are de facto barometers of success. Acceptance rates are indeed presumed to be the measure of success within OPOs and in the policy community. This presumption is clear not only in the way that OPO representatives speak, but in the way OPOs are judged relative to each other (federal policy makers assume the better OPOs have higher consent rates) and in the way the organ procurement profession seeks to improve itself. Currently, for example, UNOS is sponsoring a best-practices study in which top OPO staff from around the country are identified and studied as potential models for others. The criterion for these models of best practices is unusually high approach-acceptance rates.

That chaplains consistently rejected donation consent as a de facto measure of success indicates their adherence to something like Ramsey's distinction. Since they viewed the intended effect of their interactions with family as grief support and consensus facilitation, success could not be determined except in reference to constructive grieving and cohesive relationship building in the family. The chaplains all expected consent rates to rise with what they considered sensitive approach, yet suppressing any desire to make that a goal in itself was perceived as a professional challenge and obligation.

Differing goals may explain why chaplains so consistently identify the task of negotiating moral tensions as inherent in their provision of pastoral support to potential donor families, while such a sense of competing pulls is largely absent in the OPO community. All of the chaplains wished to resist a perceived temptation to adopt as a goal what ought be an unintended good. Yet several noted that they felt the recognized tension was itself good: "I hold onto that tension"; "I think it's a healthy tension"; "I think it is good to feel the tension." Perhaps the tension is seen as good because increased donation was deemed genuinely good, though pastoral commitments demand that it be subordinated to other allegiances. Thus the tension testifies to a multiplicity of moral goods and necessary trade-offs between them.

Of course, the goals of organ procurement staff and chaplains are not so clearly separable. OPO staff can be very genuinely concerned about the needs of grieving people they serve. At the training session I attended, for example, the instructor heavily emphasized the need to facilitate families' grieving processes. In a personal discussion after the session, he told me that he had originally been inspired by the work of certain chaplains. (Coincidentally, one of those chaplains was interviewed for this project.) Similarly, chaplains may be committed to increasing organ donation. In fact, two respondents were personally involved as trainees or board members of their OPO, and one had conducted community outreach to local churches to promote donation.

Nonetheless, I am struck by the consistency with which Ramsey's basic distinction seems to govern a fundamental difference in attitude toward approach of organ procurement professionals and chaplains. Conversations with a chaplain and an OPO representative are illuminating. I would describe the chaplain as particularly committed to organ donation and the most personally connected to her OPO. Still the contrast is striking. The chaplain described a "good, memorable" case in which a woman angry at medical staff declined to donate, then changed her mind:

> INTERVIEWER: So it was a good case because she decided to donate?
> CHAPLAIN: [Pause] Well, no. [Pause] I wouldn't say that. [Pause] I would say that it was good because she donated and felt good about it.
> INTERVIEWER: So the best-case scenario is that the person both donate and feel good about it?
> CHAPLAIN: I would say that is ideal. . . . I would want to distinguish some cases. If they donate and feel good about that, that is ideal. If they don't donate and continue to feel good about the decision, I don't personally think of it as ideal, but it is still successful. If they donate but don't continue to feel good about it, then that is not successful. It's all got to help the family with their grieving process [to be considered successful].

Contrast the chaplain's point of view with that expressed by the OPO representative:

> OPO REPRESENTATIVE: The new legislation specifically states it is to increase donation rates. . . . [W]e are ready to provide the training required by the law. . . . [W]e have been training people to get consent for years. We have been training people to get consent for years.
> INTERVIEWER: So, the goal of the approach is to get consent?
> OPO REPRESENTATIVE: [Long pause] Well, of course we *hope* for consent. But of course we respect the family. . . . A no is a no, period. . . . If we were bullies to families, that would end up hurting organ donation.

The chaplain subordinates her strong desire for organs to the goal of grief support; inversely the OPO representative's rationale for sensitivity to grief support is her instrumental desire for organs.

The distinction between intended and unintended promotion of donation, between prioritizing the need for organs and prioritizing the needs of grieving people, may also affect how those involved with potential donor families view refusal to donate. In particular, the distinction may govern whether refusal is considered negatively, and if so, whether it generates feelings of anger or of regret. One is more likely to feel anger if one feels one's intended goal has been thwarted. At a professional conference largely attended by OPO representatives, I was struck by the open expression of anger toward people who refuse to donate. Several portrayed organ donation as a matter of "civic responsibility," thus implying that those who refuse donation fail to demonstrate basic levels of civic decency. The word "anger" was repeatedly raised: "Sometimes it's hard because I get so angry at them [people who refuse to donate]." One luncheon conversation even centered on how to control such anger. In contrast, no chaplains discussed anger generated by refusal to consent. Some spoke of regret: "It's hard because I know what those organs could do for somebody who needs them. But I just have to live with that regret." Others were unwilling to ascribe any negative feeling to refusals that accorded with good grief support: "If the family made a decision they will be happy within six months, and they had consensus; hey, I can live with that."

The alternatives of nonjudgment, regret, or anger toward families who refuse donation raise issues of pluralism. Decisions about donation interconnect with the most ultimate commitments: understandings of embodiment, beliefs about afterlife, religious beliefs, conceptions of private and public good. Chaplains' language of nonjudgment or regret may signal a greater tolerance toward differences in such commitments. That language is also more consistent with the metaphor of donation as gift, a metaphor stressed in public awareness campaigns promoting donation. It is paradoxical to be angry at someone for not giving a gift.

In short, Ramsey's distinction seems to lie at the heart of a series of differences in the language and attitudes of chaplains compared to organ procurement staff. These differences are normatively question-begging. What should be the goal of organ donation approach? Are stated goals actual goals? How should trade-offs between multiple goals be brokered?

To articulate these questions is neither to indict organ procurement professionals nor to canonize chaplains. There are many potential answers to these questions; the disparity might suggest helpful complementary perspectives or, alternatively, might suggest something problematic in current chaplain or OPO practice. However these questions are answered, it is significant that listening to the voice of chaplains enabled their articulation in acute ways largely absent in public policy discourse.

It might be argued that the differing goals and commitments of organ procurement staff and chaplains tend to balance and complement each other, effecting a trade-off of public and private interest. As the chaplains repeatedly noted, they expect good pastoral care to result in increased donation. Or to consider another possibility, OPOs' instrumental interest in grief support might facilitate resource expenditures and coordination for grief support that chaplains have long advocated for good pastoral care. Through their different orientations, chaplains and OPO staff may remind each other of myriad important factors. Chaplains may promote attention to comprehensive grief support among OPOs. OPOs, by maintaining the importance of legal next-of-kin as well as of family discussion, may remind chaplains that processes of resolution are necessary when consensus truly breaks down. At the same time, chaplains may legitimately caution that a focus on legal next-of-kin may give up on the possibility of family consensus too easily. There may be various other examples of potential complementarities.

Alternatively, it might be argued that within current organ procurement processes chaplain involvement inherently risks co-optation by commitments antithetical to pastoral care. One chaplain interviewed overtly articulated this concern. Even respondents who disagreed recognized the danger. The chaplains' shared emphasis on prioritizing families' needs over the need for organs suggests that co-optation might be an increasing danger under the new federal policy governing approach, since that policy dictates that all approachers be trained by an organization committed primarily to organ procurement.

This point leads to a third possibility: The perspectives of chaplains could radically question the legitimacy of current assumptions governing public policy and OPO practice. Their construal of increased donation as a foreseeable and welcome but unintended goal, second in priority to other moral goals, may call into question current policy focused exclusively on promoting donation. Does designing approach processes *so that* donation increases fundamentally instrumentalize grieving families?

Personally I lean toward this third interpretation. I began this project concerned about potential conflict of interest for chaplains. But chaplains' reflection on potential conflict of interest has led me to wonder whether the much larger, and much less recognized, conflict of interest lies with the OPOs and with public policy more generally. Might the prevalent anger of OPO staff toward families who refuse donation reflect an unacknowledged conflict of interest? After all, OPO staff are by definition committed to organ procurement as a primary professional vocation. So how could they realistically be expected *not* to take face-to-face refusals to donate personally? Might refusal to donate threaten the professional identity of OPO staff more than it would the identity of a chaplain, nurse, or social worker? Should the general public consider organ donation as an altruistic gift, or as an expected act of civic decency? And what policies subtly promote these different alternatives?

The new legislation mandates that a grieving family be approached through an organization whose primary mission is organ procurement—in other words, an organization whose legitimate mission entails treating that family primarily as means to an end. Is that not troubling? Might it not be easier, ethically, to defend legislation that demands the primary approacher *not* be OPO-affiliated, but instead be someone committed to the family as an end in itself?

Of course there may be important ethical distinctions between using OPO staff as primary approachers and using other hospital staff who have attended training sessions sponsored by the OPO—the two options allowed by the new regulation. I have suggested that risk of a conflict of interest might be greater for the OPO staff. At the same time, there might be an admirable honesty in having families approached by someone introduced as an organ procurement professional. In one sense that affiliation openly acknowledges the community's desire for organs.

In contrast, hospital staff trained by the OPOs necessarily have professional commitments to the family beyond organ donation. At the same time they may well benefit from both the technical information and the wealth of experience offered by OPO training. Still, I find it troubling to legally *require* such OPO-sponsored training of all approachers.

In fact there may be ethical advantages and pitfalls for any primary approacher. I am reminded of the chaplains' common refrain "it is good to feel the tension," and struck by the comparative absence of such a "good" feeling of tension among institutions promoting organ donation. The voices of chaplains might be heard as prophetic, beckoning us to consider issues that are often veiled or invisible in policy forums. Listening to chaplains has made me realize that first knot in my stomach was related to a "so that" underlying the construction of all those graphs. It is a "so that" that ought be questioned, not simply presumed.

PART FOUR

ADULTS AT THE END OF LIFE

8

BOUNDARY CROSSINGS

The Ethical Terrain of Professional Life in Hospice Care

COURTNEY S. CAMPBELL

I mean, this is life and death. There's a humanness and immediacy to what I do. Nothing else is really that important when someone else is dying, so being involved in a very important time in someone's life is fulfilling, because nothing else really matters. –GC

From small beginnings in the early 1970s, hospice in the United States has evolved into a distinctive philosophy and respected practice of care for dying persons and their families. For several reasons, hospice provides a unique context for the display of the interweaving of ethics and religion in professional life. First, foundational to the philosophy of hospice is a holistic understanding of care, which seeks to respond to the needs of patients (and families) in many realms, including physical and psychological needs, social interests and relationships, spiritual issues, and bereavement support. These commitments require a diverse array of caregivers from several professional disciplines, including medicine, nursing, social work and counseling, home health, the clergy, and many others, as well as volunteers. Thus, hospice illuminates the meanings of caring for the dying within a web of multiple professional relationships.

Second, hospice care is influenced by and historically dependent on religious perspectives and practices. Dame Cicely Saunders, the acknowledged founder of the modern hospice movement, has commented that hospices evolved from the opening of homes in the fourth century "to fulfill the Christian works of mercy: feeding the hungry and thirsty, visiting the sick and prisoners, clothing the naked, and welcoming strangers. . . . [Hospice] meant both the place where hospitality was given and also the relationships that arose."[1] In Saunders's understanding, a basic motivation of traditional Christian practices—the injunction of Jesus to care for "the least of these" as one would care for Jesus (Matt. 25)—is retained in the contemporary ethos of hospice.

This history of the formative ideas and practices of hospice is acknowledged even in the literature of explicitly nonreligious affiliated hospices.[2] Indeed, while many hospices affirm independence from a religious identity, it is evident that foundational norms and practices historically embedded in religious traditions and communities have become *institutionalized within* hospice. In this respect, it is possible to argue that the modern evolution of the hospice movement offers a striking illustration of a form of "secularization,"[3] in which religious norms and values are integrated rather than separated from organizational self-identity.

This chapter will seek to provide an interpretive commentary on the embedded moral and religious terrain of professional life in hospice care, which is revealed through the stories of professional caregivers. In this respect, the professionals themselves are the formative "text" for the commentary: Their stories point particularly to themes of "boundaries" and "crossings" as substantially constitutive of the ethical terrain of hospice. In general, while religion figures prominently as a "boundary" in hospice care, it is a very problematic rationale for "crossings" of moral boundaries in the delivery of hospice care. The religious dimensions of hospice are more significant as motivations for caregiving rather than as grounds for distinctive actions. Before proceeding with this interpretation, I wish to provide some observations on the research methodology used in this study.

METHODOLOGICAL OVERVIEW

Hospice is an increasingly significant program and partner in the care of terminally ill persons. The state of Oregon has a very active hospice program, overseen by the Oregon Hospice Association. The hospice "penetration rate" (that is, the number of deaths that occur in hospice as a total of all deaths) was 28 percent in 1996, compared with the national average of 19 percent. This placed Oregon hospice programs fourth in use among national programs. Hospice is sought out particularly by persons dying from cancer, with three-fourths of deaths due to cancer in Oregon occurring in hospice care. An increasing number of persons dying from AIDS also seek hospice care, and in 1996, over one-half of the AIDS deaths in Oregon were overseen by hospice. Both of these figures are substantially higher than comparable national figures.[4]

Most of Oregon's population has access to hospice care. Some 80 percent of Oregon's 3.3 million residents live in the Willamette Valley, a 120-mile long swath of fertile landscape carved by the Willamette River between two mountain ranges. Twenty-three hospice programs provide services within this area. The largely rural and less populated portion of the state is served by twenty-seven hospices.

The "text" for this interpretative commentary was generated through interviews with hospice care providers at three respected and established hospice programs located within twenty miles of each other in the mid-Willamette Valley. One hospice is affiliated with a religious community (Mennonite), while the other two have no religious affiliation. The executive directors of the hospices were contacted through a letter describing the purpose of this research and asked to recommend individuals who might be interested in an interview. The executive directors announced the request at their respective staff meetings and provided a list of several prospective participants. These persons were then contacted and interviews scheduled.

Interviews were conducted with nine hospice professionals (three in social work, three in nursing, one in medicine, one member of the clergy, and one home health aide) and nine hospice volunteers (conducted in two different sessions). In all but two instances, the persons who were interviewed were female; the executive directors confirmed that this is characteristic of the gender representation of hospice caregivers. The interviews were taped with the consent of the person being interviewed and subsequently transcribed and returned to the participant for corrections or other emendations.

The interviews were semistructured in that general questions were used to elicit reflection and discussion on a number of themes salient to understanding the ethical terrain of hospice care (see Appendix). For example, I was interested in learning the following: how these caregivers became involved in hospice care, the personal meaning they found through their work, perceptions of a "good" or a "bad" death in the context of hospice, images or virtues of the ideal hospice caregiver, the extent and manner in which the dying (or their families) become "teachers"[5] for their hospice caregivers, the role of personal religious convictions in hospice care, and the motivations that sustain professional caregivers amid the constancy of death. Although I hoped to focus the interview on such issues, the participants were encouraged to work with a question in whatever way that was most meaningful for them. Strikingly, this often meant that an abstract question (e.g., about "the good death in hospice") was addressed through a concrete narrative about patient or family care.

While this chapter engages in a serious effort to be faithful to the narrative framing of experience and the linguistic conventions of the participants, its representation of that experience and its interpretation of its ethical terrain are inevitably methodologically limited. Nonetheless, I found that the caregivers' constant invocation of the language of "boundaries" illuminated particularly well the ethical terrain of hospice care, and that the theme of "crossings" revealed professional and religious tensions or dilemmas experienced by caregivers as they encounter boundaries. It will be valuable to construct a general typology of these boundaries and then examine specific illustrations.

BOUNDARY CROSSINGS

Encountering a boundary in hospice care implies limits to intervention and care. A crossing can occur only with some special exemption or permission, or when certain conditions are fulfilled that ensure the retention of the boundary. I want to distinguish the kinds of boundaries that are encountered in hospice care, the rationale for legitimate boundary crossings, and the implicit ethical and religious dimensions of these crossings.

A first form of boundary can be designated *boundaries of ultimacy*. Hospice exists at the edge of mortality's great boundary, that between life and death. Its defining mission is to provide compassionate care and human presence to enable a peaceful transition for both patient and family as the dying person crosses that boundary. The rationale for a boundary crossing is certainly a recognition that death is a part of and culmination of natural life processes; however, hospice care seeks to ensure a "good" death, as delineated below, which may be transformed by the presence of religious dimensions into an "awesome" death. Given this ultimate boundary of death as a defining context for hospice care, it is perhaps not surprising that hospice professionals interpret their caregiving in terms of determining the existence of boundaries and the grounds for permissible passage.

A second form of boundary, *boundaries of identity,* arises because of the core commitments and context of hospice, the professional training of caregivers, and the nature of the relationships that hospice caregivers experience. While hospice professionals criticize the "faceless technician" model of care within which many received their professional education (and which can still permeate the ethos of the hospital), they can experience tension and uncertainty about how to retain their professionalism while expressing their humanity. This tension is inescapable when providing care and presence to a dying patient who is both a person and but one of many patients for whom the professional provides care. A boundary crossing from professional technician to human presence could be justified on grounds of providing personalized care, but this strategy seems to risk loss of credibility and identity, as well as posing practical issues of burnout. However, a retreat to dispassionate distance, within which there is no legitimate rationale for crossing, risks callousness and insensitivity. I will suggest that hospice caregivers try to resolve the tensions that surround boundaries of identity through an ethical concept of "empathetic distance" and through a holistic, team model of caregiving.

In caring for patients, hospice professionals also encounter *boundaries of inti-*

macy. They are entering into space, such as a home, a bedroom, or bodily dignity, that is not theirs but that of a dying person and their family. These boundaries must be crossed for the care to be provided, but only on the invitation of the patient and family and with the condition that the space be respected, the boundary observed even as it is crossed. As particular space, such as the patient's body, reflects even deeper layers of intimacy, these boundaries can be crossed, for example, through touch, only when a profound trusting relationship has evolved between the hospice caregiver and the care recipients. In a significant respect, this space over which the hospice professional has crossed assumes dimensions of "sacred ground," terrain that may well evoke sentiments of a religious nature in the professional.

While moving within this physical space, hospice caregivers may encounter situations where they feel disposed to enter the moral space of the patient or the family. They encounter *boundaries of integrity,* where their personal or professional commitments collide with the values or practices of the care recipients. These situations are created in part because of core values of hospice philosophy, particularly a commitment to the idea that "control" over the dying process resides with dying persons and their families. Hospice caregivers have an obligation to respect these wishes and to treat these preferences as the primary interests at stake. However, control by others may limit the effectiveness or even the possibility of the hospice intervention. Thus, under conditions of last resort, hospice caregivers may enter this moral space to maintain fidelity and integrity to other core hospice values, even including—although it may be more problematic— attention to the spiritual and religious needs of the patient that the hospice caregiver believes may be neglected.

Ultimate Boundaries: Mortality and Death

> A perfect death, a good death, an awesome death is when the family is there, and the extended family, generations and grandkids; there is sadness, but also joy over a natural process; there is deep spiritual belief; there is prayer and singing, and people in the other room laughing and talking and remembering; sharing the physical care of the person—turning them, rubbing them, touching—including them as part of the entire extended family. . . . It is an awesome experience. –EC

As death looms as the overshadowing boundary of human life, as well as of professional caregiving in hospice, it is vital to understand the boundary of death within hospice and how that understanding shapes hospice care. There seems to be no dominant image of "death" among hospice caregivers or in hospice philosophy, at least none equivalent to that of "death as enemy" in curative medicine. Hospice practices presuppose an understanding of death as a natural process of human life; death therefore does not assume personification. TM, a hospice physician, describes death in the context of hospice as "a path that leads into a fog, and we can't see through or beyond the fog." The language of "path" and "journey" are important in hospice discourse and imply that the attention of hospice is directed to the process of dying and facilitating a "good death."

Notions of what comprises a good death (and correlatively, a bad death) vary from caregiver to caregiver, but some common patterns of interpretation are apparent. It is possible to identify five levels of a "good death," levels that have their own distinctive identity, but that nonetheless can build on each other in hospice discourse.

1. A first level focuses on *medical/nursing* issues, primarily *relief of pain.* The provision of palliative care and pain and symptom management are necessary features of a good death. The poor or bad death invariably occurs when pain is not controlled. With current palliative care measures, uncontrolled pain seems to be the rare circumstance; even if patients may not be pain-free, they can at least achieve "comfort." However, sometimes pain is "managed" at a tolerable level at the request of the patient or family in order that the dying person be more aware and alert as he or she approaches the boundary of death.

2. A second level concerns issues of *relational presence.* The presence of the family is deemed especially important by hospice caregivers. Family presence does not guarantee relational closure; BC echoed the comments of several hospice caregivers who indicated that past patterns of dealing with family crises, such as a divorce or loss of a job, are predictive of how a family will respond to the crisis of impending death of a family member: "We know that families will handle the crisis of somebody dying like they've handled crises in the past. So, we will try to identify how this family was functioning before they've gotten to this death." Some families are brought closer together, and some are ripped apart by the encounter with death; imminent death does not necessarily change long-standing familial patterns. Still, it is deemed preferable to have the family present than for the patient to die alone.

   To be sure, hospice professionals, especially social workers and counselors, devote substantial attention to enabling the dying to gain "closure" not only with respect to their own lives, but also in familial life. "Life review" is an important part of this process. However, counseling professionals take their cues from the patient and the family as to whether this practice is desired, rather than imposing it as part of the services offered in hospice care.

3. Family presence provides a basis for *family empowerment* regarding caregiving responsibilities. When hospice philosophy affirms that the patient and family are "in control," that doesn't merely mean professional deference to patient or familial autonomy. It has a much richer implication of the family's assumption of caregiving responsibilities. The family shares in providing physical care to the dying person and is "in control" of the dying situation—the location (home) and emotions and grieving—while the hospice professionals hover in the background, supportive and instructive, but neither dominant nor as authoritarian as a hospital physician.

An integral part of hospice, commented WS, is to "give people [the family] the skills to do the job that is *their* job to do" (my emphasis). This effort includes educating the family regarding the natural process of dying, so that, for example, they do not continue to offer food and fluids when the body's systems are closing down. The family can assist a comfortable crossing for their relative by withholding nutrition in order to minimize lung congestion and bladder retention, while providing mouth care. Withholding of food and fluids when death is imminent is considered a "comfort" measure by hospice nurses, but this practice can become psychologically confusing and emotionally traumatic for the family; moreover, the language of "comfort" may mask important ethical questions.[6] These three levels—pain and symptom control, family presence, and family empowerment—are at the core of hospice ideals of a good death. They provide legitimation for the boundary crossing from life to death. However, some hospice caregivers emphasize two additional levels that transform a "good" death into an "awesome" death. This language situates a boundary crossing within a texture of religious meaning.

4. Several professionals conveyed the first of these additional levels through the language of *"hope."* "Hope" may assume several different meanings in hospice. In one sense, it means the opportunity for patients to come to terms with issues of importance to them, some of which will concern matters of family while others address one's mortality and ultimate destiny. Hope may also refer to the dying process, as observed by NR: "Hope changes from the hope that you get better, that you will be cured, to the hope of a good death." The context of hope is also provided by presence, which diminishes the fear of abandonment in the dying process.[7] While presence is typically the province of the family, it is clear that hospice volunteers embody the message that the patient will not be abandoned. This message is "embodied" because it is often conveyed through touch, washing, bathing, or holding hands. A dimension of prospective hope is included, that is, a faith conviction or assurance about a life-to-come and the continuation of the self and family relations.

5. *Spiritual meaning* characterizes the awesome death. The spirituality of dying reflects a continuity of life processes, wherein images of birth are invoked. SL commented that "it is an honor to witness a death just the same as witnessing a birth," while TM sees her role as similar to that of a "midwife." In the setting of an awesome death, the family and dying person collectively participate in remembering, singing, praying, and reading from scripture, such as the Twenty-third Psalm, and they may discover new insights as they reflect on their shared life history and their faith tradition. In this discovery of meaning, death is viewed not as "the end," or a crossing to the unknown, but rather as a passage in a person's "journey" towards reunion with God. Patients and families receive an affirmation of transcendent presence, that they are cared for and loved by God even in the midst of pain, suffering, and separation. While sadness and grief are appropriate, such emotions are coupled with joy and an attitude of "celebration" about the person's life and death. The hospice worker, in the view of MV, simply assists in a natural process that began at birth and "shares the journey" to a new dimension of being.

Boundaries of Identity: Empathetic Distance

There are a myriad of ways these boundaries are being chipped away at, and you just have to do your best at both being professional and being more intimate. I guess that's what I've both enjoyed and agonized about this job: it's the challenge of relationship, and asking where do the boundaries exist. –GC

Against the background of this boundary of ultimacy between life and death, the provision of hospice care gives rise to other significant boundaries that direct and constrain the actions of hospice professionals. As illustrated in the previous quote, an especially demanding (and common) boundary is that generated by professional identity and role-related responsibilities while caring for dying persons and their families in all their vulnerability. For many hospice workers, professional training has inculcated a view that caregivers should aspire to be as "faceless and impersonal" as possible (GC). Yet the hospice caregiver is invited to participate in a relationship and process suffused with personal meaning, in which a human self is revealed in all its intimacy, vulnerability, and bodily and relational extremity. In such a context, the prospect arises for a professional stranger to evolve into a friend or "part of the family." Thus, many hospice caregivers find themselves trying to define and negotiate boundaries of identity, seeking an appropriate balance between intimacy and detachment, human presence and depersonalized technique, partnership and specialization.

The boundaries of identity function ethically to provide professional direction and to establish limits for caregivers. Psychologically, such boundaries enable caregivers to offer continuity of care for specific and multiple patients. Boundaries of professional identity prescribe routines that insulate caregivers from disabling grief and loss. Caregivers can cross these boundaries, therefore, only at some peril to their caregiving functions, their patients, and themselves.

One important boundary of identity for hospice professionals concerns *self-disclosure*. Given the vulnerability of the dying patient and the transparency of the family setting to the hospice caregiver, there may arise a patient or familial expectation of reciprocal self-revelation on the part of the professional. Hospice workers may receive inquiries about their general life values and interests, or, more specifically, their preferences for a certain mode of care or a certain kind of death. In these contexts, the question becomes, How much of my personal self can be revealed that is compatible with my professional presence and role?

Most commonly, it seems that hospice professionals are reticent about crossing this boundary. Indeed, self-disclosure may work against the values of patient control and familial empowerment. Caregivers are best able to provide care through disclosure of their professional knowledge, skill, and technique, rather than through disclosure of personal preferences. When a boundary of identity is encountered, the caregivers' goal is to retain their professional status and presence while avoiding the perception of impersonal care and callousness to the person's request, or toward the general plight of the dying person. Thus, if an issue or question arises in which the selves of hospice professionals may be exposed or revealed, caregivers typically seek to validate the meaningfulness of the inquiry but also to redirect the question so that it returns focus to the needs and interests of the patient and family (EC). A question about the caregiver's family, for example, will be answered, but the professional will use the subsequent conversation to remind the inquirer that the caregiver is present to assist the patient and his or her family.

With respect to boundaries of identity, it should be noted that there is a distinct difference between the attitude of hospice volunteers and that of hospice professionals. This should not be surprising, because there are differences in identity from the outset of a caregiving relationship. Volunteers do not have the training to perform specialized tasks; they fulfill domestic responsibilities, such as washing dishes, grocery shopping, or cleaning the house, that family members characteristically perform. Volunteers thereby have no difficulty understanding themselves as "part of the family" of the dying person, or as "extended family." This identity also is extended from the family to the volunteer. One volunteer indicated that when a patient was in a coma and death seemed imminent, the family called her and invited her presence, "not as a hospice volunteer, but as a friend. Hospice meant 'death' to them, and they didn't want that connection. They just wanted

Mom to go surrounded by family and friends, not hospice" (LH). This assumption of a familial identity ("aunt" or "grandma" are common titles given to hospice volunteers) helps explain why it is common for the volunteer to attend a funeral or memorial service for the deceased. That is what "family" does, after all.

The professional, by contrast, tries to maintain the boundary of professional identity and not to assume a family identity or role. This relational distance is necessary in part to carry out professional caregiving responsibilities for a particular patient efficiently, and in part so that professionals can continue to provide care for other patients. A close association with a patient or family can be professionally perilous. Such a boundary has implications for the mode of communication between professional and patient or family, including how the professional conveys to the patient the personal meaning of their relationship. In discussing her need to experience fuller closure with families with whom she develops closer relationships, GC observed, "I feel uncomfortable if I don't acknowledge to the [dying] person their value to me, and my sadness at their death. I feel a need to tell them I will remember them, but I tell them in a professional way." This professional distance, as well as other work commitments, helps explain why hospice professionals, unlike volunteers, characteristically will not attend patients' funerals.

Moreover, even after a patient's death, there is still a focus of care for the hospice professional: the family. Indeed, as the patient's condition deteriorates physically, hospice professionals direct more of their psychological and emotional support to the family. They cannot so readily assume a family identity and provide the professional care and assistance the family requires. Nonetheless, especially for hospice nurses, the relational bonds may become particularly strong so that the caregivers' identity may move from strangers or professionals to friends or family members. And, if nurses experience too many "family" deaths in a short period of time, they are likely to experience burnout. Thus, this boundary crossing can be professionally disabling.

The approach that hospice professionals have evolved to maintain professionalism, to avoid crossing the boundary between their roles as professionals and more intimate roles as friends or family members, yet still to convey personalized care is what I will designate *empathetic distance*. While immersed in facets of death and dying in their daily care, hospice professionals also are careful to not be consumed by their caregiving responsibilities and relations. Identification with the dying in a personal way could be professionally paralyzing. Indeed, BC indicated that she would find it difficult to care for dying members of her own family; however, she said, "So long as the dying is removed from me, I can relate to other people in a professional way." Thus, professionals' expressions of genuineness, empathy, and compassion are conveyed to the patient and family from an emotional distance. This balance of relational intimacy and professional identity involves professionals in what GC referred to as the caregivers' "dance with the family."

The strategy of empathetic distance, while not easily explained or articulated, is a form of coping mechanism, enabling professionals to care for all of their patients as well as for themselves and their families. "There have to be some boundaries," commented HH, "so you can be caring and be there for one person, but not become so attached that you can't continue on to care for the next person." Similarly, EC alluded to the theme of empathetic distance in describing her "full bucket" concept of the self: "You have to have a fine balance between empathy and compassion and the need to take care of yourself, too. You have to have a full bucket yourself in order to give out of that; if you are giving out of that for any other reason, you will dry up and burn out."

Because the family receives the accumulated caring expressions of an inter-disciplinary team, this distance may not be as acutely perceived by the patient or family as it is experienced by the caregivers. Thus, even though boundaries of identity are critical in the relationship between a particular professional and patient and family, the retention of disciplinary boundaries between professionals is not a priority. In contrast to the often fragmented and discontinuous care that patients may experience in other settings, hospice philosophy emphasizes a dis-tinctive team approach to caring. Thus, it is not surprising that a characteristic of the ideal hospice caregiver is being a "team player." The "team" metaphor pro-vides direction but also establishes a boundary; the success of a team is contin-gent on all members performing their roles with the skill and knowledge they acquired in their professional training and using their cumulative expertise to pro-vide holistic care for the patient. The collaboration of a hospice team implies a mutual effort toward a common goal, not a sharing of interchangeable responsi-bilities. Wisdom and care are integrated by the team, even though dispensed by particular caregivers.

The functioning of the "team" may be characterized by hospice staff through metaphors of the body. For example, TM, a hospice physician, understands other team members "as the doctor's eyes, ears, and hands; the nurses and other hos-pice caregivers see and hear what's going on, and then are the doctor's hands to help with whatever needs to be done." Similarly, HH presupposes the bodily metaphor in describing her role to be "the eyes of the nurses."

Boundaries of Intimacy

> Can you imagine going into someone's home, and sitting in some-one's bedroom? And you just learn so much from people, especially at the end of their life. . . . You learn what is really important to

people. That really fuels a passion for my work. What an honor and privilege, I tell people, to go into a person's home, and sit in their bedroom, or in the bathroom while they are nauseated. It's such an honor to be able to support them.–BC

The initiation of a caregiving relationship presents important boundaries of *intimate space* that must be respected, but also crossed, by hospice professionals. Although the professionals have been invited to perform certain caregiving tasks, these tasks occur within a context of place and in a realm of personal space. This space is environmentally and existentially different from the zone of institutional space in a hospital setting where most medical professionals feel "at home." In hospice, the context of caregiving is patients' homes, their kitchens, bedrooms, bathrooms, that is, spaces of intimacy that are typically "off-limits" to everyday strangers and guests.

Hospice professionals must cross this boundary and enter this intimate space, recognizing that they are strangers and that respect for the patient's terrain is necessary to avoid trespass or intrusion. This space is sanctified or even "sacred" space for the patient and family, set apart from the natural world outside, and only restricted access is offered to the general social world. This space of caregiving evokes in the caregiver a sentiment of appreciative respect that is somewhat comparable to the sentiments evoked by a religious sanctuary; caregivers acknowledge that they are on just that ground that bears the marks of persons' lives and has been specifically chosen by dying persons and families for the patients to spend their final days in mortality. Thus, the discourse of hospice caregivers often invokes the language of "honor" or "privilege" in describing the significance they attach to being invited into a home, a bedroom, or a bathroom, or invited to care for patients' bodies.

As the caregiving relationship proceeds, boundaries of *embodied intimacy* become especially prominent. Some hospice professionals and volunteer aids provide specialized care, such as giving baths, washing hair, and massage. The boundaries of bodily integrity must be crossed, but not without invitation, trust, and respect for a person's dignity; even with this permission, it is important to maintain professional presence. As MT commented, in this intimate context of touching the body, the objective of the caregiver is to "be professional, but also ensure [my patient has] comfort and dignity." This end is achieved in part by letting the patient direct the care, including where the caregiver's hands are placed on the patient's body. "I will ask them questions, if this is okay with them. . . . I let the patient communicate what they are comfortable with."

The expression of care through *touch*, rather than technology, can be a powerful occasion of mutuality and bonding. After inviting and entrusting hospice professionals to cross conventional boundaries into the realm of personal bodily intimacy, patients may feel empowered to "share" and "open up" the realm of emotional intimacy to caregivers as well. As MO described it, "water and touch can be a source of healing for people; there's a bond between the people that you don't get if you're just talking back and forth." A reciprocity of trust is present in these situations that permits hospice professionals to cross the boundary of bodily and emotional space that may not be accessible even to family members. In a trusting relationship, then, patients' bodily vulnerability may not be perceived as "indignity" nor as "regression" to an infantile state, but as a witness to their humanity. The shared intimacy prompted by touch, and the embodied knowledge conveyed through caring hands, becomes an occasion for patients' self-disclosure and review of their life stories.

Boundaries of Integrity

> Hospice would tell you that they do not either hasten or prolong death. That is their basic philosophy. My personal philosophy is that there are fates worse than death. And sometimes as a culture, we come to worship life so much that we become almost vitalistic, that life is to be preserved at all costs, and we fail to take into consideration quality of life. . . . Philosophically, I'm glad that physician-assisted suicide is available for someone that might choose to do that. –FC

Hospice is a distinctive form of caring in part because of its philosophical commitment to a set of moral values and its integration of spirituality within a holistic caregiving model. The value commitment to respect and facilitate patients' and families' "control" over dying directs professionals to serve patients' and families' needs as patients and families define them. However, this presumption of control in the caregiving context may create situations where some professionals, especially nurses and counselors, feel they have compromised the efficacy of their caregiving and their own moral commitments. Professionals may experience either a diminished realm of moral integrity, or a partitioning of their views into distinct realms of professional and personal, or they may contemplate crossing the moral boundary of control by the patient and family. There is no easy remedy for hospice professionals to rely on in resolving conflicts over integrity.

One common occasion for conflicts of moral integrity occurs over levels of pain medication. As noted, hospice professionals find freedom from pain to be a necessary condition of a good death. They are willing to respect choices by the patient or the family for "tolerable" pain so long as this choice serves some relational goal, such as continued communication within the family or a conscious state as the patient approaches death.

However, there are some patient or familial rationales for minimal pain medication that hospice caregivers are reluctant to accept, and they instead express a willingness to cross the boundary of integrity and control. For example, hospice professionals are willing to cross the boundary if they perceive that parsimonious levels of pain medication really reflect familial ignorance, neglect, or abandonment. Should such circumstances arise, nurses and volunteers typically provide education to the family about appropriate doses of pain medication. If the problem is not lack of information about pain control and the dying process but represents deeper family issues that are unresolved, including denial of dying, a social worker or counselor will be invited to assist other professionals in understanding the meaning behind the family's reticence, and to try to negotiate with the family to increase pain medication to a level that provides comfort for the patient. These conflicts of integrity, then, are usually soluble through education, persuasion, and a trusting relationship.

Much more dilemmatic are patient or family requests for what the hospice staff believes is inadequate palliative care for the purpose of expressing a spiritual objective, such as experiencing pedagogical or redemptive suffering. Despite the commitment of hospice to recognizing the spiritual needs of the patient, it seems evident that spiritual control by the patient is subordinated to pain control by the hospice staff. In such situations, the hospice caregiver will rely on other members of her team, especially the clergy or spiritual adviser, to engage in a probing discussion with the patient and family about the extent and purposes for pain and suffering. These conflicts are also usually resolved, although with considerably more counseling, patience, and time than in situations where the patient or family is unaware of palliative care and simply requires more education and counseling. For, in the case of religiously motivated refusals of increased pain medication, the medical conflict is merely a manifestation of a metaphysical position.

A third, and more internally divisive, context in which the boundary of moral integrity emerges is that of hastening a patient's death, which has taken on a particular immediacy for hospice in Oregon through the recent legalization of physician assistance in suicide. In its first annual report on the implementation of the Oregon Death with Dignity Act, the Oregon Health Division indicated that of fifteen patient deaths in 1998 through physician-assisted suicide, ten patients were under hospice care.[8] This report, like FC's comment cited previously, calls into question the validity of the long-standing principle that hospice care seeks neither to "hasten nor prolong death." The possibility of hastened death through a physician prescription of lethal medication has initiated an acute conflict of personal and institutional conscience for many hospice professionals and hospice programs.[9] Bouma and colleagues have developed a discussion of the concepts of "respect," "tolerance," and "cooperation" that will be valuable in illuminating the ethical terrain of hospice on the questions of hastening death and physician assistance in suicide.[10] "Respect" is an attitude that can be expressed toward a belief that meets certain criteria of intellectual adequacy, such as "consistency, clarity, comprehensiveness, plausibility, and practicability." The concept of "tolerance" refers to a behavioral response to the views or actions that a person disagrees with—in particular, a response of refraining from attempting, directly or indirectly, to interfere with the disagreeable action. "Cooperation" moves beyond tolerance by providing assistance to another person to accomplish what that person believes is morally right, while noncooperation states, in effect, "My disagreement with you is such that I refuse to help you do what you think is right."[11]

Within this framework, it seems fair to say that so long as patients' request for a hastened death conforms to the procedures of the Oregon law, Oregon hospice professionals express understanding and even respect. That is, in a caregiving context in which the inevitability of death is a defining boundary, a request for medication to hasten death, perhaps as a means to alleviate pain and suffering, is a position that can be rationally defensible, even if caregivers disagree with it on moral or religious grounds. It is especially significant for hospice, moreover, that the report of the Oregon Health Division documented concerns about intractable pain from only one patient. The requests for assisted suicide by twenty-two patients were determined to be "consistent with a long-standing belief [of the patient] about the importance of controlling the manner in which they died."[12] This personal preference can readily be interpreted as compatible with hospice philosophy's commitment to patient/familial "control." If these patient demographics continue to hold up, it should come as no surprise that hospice would become a preferred venue for patients seeking respect, tolerance, and cooperation regarding requests for assisted suicide. Differences among hospice caregivers do emerge, however, over the modes of tolerance and cooperation with such choices. Under the concept of tolerance delineated above, the views of some Oregon hospice professionals and volunteers must be characterized as intolerant of requests for hastened death. While all caregivers will seek to understand the meaning behind patients' request for lethal medication (e.g., Is the pain not sufficiently controlled? Does the patient perceive abandonment by the family? Are prospective financial losses due to life prolongation an overriding issue?), some hospice staff members indicate they would seek to persuade patients that such a request is not compatible with other values they have expressed about dying, including agreement with hospice values on dying. That is, professionals try to persuade patients by working within the framework of the patients' values. This approach expresses respect for the patients' own boundary of moral integrity but articulates a clash of values internal to this boundary that may require patients to redefine their values or the boundary. However, such professionals indicate they would not be articulating their *own* values in discussion with patients about a lethal prescription; such an appeal would not constitute a permissible boundary crossing but rather a boundary violation. This approach reflects what has been termed "soft paternalism" in medical ethics.[13] Nor would such caregivers resort to coercive measures in the wake of failed persuasion.

Further fragmentation emerges regarding the modes of "cooperation" and "noncooperation" open to hospice caregivers and programs in response to a patient request for lethal medication. Some Oregon hospice programs have clearly cooperated with patient requests to some extent, and some physicians affiliated with hospice are known to have assisted in a patient's suicide. The two nonreligious hospices represented in this study have policies that state they will cooperate at least by beginning the process of referral to a physician, as required by law. The policy of the religiously affiliated hospice is perhaps best characterized as respectful, tolerant, and "nonparticipatory": The hospice maintains it will "not knowingly participate" in a patient's request for assistance in suicide, but it will refer patients to their primary physicians should such a request be made in the context of hospice care.

This divide between religious and nonreligious grounds over the integrity of hospice on the issue of hastened death perhaps reflects a deeper issue within hospice about an appeal to religious values as grounds for boundary crossings in general. On one hand, hospice is committed to holistic care for the dying, including attention to the spiritual dimensions of dying, and to empowering and protecting patients in their vulnerability. Simultaneously, a suspicion is perceptible among many caregivers, both religious and nonreligious, that caregivers with strong religious convictions will take advantage of patients' vulnerability to engage in deathbed evangelization. A person of religious convictions who is "public" about those convictions is unlikely to be viewed as an ideal hospice caregiver; as GC noted, a hospice caregiver "can't be on a mission to save people through religion." Put another way, ideal caregivers will do well to keep personal religious values in the realm of their private, nonprofessional lives. Indeed, hospice's attention to patients' spiritual needs as part of holistic care notwithstanding, there does not seem to be a reciprocal emphasis on a holistic *professional* experience that enables religion and spirituality to be smoothly integrated into patterns of caregiving.

At one level, hospice professionals clearly work in the context of an informal and de facto prohibition on initiating conversations with a patient about religious beliefs or spiritual meaning. Repeatedly, hospice caregivers who were interviewed for this study, including those with very strong religious commitments, indicated the presence of a boundary that precludes, in the words of HH, "bounding through the doors and preaching" to the patient. At times, patients give signs or cues that they desire, or even need, to talk of religious and spiritual matters. Hospice professionals may perceive this opening as an opportunity to provide the holistic care that hospice promises. Depending on the professionals' background, skills, and personal convictions, they may invite a spiritual adviser or minister to attend to the patient's spiritual needs, or they may participate in the initial discussion and subsequently inform the spiritual adviser of the situation.

TM does engage in boundary crossing with respect to initiating conversation about spiritual meaning with patients. Her approach is to "bring up spiritual issues with my patients, certainly when they are seriously ill, absolutely if they are approaching the end of their life." TM justifies her proactive approach with the argument that it enhances the efficacy of hospice care. That is, a patient may be showing physiological or psychological symptoms of underlying spiritual distress, particularly in the quite common circumstance of depression among terminally ill patients. In addition, TM contends it is vital for "[patients] to acknowledge that spirituality is part of our humanness; if we ignore it, we won't feel whole or total. . . . Patients need to deal with [spirituality] in whatever way makes sense to them, and that will help their wholeness." While TM does not see herself as a resource for spiritual care, the interdisciplinary team approach fulfills this responsibility of holistic caregiving through the attention of a minister or spiritual adviser. Whether the opportunity for religious discourse is invited by the patient or initiated by a hospice professional, the focus is on the *patient's* needs for meaning. Hospice professionals have a pronounced reticence to share their own convictions about the religious meaning of life, the significance of death, human destiny, and religious salvation. This "holding back," as some professionals articulated it, reveals in the hospice context a manifestation of the socially constructed boundary that forbids "imposing" religious values on others. Within Oregon's hospice programs, this boundary has been reinforced by the polemics over physician-assisted suicide, which were largely conducted along the social parameters of the "culture wars."[14] In response, professional and organizational assurances have been made to patients in hospitals and in hospices that institutional mechanisms will be used to ensure that vulnerable persons, and especially the terminally ill, will not be subjected to uninvited religious discussions.

There are undoubtedly legitimate concerns about deathbed evangelization. There is a boundary of both professional integrity and personal space that should be respected. However, assuming the invitation of the patients, it may be mistaken to portray hospice professionals' candid sharing of their religious convictions with dying patients as an unjustifiable crossing of the boundary into "preaching" and "imposition." In the care of dying patients, it is possible for religious ideas or beliefs to be expressed, to be meaningful for others, and to possess consoling and

comforting influence, without assuming the coercive character that is presup-
posed in the language of "imposition." Nonetheless, the presumption against religious discourse with the patient is a defensible practice of hospice care. The
boundary should not be crossed unless upon patients' request and permission.

MOTIVATIONS

> I feel it's like having a gift to deal with people the way I am able to,
> because not everyone feels comfortable about it. It's not that I enjoy
> watching people die, but I feel comfortable with the work I do. I find
> it very rewarding and fulfilling. –HH

> I believe God gives me opportunity when He sees a need or puts me
> in places where I can help, so I welcome those opportunities. Feeling
> that God has given me permission to do this work is a belief that sus-
> tains me and gives me motivation to continue. –EC

Although religion and spirituality are integrated into the holistic care model of
hospice, this integration places the spiritual dimensions of a patient on a par with
medical, emotional, and psychosocial needs. In practice, hospice discourse seldom ventures into the religious realm, unless a patient is experiencing a "problem" with religious purpose or spiritual need. Sometimes, the patient may directly
convey religious turmoil to caregivers; in other instances, the conflict may be
communicated indirectly, as when medical, nursing, or counseling methods
appear to be inadequate because of an underlying question of ultimacy that the
patient has yet to resolve or experience closure on. In either context, in encounters
with patients, the hospice caregiver typically experiences religion as a "problem."

This perception may be quite different from the caregiver's own experience
with religious belief, which quite often provides a powerful source of motivation
for providing care to the dying. Moreover, this presence must be displayed not
merely to one patient but to a multitude. How is that humanly possible, even for
professionals who maintain empathetic distance as a psychological coping
method? It is possible to delineate nonreligious and religious motivations for
caregiving that enable hospice workers to embody ongoing compassion, presence, and continuity of care.

Some moral motivations are held in common by hospice professionals, including the fulfillment all professionals seek to "make a difference" to better the lives
(or deaths) of other people. In hospice care, even though the outcome of death is
a given, caregivers can and do make a difference in many ways. They are cog-
nizant of the little successes they achieve in the process of dying that ensure a
better death for the patient and solace to the family in the midst of their mourn-

ing. In particular, hospice professionals are especially motivated to involve the family as full participants in end-of-life care. A death that occurs when "the family does it right" comprises part of the stories of "beautiful death" that hospice staff tell to each other and that provide a source of emotional renewal for caregivers (GC).

In addition, hospice professionals express a profound awareness of solidarity with others, whether fellow workers or the family, as they engage in a collaborative effort to address something of real importance, the mortal matters of life and death. The interdisciplinary team not only provides a more humane, personalized caring context for the patient than the hospital, but it also provides caregivers with important resources of collegial support and common purpose.

These shared motivations are supplemented by motivations that are distinctive to hospice staff with religious convictions. Religious caregivers express a strong faith and trust that all experiences are under the providential care of God, including patients' dying or caregivers' felt inadequacies in meeting patient or familial needs. Prayer is an important part of the ongoing daily professional preparation for such persons, who ask for a divine blessing of strength and courage to continue in their care and to be a channel to convey the embrace of divine love to patients (CE). In their prayers, religious hospice staff express that they "turn it all over to God," with "it" having reference to the burdens of caregiving, the sharing of grief, and the ultimate destiny of the person who dies. While some professionals and volunteers read biblical passages or other spiritual literature with patients at their request, specific passages can be meaningful sources of support and motivation for caregivers as well. Some caregivers give a religious interpretation to their work through the biblical commendation of those who feed the hungry, welcome the stranger, clothe the naked, and visit those in prison, which concludes with the affirmation that "as you did it to one of the least of these who are members of my family, you did it to me" (Matt. 25: 34–40). As noted, Dame Cicely Saunders places hospice within this religious vision of compassion. Others of religious conviction derive religious meaning from the Ninety-first Psalm, which is often referred to as "the hospice 911":

> You who live in the shelter of the Most High,
>   who abide in the shadow of the Almighty,
> will say to the LORD, "My refuge and my fortress;
>   my God, in whom I trust . . ."
> Those who love me, I will deliver;
>   those who I will protect, know my name.
> When they call to me, I will answer them;
>   I will be with them in trouble,
>   I will rescue them and honor them.

> With long life I will satisfy them,
> and show them my salvation. (Ps. 91: 1–2, 14–16)

In addition, some hospice caregivers share a clear sense that their work is a "gift" from God and that in fulfilling their responsibilities, they are manifesting an embodied witness of God's love, or acting as a minister of God's presence. CE understands hospice care to be the integrating culmination of her prior professional work and her life paths; her prior experiences constituted God's way of preparing her for her responsibilities as a hospice nurse. Others express a deep sense of calling or permission from God to undertake hospice caregiving. Thus, the endeavor to join with patients and families in their encounter with the boundary of death can be no less a journey that unfolds and discloses spiritual meaning for the professional.

Hospice can assume religious significance and meaning for caregivers in several ways, including interpretations of the meaning of death's boundary and defining practices of hospice integrity, including postures of respect, tolerance, and cooperation regarding medical assistance in suicide. However, the most meaningful experiences of spirituality for hospice professionals appear to come through affirmations of trust in God, prayer, reliance on sacred literature, and a view of hospice as a gift or calling. These practices reflect distinctive motivations for hospice professionals with religious convictions to enter hospice care and to continue in faithful caregiving under the omnipresent shadow of death.

APPENDIX: INTERVIEW QUESTIONS

1. How and why did you become involved in hospice?
2. What does hospice mean to you and why is it important?
3. Does hospice have an ideal of a "good" death? Do you?
4. Could you relate an experience in which this kind of death was achieved or approximated?
5. Could you relate an experience of a "bad" death in hospice care?
6. What makes a good hospice caregiver?
7. How do you help patients find meaning in their dying?
8. What have you learned about yourself through providing hospice care?
9. What have you learned from your patients and families that you have cared for?
10. Does religion or spirituality come up frequently in talking with patients? Explain.
11. Do patients place their dying and death within some framework of a life purpose or meaning? How do they communicate this?
12. What motivates or sustains you in your caregiving?
13. Do religious values play a role in your understanding of your work?

9

PROFESSIONAL COMMITMENT TO PERSONAL CARE

Nurses' Commitments in Care for the Dying

DAVID H. SMITH

I will argue that becoming a nurse entails a change, often an enlargement, of someone's identity, and that serious work on the ethics of nursing must attempt to explicate the nature of the moral world, or nursing ethic, that the new identity entails. I found nurses particularly concerned about providing attention and offering personal presence to persons who are terminally ill. Their *professional* creed calls for a *personal* relationship with patients. In his essay in this volume, Courtney Campbell recounts some of the boundary issues raised by this orientation, but my primary concern is with the situations of doubt and uncertainty inherent in nursing identity. I will suggest that gentle opening of topics and providing opportunities for reconciliation may be appropriate dimensions of professional friendship, but that initiating prayer is not. I will defend these conclusions by using both a casuistical analysis of stories from nursing life and a set of theological arguments.

The research that lies behind this chapter comprises interviews with ten Christian nurses, conducted as part of a larger project on the role of religion in the life of professionals who care for dying persons. That project includes interviews with physicians and chaplains; at one or two points in this essay I refer to things learned in those interviews, but my focus here is completely on nurses. The nurses in this sample currently work in several hospitals. All have had experience on oncology wards, in hospices, or both; several have moved from regular patient care into administration, which gives them a complementary perspective on their professional colleagues. All are women. They range in age from their thirties to their sixties.[1]

The sample was produced by identifying a couple of key players known through my prior experience, asking for their suggestions, and conferring with other knowledgeable persons. I wanted to speak with experienced nurses who were willing to reflect with me about their experiences.

Quick profiles of four nurses may be helpful:

> Hazel is about forty. She was raised in a Christian Reform tradition, trained as a nurse, and then married. Then her life fell apart. The marriage broke up; she had to confront issues of substance abuse. She now worships in an Evangelical church, which has been an essential part of the reconstitution of her life.

> Faith was raised Catholic and has never left the church; her sisters have entered religious life. She has cared for many members of her family as they died. She attends mass regularly. She would never think of asking a priest for advice about care for the dying.

> Terry grew up in a mainline Protestant denomination in which her parents are still quite active. She can live neither with it nor without it. Her own bouts with serious illness have in some ways shaped her attitudes toward care of the dying. She sometimes goes to church because she's "supposed to" and wonders if she should get something out of it.

> Rachel's religious nurture as a child is unclear although it must have been Protestant. She now occasionally attends nondenominational community churches. She has written her own eulogy. She prays. She rides her Harley-Davidson and has attended a biker church, "the most sincere worship I have ever seen."

I haven't singled out these nurses because they are to be quoted unusually heavily or because they are in some way particularly important, but because these sketches should suggest something of the range of persons with whom we spoke.

RELIGION

I did not seek uniformity of opinion or religious orientation. In fact, although all respondents were nominally Christian, their religious orientations and practices are quite diverse. Six are members of mainline churches, three of them Roman Catholic. Two are distinctly Evangelical in their orientation; two might most accurately be described as "spiritual," by which I mean that they think of themselves as religious but are not regular worshipers in an established or stable congregation. This exclusionary use of the label *spiritual* is a little misleading, however, as more than these two nurses would probably be more likely to stress the importance of the *spiritual* than the *religious*.

All of the nurses we talked to describe themselves as religious or "spiritual."

We think they fall into three loosely identifiable cohorts. Some are evangelical Christians. Their piety is highly biblical; they read the Bible to suggest the importance of an adult conversion or act of faith and believe in a life after death with the heavenly reward conditional on adequate faith and a righteous life today. Another group is religious but more mainline in orientation. They worship in Methodist, Presbyterian, or Catholic churches; they take their religion seriously, but the Bible is somewhat decentered, and they adopt a more ironic, reflective, or selective stance toward traditional doctrines. Revelation is understood in more sophisticated terms. Traditional religion is clearly part of these people's lives, but it is put in question by things that happen at work, and it does not so clearly function as an authority. A third group is best described as "spiritual." While they may occasionally worship in some communal setting, their form of piety is eclectic and idiosyncratic. That is not to say that religion for these persons is trivial or unimportant; in fact, this more individual spirituality may be quite intense. But membership in an established community is not central to the identities of these persons, and their religious engagements have clearly been shaped by a sense of personal need or personal insight. For them, the self defines religion rather than religion defining the self.

We have very few, if any, respondents who describe themselves as completely nonreligious; few if any say that religion *as they understand it* plays no part in their lives. That is not to say that all respondents are positive about existing religious communities or practices. To the contrary, most of them offer trenchant criticisms of religion and its presence or absence in the clinical setting. But it is interesting that few, if any, self-consciously define themselves as completely outside the religious circle. (Of course, that may say something about Indiana and about our limited sample.)

Our respondents take comfort in their religious beliefs, but to varying degrees and in differing ways. The evangelical professionals live within a structure of belief that clearly sustains them. They have a strong sense of reassurance about their own destiny and that of their patients. In particular they rejoice in belief in a life after death, in resurrection in heaven. Death, "the last enemy," has been conquered by Jesus Christ, and for them that is good news indeed. Religion gives them a system of beliefs that they can use to interpret what is happening to people at the end of life, which helps them to set the loss into a larger conceptual framework. The link between religion and a particular set of beliefs is very close.

In contrast, the more mainline Christians, despite their ongoing involvements in a church, find their religious commitment more fluid on the level of ideology or dogma. Religion for them may not be primarily a matter of beliefs and ideas. Rather, it may relate more closely to a set of attitudes toward other persons and the world; to a point, it relates to membership in an ongoing community of worshipers, but even that is negotiable as more than one of these nurses modulates her attendance to the style or convictions of a particular minister. Thus, when we asked whether religion helps them in coping with death and dying, the crisp answer that the evangelicals can give is not available to the mainliners. For them, the way religion might help is not ideological or dogmatic; rather it sustains another dimension of life, one that serves both to change the subject and provide a broader and richer perspective through which tragedies at the end of life can be reenvisioned, or put into another perspective.

The spiritual nurses we interviewed have worked out a form of loyalty or connectedness that is tailored to their own needs. It would be strange if it did not provide our respondents with some help, or if it were seriously challenged by events at the bedside. For some, the spiritual may involve walking or hiking; it may involve intense recreation; it may include other people who see the world somewhat the same way.

We found it striking that religious institutions or clergy are seldom looked to for either comfort or teaching, either by the evangelicals or the mainline professionals. We discovered at least one Christian support or prayer group among the evangelicals; two of the Catholics referred to support from eucharistic life. But this response is distinct from looking to a religious community for distinctive teachings or as a moral authority. To some of our respondents, even the thought that one might find comfort or support in worship seemed alien. The absence of a sense of personal support from clergy is even more striking. Our respondents are unlikely to turn to clergy when they need someone to talk to. In some cases, they may have concluded that the clergy are ideological, inexperienced, or insecure. In others, the thought that a member of the clergy might have something to bring to the conversation may never have crossed their minds. Chaplains get better marks than the rest of the clergy, largely because they show up, and they have learned to listen and to avoid superficial platitudes. The chaplain who comes in with too strong an agenda of his or her own, unwilling to listen and spend time, is quickly written off. Chaplains themselves feel that they must have come to terms with their own morality, and then be willing to listen. As one told us, "I make a fairly good living not knowing what to say next."

One of the chaplains we talked to clearly defined his role as support for nurses who were, he thought, the primary ministers in health care. This didn't mean that he stopped ministering to patients himself; it meant that he knew the amount and quality of patient contact he could have is limited. Good stewardship of his time meant investing it in a way that would have the most significant impact on patients, and that meant providing pastoral support for nurses. This seems to us to be a suggestive insight not only for chaplains but for religious congregations of all sorts.

NURSING AS FAITH: BAPTISM INTO DEATH

In Christian tradition, baptism is the ritual that acknowledges the Christian's new identity. Baptism may follow an experience of conversion, or it may be seen as an acknowledgment of a fundamental reality: the adoption of the baptized as a child of God. Becoming a nurse includes a qualification of someone's identity that is similar to the process of conversion. Working as a hospital nurse forces one to begin to look at things, including "last things," in new and different ways. Daniel Chambliss's sociological study of nursing, *Beyond Caring*,[2] is helpful on this point; the nursing analog to conversion is *routinization*.

Chambliss notices that outsiders coming into or inquiring about hospital work always assume that it must be very stressful, "[b]ut the layperson has not seen the routinization of activities and the parallel flattening of emotion that takes place as one becomes a nurse" (12). Morally ambiguous tasks become routine as they are repeated. "Every day nurses respond to and share the most intense emotions with total strangers" (18). Deaths and surgical events are repeated again and again; the bodies of others are viewed and handled with detached concern. "Even when professionals are respectful (and many of them always are), the effect on patients is one of secularization of their own flesh" (26). The normally sacred is profaned; "nothing is sacred" (28). This process takes time. One must learn to find one's way around the physical space, learn to speak the new jargon, learn a distinct set of techniques and technical skills, and learn to classify and understand patients' recurrent medical problems and personality types (30–38). Once those things have happened, a "qualitative transformation of consciousness, a *routinization of the world*" is possible (39). This conversion (my word, not Chambliss's) is not automatic; it may not happen. But if it doesn't occur, ongoing work in the hospital will be well-nigh impossible.

The conversion creates a new moral world. Each nurse who inhabits this new moral world "has limits to the sights she can tolerate, to the work she will carry out," (55ff.) and those limits vary from field to field (e.g., from pediatrics to oncology to intensive care to psychiatry) as well as from person to person. But for any one field, and for any given individual, the nurse's identity "has a distinct moral landscape, with a distinction of 'tolerable' and 'too much.' . . . Their limits are professionally different than ours, but they have limits nonetheless" (58ff.).

What moral implications follow from the sociological fact of identity transformation? We can distinguish Chambliss as moralist from Chambliss as sociologist. Chambliss's own moral concern is with the issues that are concealed by the routinized identity. "The great ethical danger . . . is not that when faced with an important decision one makes the wrong choice, but rather that one never realizes that one is facing a decision at all" (59). He goes on to argue that nurses only

rarely face "dilemmas," which he understands to be conflicts among the values
they hold; rather, the moral pathos of nursing is associated with "problems" that
nurses have with people and social structures. "Powerful people—for instance,
traditional solo practice physicians—have dilemmas; the rest of us have problems" (118).

The language of *dilemmas,* Cambliss claims, "individualizes ethics" and
"diverts attention from the structural conditions that have produced the problem
in the first place" (92). But moral *problems* are "symptoms of occupational group
conflicts in the hospital in which moral arguments are weapons in a fight, usually
decided in favor of the greater power. [They are] not so much dilemmas of conscience but practical problems dumped on nurses from other units, other institutions, and from the society at large. . . . [N]ursing finds itself at the intersection
of competing occupational groups and moral ideologies, and this competition is
the source of its ethical problems" (93).

Chambliss is getting at something profoundly right in these claims. People's
moral worlds are shaped by their social locations. One's power does constrain the
range of "dilemmas" or value conflicts one may confront; insofar as social problems can be solved, key components of the solution must include systemic change
and the redistribution, or at least the rebalancing, of power. It is possible that
some serious and important work in medical ethics has been insufficiently attentive to these social realities.

But the effect of Chambliss's moral modesty is to allow moral analysis to
avoid engaging the issues as nurses themselves perceive them. He seems to think
that a moral issue must be *either* a conflict of values or ideas *or* a conflict of
power or interest, and that the conflict of power or interest is the more basic of
the two. Thus, disputes between nurses and physicians over end-of-life care
reduce to a power struggle between these two professional groups. A loss of
power by physicians in the past quarter century means they are not winning all
these battles, but, as the dominant group, they retain the ability to set the terms of
the discussion.

Even if this analysis is correct, it is mistaken to think that the discussion of biomedical ethics in the United States in the past quarter century has concerned only
"dilemmas" for the powerful. The concept of informed consent, so central to most
components of that discussion, is a highly political concept, which requires lim-
iting the power of physicians and researchers. It may or may not be an adequate
concept to ensure justice and respect for persons, but it is scarcely an abstract or
private idea. Indeed, thinking that one must choose between sensitivity to group
life and conflict, on the one hand, and attention to serious philosophical analysis,
on the other, seems an unfortunate way to begin. We should try our best to have
it both ways.

An alternative development of Chambliss's insightful characterization of routinization is to attempt more systematically to investigate the new professional world of a nurse: to see what the nurses see to be issues and to take those issues seriously.

CONFLICTS WITH PHYSICIANS

Everyone who has been a nurse, talked to a nurse, or read about nursing knows that conflicts with physicians are a significant part of a nurse's agenda. One dimension of this conflict concerns quality control in medical care. Nurses have an increasingly high level of scientific and technical preparation and competence, and they think this technical competence is the sine qua non of their professional work. They may find themselves able to correct a physician's orders and prevent mistakes. For example, we were told of an incident in which a physician had written an incorrect prescription. When a nurse caught the mistake, the physician's first response was a raw exercise of authority: "Do it!" But the nurse persevered and involved her supervisor, who raised the issue again offstage with the physician. At last, the physician admitted her mistake and apologized.

In this probably recurrent kind of conflict, we see the importance of courage and diplomatic skills in a nurse's set of virtues. Without courage, the nurse would not have pointed out the mistake, and the patient might have been harmed or even killed. Without diplomatic skills, conflict with physicians would lead to acrimonious standoffs. Sometimes diplomacy breaks down, as we will see, but without it the workplace community would suffer. But courage and diplomacy are necessary in many forms of conflict; in particular they are necessary in conflicts among physicians. Important as it is that nurses are courageous and tactful, we don't learn much about the distinctive perspective of nurses from studying this form of conflict.

More interesting for our purposes are nurses' conflicts with physicians that involve perceived differences in professional values. Consider these two stories:

> [W]e still have physicians who think it's bad medical practice to keep people comfortable with morphine. They truly believe that. . . . I had a doctor . . . [who] had his patient on the floor. And his patient had bladder cancer, and he was in so much pain because it had metastasized. And I said to him, "Let's give him a morphine drip." And he said, "Oh, no." And I said, "But, doctor, he's in so much pain." So he said, "Okay, fine. Tell me what I need to order and how much I need to order." So we told him how much to put in, and then he whispered as he left, "Don't tell anybody I did this *thing*." But the next day that patient was alert, talking to him and everything. And he said, "This is

it. This is not bad medical practice." [Laughs] So. But they were taught that way. And if you give morphine all the time, that's *bad.* But, boy, it's certainly not bad where the patient's concerned. When they get free of pain, they can talk and move, and it's great.

Or, again:

> NURSE: Our patient had radical neck surgery for carcinoma. And over the time of his year of coming in and out for chemotherapy and radiation, I would talk with him about what he would want at the time of his death . . . if he would want to stay alert at the end or be sedated, et cetera, those kinds of ideas. He was very much wanting to stay as alert as possible at the time of his death. So I did talk with him about the fact that he would have a high percentage that some type of bleeding would cause his death. From a carotid bleed, actually, is how it all ended. But he was very clear, all the way through that, that he wanted to stay awake as long as possible. In the end, he did have a very slow carotid bleed. And so through that last probably few hours of his life, we did not sedate him. He was not in pain. He simply was losing consciousness over time. So he died then very quietly and very peacefully with that. But very much with his eyes fixed on us. And we had learned to communicate a lot with him through eye communication over the last month of his life. So there was that sense of connectedness until he died.
>
> Now, that was fraught with some issues. The physician did want to sedate him.
> INTERVIEWER: Why?
> NURSE: Well, the doctor wouldn't say. He was more angry than anything, because he realized that we would not sedate him at that time. He felt that it would take the man out of his suffering. . . . I talked with the doctor, though, and said, "No, that wasn't his wish. His wish was to remain as conscious as possible." I said, "He's not uncomfortable. He's not in pain. And he knows what's going on. So we can't give him anything." That worked out. I mean, the physician walked out and that was it.

I focus my discussion of these cases on the way the situations are perceived by nurses. It may well be that they misperceive or oversimplify. They may have misunderstood the physicians with whom they were interacting. My data do not allow me to try to sort that out, nor would it be to the point. My concern is with the moral world the nurse inhabits, with the values she thinks important and may have to defend.

And it is indisputable that many nurses disagree with many physicians about priorities in care for the dying. Our respondents perceive a difference in the socialization and public expectations of the professions: "[F]or physicians . . . it's harder to let go. Because they are supposed to be saving people, not letting them die"; "Nurses are always concerned about symptom management . . . comfort . . . Physicians are trained to look at the medical management of the condition. . . . [W]e get into some pretty lively discussions with physicians."

Nurses believe that our expectations of the two professions are quite different. No one will fault a nurse for the fact that someone dies under her care—so long as the technical assignment has been handled properly—but they will certainly fault a physician for an unanticipated death. It is obvious that serious conversations about modulations of treatment are daily matters for these nurses. They are not passive but effectively assertive with physicians. Many of the physicians agree with the nurses about terminal condition and shifting care modalities, but not all do, and disagreements are common.

What are the nursing values that nurses believe compete with those of physicians? Our respondents regard the nurse's ability to provide personal presence as the single most important contribution they can make to the care of the dying. They define the patient's biggest expectation as "our attention," and they find that expectation entirely reasonable. "[T]he most they expect is a sense of presence. Just a moment to be engaged with the patient and family. . . . [S]ome families . . . [want] a lot of information and data . . . [but] once you have given them that and they realize that there is no other place to go except be here, then it is a matter of presence and just being with them."

This personal presence entails the creation of something like family bonds. "I have become friends with a lot of patients that I take care of often. . . . [W]e tend to latch on to those that are our age, that we can relate to. . . . We get to know their . . . children by first name, and their parents and brothers and sisters, and it's kind of a family." This level of involvement can become "protective," as when the nurses speak of someone as "*my* patient," signaling the special bond that has been formed. Seriously ill patients become comfortable with a given nurse, and "we want these patients to be ours, not a float nurse who probably doesn't understand or really, truly love . . . the field that we are in." It is not clear that all the nurses in our sample have or want to have this level of relationship; it is clear that they all think that personal caring and the presence that it connotes are central to quality nursing care for the dying.

The nurses are frustrated that they cannot always meet that expectation. Probably the most experienced nurse in our sample regrets that nurses no longer do enough of the "good old basic emotional, physical care . . . [for example] if you're in pain, instead of running and getting you a shot, maybe giving you a back rub, sitting down, holding your hand. And it's not that nurses don't want to do

that. We just don't have the time anymore." Another thinks patients don't understand the strains that nurses are under; it's unreasonable in the present context "if
they want us to be in the room a lot. And I find myself apologizing to them that I
can't be there more for them." Another nurse commented, "[O]ne of the biggest
frustrations for all of us is that we don't have time to take care of our patients. To
sit down and talk to them. I mean more about what's going on with them emotionally and then spiritually. Because you are passing pills and doing treatments,
and you've got people throwing up and people who are in pain."

There are other systemic problems: Patients are moved from unit to unit,
breaking continuity of care; or they may be assigned to an inappropriate unit.
Even if they stay on the same floor, many nurses now work twelve-hour shifts,
working only three days a week: "[E]specially with nurses working twelve-hour
shifts, I don't think you have that bond with *a* nurse anymore, if you're a patient.
Because you have different nurses all the time." Some issues are peculiar to
tertiary care settings, where patients may have unrealistically high expectations
of miracle cures. In general, nurses increasingly find themselves serving as
managers.

We asked our respondents if they would advise one of their own children to go
to nursing school. "No," one answered flatly. "I think it's too hard to be a good
nurse in this health care world . . . [because] a lot of what nursing is right now is
managing people and things. And if they are going to manage people and things,
they might as well work Monday through Friday, eight to five, in an office and
make a lot of money doing it."

A nurse could not establish those "familial" relationships if she had not gone
through the routinization process that Chambliss so effectively describes. It
would be too painful. And sometimes the protection afforded by routinization
breaks down. The pace of work is such that there is "no time to grieve" for one
patient before the next appears.

Although many physicians may share nurses' commitment to providing personal presence, attention, and comfort, many of them encounter more acute logistical problems in providing those forms of care than do nurses. Whether from lack
of time or lack of interest, it is more unlikely that physicians can offer that kind
of care. This fact explains many nurses' conflicts with physicians over care for the
dying. The first of the two cases that I cited at the beginning of this section illustrates the point. Here, the nurse, who knew the patient and his situation, acted as
patient advocate against a physician who she thought was insufficiently concerned with patient discomfort. (My data do not reveal whether her perception
was accurate.) Nurses are used to thinking about and handling this kind of problem. It is complicated for them by the fact that some physicians are discourteous
and disrespectful: "[T]here are a number of physicians out there that treat nurses

like dirt. . . . Now there are lots of them that are very, very good. But those couple that are really, really bad, that are in your face every day, can be. . . ."

The story of the patient who opted against sedation is particularly interesting in this respect, because the physician was not urging additional therapeutic treatment; compassionately, he wanted to assure the patient's comfort. Even on a completely unsympathetic reading, the physician was not uncaring. But the nurse knew the patient better, and she insisted on the priority of the patient's choice over this paternalistic action. Obviously, nurses aren't always right about these things; physicians may know their patients better than nurses do. What is clear is that the nurses we spoke to believe that this kind of knowledge of patient preferences and commitments goes to the heart of what they are about, and that they perceive this priority to differ from that of many physicians.

I do not dispute that many hardworking nurses resent physician power, especially the power of insensitive physicians. But that fact should not lead students of morality to gloss over the specific issues nurses and physicians argue about. The disagreement over care for the dying is not simply a mask for some "real" power issue underneath it; it *is* an issue that must be worked through. To resolve the problem, the parties need to engage the issue of the requirements of proper care for the dying—something they are both capable of talking about. This issue must be worked out in individual cases, and it is not clear that the "working out" is advanced by translating it into a question of professional power.

The interviews we conducted suggest that a particularly helpful reform would be creation of contexts and forums in which physicians and nurses talked across professional lines about proper care for the dying. As one of our respondents put it, nurses are good professional advocates, but they need a forum in which to express themselves. Our sample turns out to include people whose ideas—and power—have made a difference, but not as much difference as they could or should.

CONFLICTS WITHIN FAMILIES

The nursing ethics focus on concern for patient particularity—patient comfort and patient choice—extends to patients' families. All of the nurses we spoke to think of the patient and family together as the unit for which they are caring. To start with, that means that "[w]e definitely do things we know are futile. We do extra measures sometimes to make the family feel like we're doing something for that patient . . . [e.g.,] keeping an IV running on someone, or keeping their oxygen on." The nurse who said that doesn't mean that these procedures harm the patients; she is thinking of patients for whom they are indifferent. But she is clear in her mind that it is right to treat patients in these ways for the sake of their families.

For nurses, the personal is the social, and the key social unit involved in a death is often the family. But many families are driven apart as death approaches, and nurses regularly find themselves in conflicts among dying persons and families. Sometimes a nurse can stand outside that conflict, but she may be drawn in because of her concern for the dying person. Although respect for independent decision making by patients or families is a fundamental value for nurses, some of them will trump that value with an intervention if it becomes clear to them that independence is leading to suffering. Indeed, they are willing to go to considerable lengths to assure that families are helped.

For example, nurses may work to make sure patients confront crucial facts. A nurse may think her patients have come to terms with their condition, only to realize she was mistaken. Nurses will tell physicians they must inform, talk to, or meet with patient and family; they also may tell the family that they "need to have a meeting with the physician. He needs to tell you where your mother or father is at with their disease and what's expected next." Obviously, this remark reflects some of the tensions between physicians and nurses that I just discussed. But the tone also suggests dissonance between the nurse's perception of what the family should do and what is actually happening. In that situation, some nurses will be proactive in making patients face up to things. They need to help "make . . . patients come to terms with it." As one respondent related,

> Tim . . . was in denial. And about a month and a half before he died, he was in the hospital. And I talked about it. And his wife wasn't there, because she found it difficult to talk about it. And I said, "Tim," I said, "this isn't going to get better." I said, "And you and Carolyn need to talk about it. And then after you talk about it you don't need to talk about it any more. But you need to talk about it at least a little bit. About what you want and what's going to happen. And then you don't have to think about it any more, and you can deny it. But you've got to talk about it."

After this intervention, our respondent went on to say that the most important virtue for a nurse is "sensitivity to the family, kind of picking up on where they are, what they want and not imposing what we think is the way it's supposed to be. . . . [S]o far I don't think I've imposed that on anybody."

Of course, some might describe this nurse's intervention in a family process as an imposition. The hard issue arises when the nurse picks up family denial. Should she simply leave that alone? Several (although not all) of our respondents clearly think a nurse should take a therapeutic role in the family dynamics. If the family is hurting, according to this way of thinking, the nurse should act to help facilitate communication.

We should be troubled by anyone who finds this question of nurse interposition an easy issue. It is easy to criticize the proactive nursing ethic as paternalistic. People should have a right to die as they wish; respecting patients for who they are means respecting choices that seem to us destructive as well as those that are compassionate and liberating. According to this logic, nurses have no business telling their patients that they have to "face up to it" or "talk about it." It doesn't take much imagination to see that mistakes are sure to be made and patients pushed to talk about things that they might prefer to avoid or deny. For some patients and families, the chosen coping mechanism is silence.

On the other hand, there is the power of denial, the fear of death, and the fact that reconciliation delayed may be reconciliation denied. Consider this story, paraphrased from one of our respondents:

> An important death occurred when I was in hospice. The patient was a frail, little woman, debilitated by cancer. When she came in, she didn't want any more intravenous therapies or nutrition or anything. She just wanted to have comfort measures and those kinds of things. So we proceeded to take care of her in hospice. But the woman lingered and lingered and lingered, far beyond what we thought physically possible. I asked the social worker to go in, and I said, "You've got to go in and find out why she is staying on. There is something she is hanging on to. Please go in and find out what that is." It took a few visits, but finally the social worker told me, "She has a son who lives in California, and she needs to see him before she dies." So we contacted him. We did not know about him up to this point. He flew in right away, knowing his mother was dying. When he came in, you could tell he was very uncomfortable. And obviously, there was something going on for us not to have known about him until now. She appeared not to really have any other family. When he arrived, the social worker explained the situation that the mother finally had asked him to go and sit with her. And he did so. About a half an hour later, he came out of the room; he had been crying. He walked away with the social worker, and they spent a couple of hours together. And during that time, the woman did die.
>
> But what we came to find out was when he was twelve years of age, his father committed suicide and did it in the basement of the home he lived in. Well, he was playing in the neighborhood. And when he came home, his mother simply told him that his father had left. Never explained to him that the father had died or how he had died or anything. That he was simply gone. That's the way she handled it. Well, in the course of the next few days in the neighborhood, the children all knew. Except him. So at that point on, he simply

separated himself from his mother and just went the other way. So what he came back and did in that brief thirty minutes was to forgive her and to let her know that she could die in peace. That he did love her. That whatever happened, happened.

Both this and the "face up to it" intervention only make sense when we think of selves as essentially social and recognize that the nurse's responsibilities to her patient require her to be involved with other persons. It may not be possible or desirable to care for someone approaching death without some level of personal involvement. But involvement entails a willingness to take responsibility, and in a sense it is an "imposition." I think it clear that the nurse's intervention in this last case was justified, even though it may contradict theories that suggest that imposition is always wrong.

But not all interventions are equally justified. There is a difference between telling a patient that he and his family have to "face up to it" and taking the initiative to provide an opportunity for reconciliation, as in the last narrative. In the "face up to it" story, the nurse is sure that she knows what needs to be done and tells the patient the right answer; in the family reconciliation story, the nurse knows something is wrong and creates space to enable the concerned parties to work things out. That is a much more modest form of intervention. For that reason, it is a safer model than that offered by the "face up to it" story.

The reason the second intervention is safer relates, theologically, to humility—to an acknowledgment that one is not God and that one's insights, such as they are, are highly fallible. Caught as they are between strong conflicting professional loyalties, nurses may find it easy to underestimate their power and so focus more on their own sins or errors of omission than on errors of commission or of taking on too much responsibility. This may be a particular danger for a decisive and energetic personality reinforced by a form of piety that minimizes doctrinal ambiguity. Decisive people armed with certainties are more willing to cut through an impasse than are others. Occasionally, this may be salvific; as a rule trust in God and recognition of the complexity of human relationships argue for the more modest course.

RELIGIOUS CONFLICT

The issue of interposition in people's lives also comes up with respect to the religious commitments or loyalties of the nurse and her patients. Several of these nurses discussed problems for their faith created by death, especially untimely and protracted death. I will consider only the bedside problems here. Two kinds of experience stand out. On the one hand, the nurses can see religion as intrusive, inappropriate, and socially dysfunctional:

> We had one situation one time with a fellow who was of the Pentecostal faith. And they came into his room, and they were standing him up when he shouldn't have been stood up, and they were hitting him and praying for him and stuff. And that was very hard for me, because I felt like they were compromising his care. But on the other hand, for him, that was his background. That was real important for him. You know, you want to say, "Put him *down!* What are you *doing?*" But [when I was] talking with him later, [he said] it made him feel better.

The nurse tolerated this religious intervention, but she found it troubling because the patient might have been harmed. This obviously raises the question of just how far respect for difference should go in hospital care.

Our respondents tell some remarkable stories of their efforts to provide spiritual support for persons from cultures or traditions different from their own. These stories range from a Protestant's befuddlement with rosary beads through elaborate struggles to provide special clergy, dietary assistance, and consultative procedures. All of the nurses agree that they must respond sensitively when a patient asks for spiritual support, for example, if they are asked by patient or family to pray or join in prayer. Whatever the professionals' own beliefs may be, they agree that that is not the time to educate patients on the limits of their religious perspective. At a minimum, the nurse can be respectfully silent or can offer to pray in her own way.

The clearest case we discovered of a practice that was not supported was animal sacrifice. It is not clear what grounds there are in the nursing ethic of attentive care to oppose that practice. Perhaps the rationale related to public health and hygiene, perhaps to conscientious rejection of the practice by relevant nurses.

What about caring expression of the nurse's own religious views? It is important at the beginning to narrow this issue in a couple of ways. First, we spoke to no one who favored or even tolerated coercion or conversion attempts at the bedside. One of the more evangelical nurses was particularly clear about that. "Whatever helps them at this point in their lives is fine with me," she said. "I may regret that they haven't the hope I do, but that is their business." We did hear of one instance of attempted evangelism, but that went hand in hand with the comment that the offender had lost her job. The people we talked to recognize the reality of religious pluralism, and they respect difference. The hardest case seems to be volunteering to pray with patients when that has not been explicitly requested.

Why might someone offer a prayer when he or she wasn't asked to do so? The strongest case arises from a desire to provide voice and focus for patient's or family's feelings and thoughts that are troubling but unexpressed. We saw in the previous section that nurses may help a patient to articulate uncertainties about prognosis or treatment, so they may see a time when a patient or family need spiritual help or facilitation. It seems insensitive and overly guarded to refuse to offer that help. If honestly sharing a patient's grief in tears is understandable, even sometimes wonderfully helpful and supportive, why should prayer be ruled out? Consider this story, adapted from one provided us by a respondent:

> Richard J was raised in a mainline religious denomination. He remained episodically observant throughout his adult life. He was diagnosed with metastatic carcinoma and, estranged from some members of his family, he flew to Mapleton for treatment so as to be with those family members best able to provide him with support. Thus, as his condition deteriorated, he found himself in a medium-sized hospital in a strange city. He is intermittently conscious, and it appears that the end is near. Adult children have flown into Mapleton and have gathered at the bedside. They are as religiously diverse as any modern American family. They are virtual strangers to the local family, and they are uncomfortable talking about religion.
>
> Sarah K is a nurse on the oncology ward where Richard is a patient. She is a highly competent nurse and a thoughtful and reflective person. Her life has had its own share of tragedy and heartache, and she has returned to the evangelical Christian tradition in which she was raised. This renewed allegiance has helped to restore order in her personal life.
>
> Richard is unconscious, but he moves as if he were uncomfortable. As Sarah enters the room she hears someone say, "Oh, my God, how long can this go on?" Deeply moved, she turns to the family and says, "Why don't we pray?" She takes the hand of the family member nearest to her and says, audibly but quietly, "Oh, God, we don't understand what is going on, and it seems bad. Help us and Richard at this difficult time." She then drops the family member's hand, quickly completes her check on Richard's vital signs, gently pats another family member on the back, and leaves the room. Members of the family are surprised, but no remarks are made.

Did Sarah make a mistake? If prayer was the wrong response to this situation, what, if anything, should Sarah have done? The nurses we spoke to are divided on this issue, but despite the consideration in favor of Sarah's action that I offered before presenting the case, there are some strong arguments against prayer offered by nurses. One of them has to do with difference. Nurses see patients at a time of great vulnerability when pretense is swept away; this context may offer unusual insight. On the other hand, this moment is only a snapshot of the life of patient and family. Intuitions about what people need may turn out to be brilliant, but they can also seriously miss the target. This risk occurs even among persons whose religious nurture or convictions are quite similar.

Some of these problems may be alleviated if the professional *asks* rather than simply offering the prayer. For example, "Do you mind if I pray?" or "Should we pray?" That approach is certainly gentler than assuming that someone wants to participate in a prayer, no matter how honest, modest, and innocuous the prayer might be. But even that strategy has its problems.

To start with there is the problem sometimes called the "tyranny of the gift." Offering this favor—and it is surely meant as a favor—imposes obligations on someone. At a minimum, the patient or family disposed to refuse the offer may worry about hurting the professional's feelings or about implying disrespect for his or her religious commitments. The patient may go along with the prayer out of consideration for the professional's feelings. That is not what was hoped for!

Other, less subtle issues may arise. Patients may accept the prayer because they don't want to risk antagonizing a caregiver who has their lives in her hands. Patients in adjacent beds or rooms who see what happens may wonder if patients who will pray with the caregiver are favored. These issues may be complicated in a religiously affiliated hospital.

Thus, apart from an explicit invitation, the burden of proof is clearly on a decision even to offer to pray with patients or families. Religiously committed persons will find this conclusion difficult, even if it is correct, for it seems to suggest the priority of the ethics of the economic or professional role over the demands to religious loyalty. "Here I stand!" Unless standing here may happen to offend you. Deferring to arguments of the sort I have offered may seem wishy-washy.

There are two dimensions to an adequate theological response to this objection. The first is to note that the nurse is not in a position of a bystander or old friend; she is a professional with expert knowledge and power over the patient—however much she may be aware of the limits of that knowledge and power. Standing up for principle as Luther did at Worms is very different when one is vulnerable than when one is in a position of power. We often take the former, and Luther, as a paradigm of courage; the latter as a paradigm of tyranny. Sensitivity is particularly important in a culture with a historically Christian vocabulary and an increasingly diverse population. The committed Christian may see the vocabulary as an irrelevant veneer; someone else may see form and offered prayer as part of a thoughtlessly dominant culture.

More deeply, the objection may rest on an overly simple understanding of the relationship between professional identity and religious vocation, or between a traditional religious loyalty and the religious analogue in a nursing identity. The two identities or vocations may not be simply competitive; the Christian trust and loyalty that motivates one to care for others through nursing may warrant acceptance of the constraints of the nursing role as mandates or ordinances of God—not to be accepted when they become idolatrous, to be sure, but provisionally certain enough to be credible guides for conduct in the day-to-day work of nursing.

This point is reinforced if we take seriously the fact that becoming a nurse is a kind of identity-shaping experience comparable to what religious traditions call conversion. While loyalty to the one God will surely contextualize and displace that loyalty, it cannot completely replace it without blotting out the identity of the nurse. In fact, it is plausible to argue—as one chaplain cited previously has done—that work as a nurse, constraints and all, is the truest form of Christian ministry to the terminally ill that is possible in the United States today. The uncertainty about whether to volunteer to pray is best seen not as a dilemma pitting the demands of faith against those of the world; it is a question of the most caring implications of faith. As I have argued, insisting on the privilege of unsolicited prayer too easily comes through as uncaring to be a credible requirement of love.

CONCLUSION

Nursing ethics must take seriously the identity change that nursing work entails; it must engage in a casuistry of cases about problematical forms of care, and it should not hesitate to join arguments in religious terms insofar as that is the way nurses see the issues. Neither philosophical abstraction nor sociological translation of issues should justify avoidance of these levels of intellectual engagement.

10

"APART AND NOT A PART"

Death and Dignity

GILBERT MEILAENDER

We're paying more attention to dying than to death. We're more concerned to get over the act of dying than to overcome death. Socrates mastered the art of dying; Christ overcame death as "the last enemy" (I Cor. 15:26). There is a real difference between the two things; the one is within the scope of human possibilities, the other means resurrection.[1]

They were silent for a while. Then the first leaf said quietly to herself,
"Why must we fall? . . ."
The second leaf asked,
"What happens to us when we have fallen?"
"We sink down . . ."
"What is under us?"
The first leaf answered,
"I don't know, some say one thing, some another, but nobody knows."
The second leaf asked,
"Do we feel anything, do we know anything about ourselves when we're down there?"
The first leaf answered,
"Who knows? Not one of all those down there has ever come back to tell us about it." . . .
"Let's remember how beautiful it was, how wonderful, when the sun came out and shone so warmly that we thought we'd burst with life. Do you remember? And the morning dew, and the mild and splendid nights. . . ."

A moist wind blew, cold and hostile, through the tree-tops.
"Ah, now," said the second leaf. "I . . ." Then her voice broke off.
She was torn from her place and spun down.
Winter had come.[2]

To struggle with death and dying is nothing new in human experience. That struggle has taken on a peculiar tone in our society, however. On the one hand, we seek a certain control and mastery over our fate. On the other, we are increasingly asked to find ways to accept death as no affront to our dignity and as a natural part of life. To learn to think this way is itself, of course, to exercise a certain kind of "control." Indeed, it has in some ways been the burden of a quarter century's bioethical reflection to teach us the acceptance of death free of intrusive, high-tech medicine. By contrast, Felicia Ackerman has recently suggested that the "philosophy of hospice," which affirms the importance of accepting death, is "a highly questionable ideology" that may "attempt to export religiously based attitudes . . . into a context where the religious grounding that justifies these attitudes is lacking."[3]

I want to reflect upon some stories about dying to see what we can learn from them, but I suspect that just looking at how people die or telling their stories will not determine for us whether death is an enemy against which we ought to rage and struggle, or whether it is a part of life that comes naturally and ought to be accepted. What we think about such questions is likely to depend on what we think about quite a few other matters. I will, therefore, reflect upon these stories against the background of more systematic consideration of the significance of death.

The stories I will draw from Ira Byock's widely read book, *Dying Well: The Prospect for Growth at the End of Life.*[4] As a hospice doctor, Byock has cared for many suffering patients in their dying. Moreover, he believes deeply in the importance of accepting that dying and making it—as the book's subtitle indicates—a time of personal growth. But I will place these stories in the context of a pair of essays that are now more than a quarter-century old: Paul Ramsey's "The Indignity of 'Death with Dignity,' " and Leon R. Kass's rejoinder, "Averting One's Eyes, or Facing the Music?—On Dignity in Death."[5] The Ramsey/Kass exchange will serve to remind us that what we make of Byock's stories depends in some considerable measure on beliefs—even metaphysical and religious beliefs—that we bring with us when we read them. Our moral reflection on the meaning of death seems almost to require that we move back and forth between 1) particular cases, and our response to them, and 2) the larger patterns of belief that frame our response to cases and, in part, shape what we see. We cannot simply reflect on cases as if ours were a view from nowhere in particular. Neither, however, should we suppose that our beliefs about the meaning of death remain entirely unaffected by the experience of dying patients.

IS DEATH AN ENEMY?
REVISITING AN OLD DEBATE

In arguing that death itself is an affront to human dignity and that, therefore, the shibboleth of "death with dignity" can also readily become an affront, Ramsey wants to make place for the attitude exemplified in the oft-quoted passage from Dylan Thomas, which he himself also cites: "Do not go gentle into that good night. . . . Rage, rage against the dying of the light." In making this claim he does not deny that death might sometimes, by some people, be accepted with serenity (48). He does not deny that, weighing the "comparative indignities" of different possibilities, one might sometimes conclude that continued personal deterioration was more fearful than death (51f.). His central contention is summed up in a sentence such as the following: "The more acceptable in itself death is, the less the worth or uniqueness ascribed to the dying life" (56).

Why might one hold such a view? Underlying Ramsey's position are beliefs that he draws from Christian faith but also understands to belong to any "true humanism"—in particular, 1) the belief that we are bodies extended in time, that human life is biological and historical in character, and 2) the belief that each person is unique and cannot be replaced by any other, because each is made for God. These are the two grounds of our individual worth.

We are finite bodies, located and connected in a particular time and place. Something of what this means is nicely expressed by C. S. Lewis in a passage discussing the way Christians tend sometimes to depict death as simply a good thing—the transition to a new and better life. Lewis does not deny that belief; he simply points to what has been lost—and seemingly lost forever—to the alien power of death.

> If a mother is mourning not for what she has lost but for what her dead child has lost, it is a comfort to believe that the child has not lost the end for which it was created. . . . A comfort to the God-aimed, eternal spirit within her. But not to her motherhood. The specifically maternal happiness must be written off. Never, in any place or time, will she have her son on her knees, or bath[e] him or tell him a story, or plan for his future, or see her grandchild.[6]

But we are not only embedded in nature and history. We are not just "a part" of it. Called into personal communion with God, we are "apart and not [simply] a part" of the natural world (55). It follows, therefore, that death, in cutting off a particular "human countenance," is the enemy. My death may be part of the natural cycle of birth and death; it may seem necessary for future generations to flourish; it may bring to an end "comparative indignities" of suffering and deterioration that were themselves even more fearful; but, nonetheless, it does not bring my life to completion. It is "*finis*, not in itself *telos*" (53).

For both reasons, then, death is the enemy of our individuality and our worth. Hence, when caring for one who is dying, or when facing our own death, we need "to acknowledge that there is grief over death which no human agency can alleviate" (62). This will be true, on Ramsey's account, not only when a child dies prematurely (as we would say) but also when someone dies "full of years." If we try to ignore or deny the loss that every death brings, we miss the dignity of the dying person. We cherish him too little if we seek "dignity" in death as a way of removing its sting, as if any "human agency," any theory of ours, any care (even the most dedicated) that we might give, could itself "alleviate" the loss of this "human countenance."

None of this means, of course, that there are not comparatively better and worse ways to die. None of this means that specific deaths might not be comparatively more or less dignified. It means only that, even in the most dignified of deaths, we need to recognize the presence of a hostile power, the "last enemy" from which Jesus himself shrank, a power that cannot be overcome simply by mastering the art of dying. Something like that is Ramsey's understanding of "the indignity of 'death with dignity.' "[7]

Kass's response, although largely agreeing with respect to some of the deformations brought to our experience by notions of "death with dignity," nevertheless turns in a very different direction. In part, Kass argues for an understanding of dignity as a human achievement and, hence, not just a universal human possession. The dignity that we do sometimes attain is dependent not on what uniquely individuates each of us but on the way we exercise those generic qualities that distinguish the human species from others. Moreover, in his view, death is not a hostile power; it is simply the natural conclusion to the trajectory of a human life and, still more, a possibly necessary condition for the display of much that is noble in our life (68f.). It is a good, even if sometimes an "evil good."

This is, in many respects, Kass at his most Aristotelian—set over against Ramsey at his most existentialist. For Kass our nobility lies in the exercise of the most characteristically human capacities—presumably, although he does not specify them precisely, a yearning for what is true, and good, and beautiful. For those human beings who achieve such dignity, death, simply in and of itself, cannot be an indignity—a judgment for which Kass offers several reasons. He suggests, for example, that—whatever we may say of the child who dies prematurely—we do not regard death as an affront to dignity when it takes one who dies "full of days after a rich and worthy life" (74). We may pause briefly to reflect on this claim in contrast to Ramsey's view. Certainly it is true that we react differently to the death of an old woman than to the death of a young girl. That much one must surely grant to Kass. But it is harder to know how to decide whether the death of the old woman—even if painless and at a ripe old age—should be counted an affront, a defeat by a hostile power. Simply observing such deaths will not, I suspect, make the distinction for us. Kass himself, after all, can understand a sense in which any person's death—the sheer fact of mortality—could be considered an indignity: "Only if dignity were synonymous or coextensive with life itself could we even begin to make such a case" (73).

But, of course, precisely such "coextensiveness" is integral to Ramsey's case. What sets us "apart" for him is, first, the particular web of relationships and loyalties that constitutes this bodily life, to which death brings a *finis*. What also sets us "apart," and makes us more than just "a part" of nature, is that each is called by God to himself. That is an alien dignity conferred or bestowed from outside; it is not a matter of human achievement. Each person has an individual dignity that is snuffed out by death. For Kass, at least the Kass of this essay, it is universal form—the generically human rather than particular matter—that really makes for human dignity (76). And death is the end point of the decay and decline built into life, not a personal force that confronts us from the outside, opposing itself to the call of God. There is no way to read the differences between Ramsey and Kass apart from these differences in worldview. Neither confronts the fact of death simply as an event to be observed. Each sees in death an event shaped by the (Aristotelian or Christian existentialist) metaphysic he brings to it.

Kass also offers a variety of angles from which we may see death as necessary to a world in which virtue and nobility are present. Heroes and martyrs demonstrate how death can provide "the occasion for the display of dignity. . . . Far from undermining their worth, their death—like the life it terminates—is a necessary condition for the display of dignity" (74). In addition, the simple fact of our mortality may be a kind of "necessary spur" to excellence, pressing us along the way by reminding us that we may not, in fact, have "world enough and time" (74). And without death, without the withering and dying of the old, there could be no place for the next generation, for the young with their vibrant sense of hope. In all these ways death may serve human well-being and enhance human dignity.

Finally, death is, on Kass's view, simply a natural event, a limit set within the very principle of life: "How can death be an indignity if it is the natural and necessary accompaniment of life itself?" (75). Against Ramsey's suggestion (48) that suffering, which we think it right to oppose, is also a natural part of life, Kass argues for a difference. Disease—and the suffering it brings—are "*fought* by nature working within, whereas decline is *produced* by nature working within"

(75f.). Hence, "unlike all those other things which *occur* in life, decline and death are a *part* of life, an integral part which cannot be extruded without destroying the whole" (76).

There is, however, one sense in which we might wonder whether Kass is quite Aristotelian enough here. For Aristotle the "natural" is not simply what happens regularly and, even, inevitably. The "natural" is whatever is appropriate to a thing of a particular kind, whatever constitutes its flourishing. It is, then, a normative concept, and that opens up space for Ramsey's view of what is fitting and appropriate for beings of our kind, when he writes, "But the man who is dying happens not to be evolution. He is a part of evolution, no doubt: but not to the whole extent of his being or his dying. A crucial testimony to the individual's transcendence over the species is man's problem and his dis-ease in dying. Death is a natural fact of life, yet no man dies 'naturally . . .' " (49).

In Ramsey's view, in other words, human self-transcendence is a sign that we are made for the living God—and that death is an affront to the "nature" of such creatures. The lesson to be drawn is one I need not belabor further: The different responses of Ramsey and Kass as they stand at the bedside of a dying man may not be explicable apart from the respective webs of belief which they carry with them to that bedside. Their respective attitudes toward the man's dying will be shaped by their metaphysical accounts of human nature. That said, we are ready to consider Ira Byock's stories of the dying.

THE DYING OF THE LIGHT

Chapters 10 and 11 of *Dying Well,* the last two stories narrated by Byock, form a pair. The first (the story of Terry Matthews) illustrates what he regards as a bad death, and the second (the story of Maureen Riley) offers his image of perhaps the best possible death. Yet he is willing to say that each of these women "died well" because each died in her own chosen way. In general, this seems to be the key to his evaluations. Having first, as he tells his readers, been drawn toward the concept of a "good death," he rejected it in favor of the idea of "dying well" (32). Focusing on a "good death" may not be helpful. For one thing, most people will describe it only negatively—in terms of the evils they hope to avoid in their dying. Moreover, "it tends to blur the distinction between death . . . and the preceding time of living" (32). "Dying well," by contrast, "expresses the sense of living, and a sense of process" (32). It invites us think about what we may yet accomplish in our dying and sees that dying as another stage in a lifelong process of human development.

Terry Matthews was twenty-four years old and the mother of a toddler when she had a growth on her right kidney removed. To her physician's surprise, the growth turned out to be cancer of a kind difficult to cure. She undertook a course of chemotherapy, however, went into remission for a time, conceived and gave birth to a second child, and (with her husband Paul) adopted a third. Thus, she was a mother of a son and two young daughters, and she devoted herself whole-heartedly to being that. After six years, however, she developed a persistent cough and occasionally spat up blood. Lung X-rays showed that, after years of lying dormant, the cancer "had returned with a vengeance" (195).

Over the next nine months Terry struggled with her own vengeance against her illness and in the face of "unbearable pain."[8] Even in the midst of such pain, however, she hung grimly to life. Byock recounts a conversation Terry had with Vickie Kammerer, the hospice social worker assigned to help her. The issue was whether Terry should enact a directive stating that she did not want CPR if she should undergo cardiac or respiratory arrest:

> Though Vickie knew of Terry's fierce drive to stay alive, the topic required discussion. As she had with hundreds of patients with advanced cancer, Vickie gently explained to Terry, "If you had a mas-sive heart attack in your current condition, it might be somewhat futile even if you could be briefly revived." Terry's reaction said it all: "If they could bring me back to life and if I could have one or two more days, that is what I would want" (200).

Why? Why would she rage this fiercely against the dying of the light?[9] Because she loved her husband and her children. Byock says of her case: "By the end of her life, Terry's pain was as bad as it gets, as severe as I have ever wit-nessed" (215). She "was absorbing—and her pain all but ignoring—more than nine hundred milligrams of morphine per hour," yet she clung to life (207). Indeed, in choosing every possible life-prolonging option she certainly brought upon herself—and willingly accepted in return for life—much greater pain than might otherwise have been hers. "She clung to life far beyond the point at which most people surrender to the inevitable. Her connection to her family, being with them, was more important than the pain—and her resistance to letting go gave the disease more time to inflict its cruel torment" (214f.). Even this, however, does not tell the whole story of her suffering or the reasons for it. Byock can write that "while the physical aspects of her distress were enormous, I have no doubt that Terry's blinding grief at the thought of losing her husband and three young chil-dren contributed to her pain" (214). Clearly, hers was, in Ramsey's words, a grief that "no human agency can alleviate."

In the end her pain could be relieved only through permanent sedation, which gave her troubled body the peace of "twilight sleep" until she died thirty hours after the barbiturate drip was begun. Even in the last hours before she was thus sedated, in the midst of almost unspeakable suffering, she spent her time making notes of her last wishes for her children, worrying about what they would wear at her funeral, and expressing to her husband her sorrow at leaving him (210). "Life had to be plucked from Terry; she never did let go or turn inwardly to leave the way most dying people do. This was the crux of her life: she died with arms open and outstretched toward her family. Her reluctance to leave will always be part of her legacy to them" (212).

Byock's own assessment of the death of Terry Matthews is clear. He will not deny a certain authenticity to her dying. Because she died in her own chosen manner, she did, in a sense, "die well." Nevertheless, he will not call "good" a death in which one never lets go, in which life is forcibly taken by the power of death:

> Terry's was not the way I would choose for a relative or loved one to die. By my personal values, Terry did not die a "good death." Yet how Terry and her family felt, not my values, is what ultimately matters. In this respect, she died well, because she died her way—fighting for life and time with her family. In her dying, she remained true to her spirit and true to her values. It was her way, thus the only way (193).

Surely there is something to such a response; yet, if this is where telling stories leads, it may have deleterious consequences for ethical reflection. One of the themes of *Dying Well,* for example, is that euthanasia is never necessary or choiceworthy. Physical suffering can always be relieved, and dying can become the occasion for one last stage of personal growth. Yet, if what counts most is that we each die in our own way, true to our values, it is not clear how a judgment against euthanasia can be sustained. Byock does not recommend Terry Matthews's kind of death, but he is willing to stand by her throughout it and do everything he can to care for her—because it is "her way" and "thus the only way." Analogous reasoning might seem to commit him to provide assistance also to those desiring euthanasia—which would undercut one of the themes of his book and, perhaps, the point of the care he has rendered to so many of the suffering dying.

If that is not where we want the argument to lead, we must step back and ask whether there is not something more positive to be said of Terry Matthews's dying. On Ramsey's terms, of course, her rage against the dying of the light, however hard it might be for many of us to emulate and however true it may be that it is not the only acceptable way to die, can be praised. In its appreciation of the moral and personal significance of her embodied life and individuality, her rage and her struggle may manifest a "true humanism." Even on Kass's terms, there is room here for praise. She neither averts her eyes nor refuses to face the music. When the time comes, when she is compelled no longer to avert her eyes, she and her husband tell their children what is soon to happen. She will not regard her death as anything other than an evil. Not for her Kass's sense that the death of individuals may contribute to the good of the species. Yet I think it fair to say that any reader of Byock's chapter 10 will conclude that she makes of the occasion of her death an opportunity for the exercise of nobility. And finally, in saying good-bye and accepting sedation when she can bear no more, she gives nature its due. It is a more grudging acknowledgment than Kass might wish—more in the spirit of Ramsey. But it has about it an undeniable nobility that Byock's account captures quite well. As one who had won "the lottery from hell" (215), Terry Matthews seized the occasion to turn outward and die "with arms open and outstretched toward her family" (212). In that sense, though she would not agree with Kass that death could be an "evil good," she made of it a "good evil."

The death of Maureen (Mo) Riley was very different indeed. For her it was a good and hardly, even, an "evil good." Of her Byock writes,

> Everything this woman did in her dying days reflected not just acceptance of her impending demise, but curiosity, anticipation, and even pleasure. She typified full, rich living through her very last breath. Mo also showed me how someone who is dying can transform herself from a vibrant, loving mother and person living in the world into an almost lofty being of beauty and spirit. . . . Mo epitomized a blessedness that comes with letting go of both the burdens and the delights of daily life—ultimately letting go of life itself and willingly slipping into another realm (217).

She is, in short, the very epitome of his notion of "dying well," for hers is a death that takes seriously the possibilities for personal growth in the process of dying. If part of Byock's problem with Terry Matthews's dying was that she focused entirely on "a deeper love for her family" rather than "experiencing a deeper love of self" (212), the same cannot be said of Mo Riley. She, by contrast, seemed "to flow smoothly out of worldly concerns and relationships and toward an ethereal, spiritual state" (218).

Sixty-five years old and retired, with six grown children and also grandchildren, Mo Riley learned that she had "a very fast-growing cancer lodged at the top of her spine and entwining the base of her brain," and was told that she probably had only weeks to live (220). She initially accepted radiation therapy to shrink the tumor and ease her pain. Her twenty-six-year-old daughter Emily, although seven months pregnant with her own first child, moved back in with her to provide care during her dying, and Mo accepted no further radiation therapy or chemotherapy. She seemed remarkably calm at the thought that she would die soon, showed little inclination to regret anything, and even felt no strong urge to stay alive long enough to see Emily's child born. " 'Actually,' she reflected, 'I've been ready for a while' " (224).

As it turned out, Mo lived longer than her doctors had predicted—some three months, and long enough to see the birth of her granddaughter. When she lost control of her bladder, she accepted with equanimity the fact that Emily had to "change" her as she did the baby. "Out of necessity, Mo had shed her modesty as one might set aside a favorite wool coat for the spring" (228). We could overstate the case, however. Byock does, for example, recount an occasion when she expressed concern about being a burden to her children and was overcome with tears at the thought of what they had to do for her (231). The last time he saw her, only hours before her death, he could still see, however, that "her spirit was strong and soaring" (234). He writes of her, "As much as any patient I have known, Mo personified the possibility of a joy within the process of letting go, transcending this world, and growing into an unexplored, spiritual realm" (234).

Here is one who did not rage against the dying of the light; nevertheless, her case, at least as Byock describes it, demonstrates how complex are the questions we are considering. Mo Riley did not appear to recognize death as an indignity or an enemy. Shall we, therefore, read her death as closer to the model Kass recommends? Perhaps in part, but only in part. The death that is "the natural and necessary accompaniment of life" on Kass's account is one that involves "decay and decline" (75). Consciously following Aristotle at this point, Kass sees human beings as, in this respect, like all living things: built into their life is "a principle of growth *and decay*" (75). And, although Kass would no doubt understand something of what Byock means when he speaks of continued possibilities for growth in dying—Kass himself, after all, sees death as the occasion for display of nobility—the account Byock gives of Mo Riley's death does not seem to make much place for decay and decline.

> At the edge of the transcendent—in the midst of "letting go"—a person who has completed the work of development does not disintegrate in dying. Rather, she *dissolves* out of life, becoming increasingly ephemeral—less dense or corporeal—but no less integrated, in the passage from life. Personhood becomes gauzy and translucent (238).

One begins to lose here not only Ramsey's sense that death is an enemy but also Kass's sense of our finitude and materiality. And if not everyone can or does die as Mo did, Byock is clear that becoming "increasingly ephemeral"—less body and more spirit—is, in his view, what it means really to die well.

Thus, at least at certain moments, Byock seems to see death neither (in Kass's terms) as the necessary decline of mortal beings, nor (in Ramsey's terms) as the enemy that is the wages of sin. One can only respect the work that Byock does, and he has surely served the well-being of many suffering patients. But one would like to know more about the metaphysical underpinnings of what he thinks he sees in death; for ultimately we seek not simply comfort but the comfort of truth.[10] It is not clear, to me at least, why we should be encouraged to seek continued growth—into ephemerality—in our dying. If I would not quite, with Ramsey, brand such exhortations themselves as always an additional "indignity" heaped upon the dying, I think they can be. Terry Matthews rightly recognized an enemy in death, an enemy to her continued "growth" as a human being, and she was not, I think, wrong to fight it.

Byock himself has moments when he seems compelled by the stories themselves to agree. Writing of Janelle Haldeman, a high-school-age girl who suffered from a rare, juvenile-onset form of Huntington's disease, whose mother constantly battled the health care system and the school system on behalf of her daughter, he can say, "Janelle's battles were more directly with her illness, which was an unprincipled, vicious enemy" (120). Perhaps he needs a bit more of this language. Many of the powerful stories recounted in *Dying Well* involve severe pain or the suffering that comes with dementia, and, precisely because they are powerful, they might cause us to wonder whether Kass's vision takes full account of them. Ramsey had noted that advocates of "death with dignity" were not as inclined to speak of "suffering with dignity" or of suffering as simply a natural part of life (48). To this Kass responded, in some ways reasonably enough, that disease and injury are not "as natural, necessary, and inextricably bound up with life as are death or decay" (75). Even in the case of disease, which might seem most natural, he notes that "disease is *fought* by nature working within, whereas decline is *produced* by nature working within" (76).

The contrast between disease and decline is worth our attention. In a finely wrought essay, Lewis Thomas once developed a similar distinction, relying on Oliver Wendell Holmes's poem about a carriage made by a deacon.[11] Thomas used it to distinguish between a life that *breaks down* and a life that *wears out*. The deacon in the poem fashioned his carriage with such care that it was the "perfect organism," each part as good as all the rest, with no weak link. Had there been a weak link, and had that link broken down, the carriage might have halted prematurely, before its time. But instead, since it never breaks down, the whole gradually wears out. As the poem puts it, "A general flavor of mild decay, / But nothing local, as one may say." Finally, one day, it simply goes to pieces: "All at once, and nothing first." This is not Ramsey's vision of death as enemy. It is not Byock's vision of death as transition to ephemeral spirit. It is, though, quite close to Kass's vision of death as the end point of decline. And such a vision is not without its attractions.

The problem, though, as the narratives in *Dying Well* make clear, is that many of us will not die this way: "A general flavor of mild decay, / But nothing local, as one may say." In chapter after chapter Byock tells us of patients who wrestle with dementia; ALS or MS; pancreatic, colon, or lung cancer; AIDS . . . the list, of course, knows no real end. In the face of these narratives we may need to choose between death as enemy or death as transition to ephemeral spirit, between raging against the dying of the light or encouraging growth and progress throughout the process of dying. Kass's vision, powerful and appealing as it is, helpful as it is in certain instances, will not do justice to what we see in these stories.

Perhaps I need to qualify that claim. In the face of great suffering, the patients depicted in *Dying Well* do often claim for themselves a measure of nobility. To that extent Kass remains on target: Dying can be the occasion for the display of much that is praiseworthy and noble. But it is an awful price some of these patients pay for that opportunity, and I am not sure many of us would wish for the chance to be this heroic. Moreover, the nobility displayed by these patients seems to depend in part precisely on the viciousness of the "enemy" they face. They are not just dealing with "decay and decline."

Time after time throughout his book, Byock emphasizes that dying is not inherently undignified. What he means by this—namely, that it is possible to provide dying patients with the kind of support they need to retain some sense of their own worth—is generally clear. Thus, for example, he writes,

> Dignity is important to everyone, but especially to someone who is dying and has already begun losing control over much of his life. And while many people think of dignity in terms of appearance, independence, and personal embarrassment, people close to a dying patient seem to know intuitively that their loved one's dignity does not depend on these. Dying is not inherently undignified, it is simply part of being human. With supportive family and friends, even needing help with basic bodily functions need not diminish dignity (72).

In thinking of death as part of life, Byock here is like Kass. In seeing that personal dignity should not depend on control or independence, he is not unlike Ramsey, for whom human dignity is essentially an alien dignity bestowed by God.

Exactly how Byock holds these several emphases together is not always clear. In one, quite simple sense we may say that he always looks for goals that the dying person can meet, tasks that can still be undertaken—if only, on occasion, the task of allowing others the satisfaction of caring for oneself. More centrally, but, I think, more problematically, he often seems to ground dignity in "the remarkable achievements in personal growth that can occur while someone is dying" (86). Yet he looks for dignity even in the stories of patients who do not really seem to achieve the kind of growth he praises. Hence, his narratives seem themselves to press us beyond his own conceptual scheme—seem to press us toward a dignity that is bestowed rather than achieved. But the conceptual resources needed to develop such a notion are not really on display in *Dying Well*—and one wonders, therefore, whether the practices of care to which Byock is committed can be sustained indefinitely without a firmer grounding.

THE ART OF DYING? OR OVERCOMING DEATH?

To recapitulate, I began with two views of death: as an enemy to be opposed or as the end point of natural human decline, to be accepted with as much dignity and nobility as we can muster. I then considered Byock's stories of dying patients within the framework of these alternatives. His stories suggest, at least to this reader, that we should not—and perhaps cannot—look at death with quite the equanimity that Kass's view intimates. Dying as many people experience it is not just the result of the decline and decay that are natural for living organisms. What they experience in their dying is something more like an assault on the integrity of their person. (And in facing that assault they are, in many respects, fortunate to have Byock at their side.) This much, perhaps, we can say at a purely phenomenological level—without importing too much by way of metaphysical baggage.

But that is what they experience "in their dying." With respect to death itself, however, Byock and Kass may not be too far apart. Neither sees it as an enemy, as a loss which, in Ramsey's terms, "no human agency can alleviate." For Kass, it would be strange to talk of alleviating what is inherent in our nature and per-haps necessary for the display of our nobility. For Byock, it would be strange to speak of such grief in connection with a moment so rich in possibilities for per-sonal growth. For Ramsey, by contrast, our ultimate problem is not dying but death. Death assaults our person, in part, precisely because we are not ephemeral beings but bodies with location and attachments. Death assaults our person, in still larger measure, because we are "apart and not [simply] a part" of the natural world. As self-transcending creatures made for God, we experience "dis-ease in dying," however commonplace and "natural" death may seem to be.

If that is true—and here we must decide what metaphysical baggage we want to carry—then we do indeed, as Ramsey put it, heap additional indignities on the dying if, in our care, we do not penetrate to a problem even deeper than dying— the indignity of death itself. Powerful as Byock's narratives are, they are told by one who is still among us, and they are therefore confined to the experience of dying. None of the subjects of these stories can come back to tell us about death itself. That is not within the scope of human possibilities, and our judgment about the meaning of death inevitably draws us beyond the limits and terrain of such stories. At least it must if we want to pay as much attention to death as to dying.

I conclude that Ramsey had his sights set on something very important; namely, that (not just dying, but) death is an enemy that assaults us. This, in turn, means that Terry Matthews cannot have been simply wrong to rage, as she did, against the dying of the light—and I trust that my account of Byock's account has made clear my admiration for her "reluctance to leave." This does not mean, however, that we should simply affirm her attitude toward death. Byock says that "[l]ife had to be plucked from Terry." But perhaps there should sometimes come a point at which—without denying that there is grief in death that "no human agency can alleviate"—we should cease to oppose our death or that of another. If the "dis-ease" that we experience in dying is rooted, finally, in the fact that we are made for God, then God must constitute the limit to our struggle against death. It must be death that we oppose—not God. "There are two attitudes towards Death," C. S. Lewis once wrote, "which the human mind naturally adopts":

> One is the lofty view, which reached its greatest intensity among the Stoics, that Death "doesn't matter," that it is "kind nature's signal for retreat," and that we ought to regard it with indifference. The other is the "natural point of view, . . . that Death is the greatest of all evils. . . . The first idea simply negates, the second simply affirms, our instinct for self-preservation; neither throws any new light on Nature, and Christianity countenances neither. Its doctrine is subtler. On the one hand Death is the triumph of Satan, the punishment of the Fall, and the last enemy. . . . On the other hand, only he who loses his life will save it. We are baptized into the *death* of Christ, and it is the remedy for the Fall. Death is . . . the thing Christ came to conquer and the means by which he conquered.[12]

Thus, death is never to be embraced—because it is an evil. But it must sometimes be acknowledged—because it is not the greatest evil.

"What madness it is," St. Augustine writes, in his famous account of the death of a friend, "not to know how to love men as they should be loved"[13]: loved, that is, as creatures—genuine goods, but not the highest good. "The good that you love is from Him; but its goodness and sweetness is only because you are looking toward Him; it will rightly turn to bitterness if what is from Him is wrongly loved, He himself being left out of the account."[14] How must we think if we do not leave God "out of the account"?

We should remember that Paul Ramsey's assertion of "the indignity of 'death with dignity' " was quite self-consciously put forward not as the whole truth but as a correction. At the outset of his essay Ramsey notes that he himself, only a few years earlier, had argued that our responsibility to care for the dying should lead to "the acceptance of death, stopping our medical interventions for all sorts of good, human reasons, *only* companying with the dying in their final passage" (47). Suddenly, however, it seemed to him "that altogether too many people were agreeing with me" (47). They had grabbed hold of only one-half of his view—thereby distorting it and heaping new indignities upon the dying with their talk of death as natural, or as friend, or, even, as something beautiful.

In chapter 3 of *The Patient as Person,* a treatment that remains one of the classics of bioethics literature, Ramsey had characterized our obligation toward the dying as one of "(only) caring." That is, faithfulness to patients requires that we never cease in our efforts to care for them, while recognizing that at some point proper care means precisely ceasing from any further efforts to cure disease or to struggle against death. And Ramsey then depicted "two opposite extremes" from which this morality of caring (but only caring) for the dying would be resisted.[15] Some would argue that if death could sometimes rightly be acknowledged, it should also sometimes be chosen and sought as a good thing. Others would argue that if death was an evil to be opposed, it should never be acknowledged or accepted. For the first, death might actually be, not an enemy, but a good. For the second, death became not just an evil, but the greatest evil, and life not just a good, but the greatest good.

Insofar, then, as Mo Riley seems (on Byock's account) to embrace, and not merely acknowledge, death, she is wrong to do so. Insofar as Terry Matthews seems (on Byock's account) to embrace temporal life not just as a creaturely good but as the greatest good, she is wrong to do so. Which mistake is the more serious? That is probably a question we cannot answer without a context. The more serious mistake is the one to which our culture is more drawn and by which we are tempted at any given moment. Judged in that light, I must say that our present temptation is to welcome and embrace death—to view it as a good to be seized and sought. We should be clear that Byock does not exactly recommend that, since, for example, he so clearly sets himself against the practice of euthanasia. Nonetheless, his stories may draw us in a direction he does not anticipate unless we are more self-conscious than he is about the background beliefs that shape our understanding of death and dying.

The question, finally, that is raised by looking at Byock's narratives in the light of the Ramsey/Kass exchange is this: Can a vision that pictures dying as "a part of full, even healthy, living" sustain over time the sense that care for the dying is "a valuable part of the life of the community" (246)? If death is simply "a part" of life, and the individual who dies "a part" of the natural cycle of living and dying, it may be harder than we suppose to retain the sense that the human being who dies is "apart" from all natural cycles and quite properly experiences dis-ease when facing death. It is that dis-ease, the sense that we do stand "apart" from the natural world that best captures our individuality. It teaches us that the dying person can never be replaced and that, therefore, death blots out an utterly unique individual. If hospice were to teach us too readily to accept another's death, we might learn lessons that could not easily be unlearned. We have, therefore, good reason not simply to reflect on stories of the dying but to contemplate how the meaning of the stories may depend in good part on the moral vision we bring to the reading of them. We have good reason not merely to try to master the art of dying but also to reflect upon the meaning of death—even if, in such reflection, we run up against the limits of human possibilities.

NOTES

Introduction

1. Courtney S. Campbell, "Bearing Witness: Religious Resistance and Meaning" in Dena S. Davis and Laurie Zoloth, eds., *Notes from a Narrow Ridge: Religion and Bioethics* (Hagerstown, Md.: University Publishing Group, 1999).

2. See, for example, Robert Zussman, "The Contributions of Sociology to Medical Ethics," *Hastings Center Report* 30 (January–February 2000): 7–12; James Lindemann Nelson, "Moral Teachings from Unexpected Quarters," *Hastings Center Report* 30 (January–February 2000): 12–17; Tod Chambers, "Centering Bioethics," *Hastings Center Report* 30 (January–February 2000): 22–29; Barry Hoffmaster, "Can Ethnography Save the Life of Medical Ethics?" *Social Science and Medicine* 35 (1992): 1421–31; John Van Maanen, *Tales of the Field: On Writing Ethnography* (Chicago: University of Chicago Press, 1988); Bruce Jennings, "Ethics and Ethnography in Neonatal Intensive Care," in George Weisz, ed., *Social Science Perspectives on Medical Ethics* (Dordrecht: Kluwer Academic Publishers, 1990), 261–72; William Sullivan, *Work and Integrity: The Crisis and Promise of Professionalism in America* (New York: HarperBusiness, 1995). See also "Bioethics and Beyond" (special issue), *Daedalus: Journal of the American Academy of Arts and Sciences* 128 (Fall 1999).

3. Robert N. Bellah, Richard Madsen, William M. Sullivan, Ann Swidler, and Steven M. Tipton, *Habits of the Heart: Individualism and Commitment in American Life* (Berkeley, Calif.: University of California Press, 1985).

4. Alasdair MacIntyre, *After Virtue: A Study in Moral Theory* (Notre Dame, Ind.: University of Notre Dame Press, 1981), American Ed., chap. 14, "The Nature of the Virtues," 169–89.

5. I want to thank Richard B. Miller for this very useful metaphor.

Chapter 1: Religion, Ethics, and Clinical Immersion

1. For a recent discussion, see Margaret A. Farley, "The Role of Experience in Moral Discernment," in *Christian Ethics: Problems and Prospects*, ed. Lisa

Sowle Cahill and James F. Childress (Cleveland: Pilgrim Press, 1996), 134–51.

2. For brief mention of several ethicists whose work has been informed by clinical immersion, see Albert R. Jonsen's magisterial study, *The Birth of Bioethics* (New York: Oxford University Press, 1998), 365–67. Jonsen also recounts his participation in various commissions, symposia, and informal meetings as an important source for his work in bioethics.

3. Daniel F. Chambliss, *Beyond Caring: Hospitals, Nurses, and the Social Organization of Ethics* (Chicago: University of Chicago Press, 1996), 6.

4. Daniel Chambliss, "Is Bioethics Irrelevant?" *Contemporary Sociology* 22 (September 1993): 648–50.

5. Arthur Kleinman, *Writing at the Margin: Discourse between Anthropology and Medicine* (Berkeley, Calif.: University of California Press, 1995), 49–50.

6. Ibid., 51.

7. Notable ethnographies in medicine include Charles L. Bosk, *Forgive and Remember: Managing Medical Failure* (Chicago: University of Chicago Press, 1979); Bosk, *All God's Mistakes: Genetic Counseling in a Pediatric Hospital* (Chicago: University of Chicago Press, 1992); Fred M. Frohock, *Special Care: Medical Decisions at the Beginning of Life* (Chicago: University of Chicago Press, 1987); Melvin Konner, *Becoming a Doctor: The Journey of Initiation in Medical School* (New York: Penguin Books, 1987); Arthur Kleinman, *The Illness Narratives: Suffering, Healing, and the Human Condition* (New York: Basic Books, 1988); Anne Fadiman, *The Spirit Catches You and You Fall Down: A Hmong Child, Her American Doctors, and the Clash of Two Cultures* (New York: Farrar, Straus & Giroux, 1997); Kathryn Rhett, ed., *Survival Stories: Memoirs of Crisis* (New York: Anchor Books, 1997).

8. I borrow the phrase "experience-near" from Clifford Geertz, *Local Knowledge: Further Essays in Interpretive Anthropology* (New York: Basic Books, 1983), 57.

9. Richard B. Miller, "Love and Death in a Pediatric Intensive Care Unit," *Annual Society of Christian Ethics* (1994): 21–39.

10. Paul Ramsey, *The Patient as Person: Explorations in Medical Ethics* (New Haven, Conn.: Yale University Press, 1970), xiii (emphasis in original).

11. Ibid.

12. Ibid., xvii.

13. For a discussion of specification, see Henry S. Richardson, "Specifying Norms as a Way to Resolve Concrete Ethical Problems," *Philosophy and Public Affairs* 19 (Fall 1990): 279–310; Richard B. Miller, *Casuistry and Modern Ethics: A Poetics of Practical Reasoning* (Chicago: University of Chicago Press, 1996), 17–25; James F. Childress, "Moral Norms in Practical Ethical Deliberation," in Cahill and Childress, *Christian Ethics: Problems and Prospects*, 196–217.

14. Richardson, "Specifying Norms," 283.

15. Ibid., 296.

16. Ibid., 294.

17. I do not mean to suggest that Ramsey discovered the idea of specification in *The Patient as Person*. See Paul Ramsey, "The Case of the Curious Exception," in *Norm and Context in Christian Ethics,* ed. Gene H. Outka and Paul Ramsey (New York: Charles Scribner's Sons, 1969), 67–135.

18. Ramsey, *Patient as Person*, xvii.

19. Ibid., 153 (emphasis in original).

20. Ibid.

21. Ibid., 11–40, 101–12, 157–64.

22. Ramsey, "Curious Exception," 125–26.

23. Ramsey, *Patient as Person*, xx.

24. Ibid.

25. Ibid.

26. Ibid., xi–xii.

27. Ibid., xii.

28. Jonsen, *The Birth of Bioethics*, 48.

29. In his medical ethics Ramsey's commitment to selfless care is qualified by considerations of the good of physical life. This structure finds parallels in Ramsey's political ethic, in which the requirements of selfless love are qualified by considerations of political realism and the relative good of political life. I discuss the latter as it bears on Ramsey's ethic of political duty and nuclear deterrence in *Interpretations of Conflict: Ethics, Pacifism, and the Just-War Tradition* (Chicago: University of Chicago Press, 1991), chap. 6.

30. Ramsey, *Patient as Person*, 194.

31. Ibid., 195. It is not easy to say whether these qualifications require Ramsey to weigh and balance rival demands against each other, since Ramsey wishes to incorporate the good of embodiment into his account of charity. Even if we were to grant Ramsey that qualification, it is still true that his attempt to specify the implications of charity require him to weigh and balance goods like autonomy against goods of patient benefit. James F. Childress shows in *Who Should Decide? Paternalism in Health Care* (New York: Oxford University Press), 164–65, where this tension materializes in Ramsey's thought and how Ramsey produces paternalistic positions regarding refusal of life support.

32. Ramsey, *Patient as Person*, 188–97.

33. Ibid., 5.

34. Ibid.

35. Ibid., xv.

36. Ibid., 5 (emphasis in original).

37. Ibid., 11. Later Ramsey argues that autonomy is only a relative right in cases of medical care. But to the best of my knowledge he never wavers about the

restrictions that autonomy imposes in cases of medical experimentation. See Paul Ramsey, *Ethics at the Edges of Life: Medical and Legal Intersections* (New Haven, Conn.: Yale University Press, 1978), 156; see also note 29.

38. Ramsey, *Patient as Person*, 13.

39. Ibid., 14.

40. This sentence presumes an understanding of, and argument about, competence and childhood that I cannot pursue here. For discussions, see Gary B. Melton, Gerald P. Koocher, and Michael J. Saks, eds., *Children's Competence to Consent* (New York: Plenum Press, 1983); Allen E. Buchanan and Dan. W. Brock, *Deciding for Others: The Ethics of Surrogate Decision Making* (Cambridge: Cambridge University Press, 1989), chap. 5.

41. Ramsey, *Patient as Person*, 11–12; see also Ramsey, "Curious Exception,"130.

42. Ramsey, *Patient as Person*, 13.

43. I do not mean to say that all nontherapeutic research on children is impermissible, only that it shoulders an additional burden of proof when compared to therapeutic pediatric research.

44. I am not suggesting that beneficence is the only relevant norm in pediatric ethics, as my previous note is meant to make plain. My critique of Ramsey is internal to his own logic.

45. Thus, I disagree with Richard McCormick, who, in arguing against Ramsey nonetheless grants Ramsey his initial premise about the centrality of consent. In developing his position on proxy consent and experimentation on children, McCormick writes that "consent is the heart of the matter." See Richard A. McCormick, *How Brave a New World? Dilemmas in Bioethics* (Garden City, N.Y.: Doubleday & Co., 1981), 60.

46. James M. Gustafson, *The Contribution of Theology to Medical Ethics* (Milwaukee: Peré Marquette Lecture, 1975), 4.

47. Ibid., 5.

48. Ibid., 7.

49. Ibid., 25.

50. Ibid., 31, 33. Gustafson develops this view more fully in *Ethics from a Theocentric Perspective*, 2 vols. (Chicago: University of Chicago Press, 1981, 1984).

51. Gustafson, "The Contribution of Theology," 13–14. See also Gustafson, *Ethics from a Theocentric Perspective*, 2: 1–22.

52. For a survey that includes Gustafson's writings, see Douglas F. Ottati, "The Reformed Tradition in Theological Ethics," in Cahill and Childress, *Christian Ethics,* 45–59.

53. For a discussion of Gustafson's role in the rise of modern bioethics, see Jonsen, *The Birth of Bioethics*, chap. 2 and passim.

54. See Jonsen's discussion of how this and related cases were received by ethicists, the press, and the medical community in ibid., 244–49.

55. Gustafson adopts the same strategy in an essay on abortion. See James M. Gustafson, "A Protestant Ethical Approach" in *The Morality of Abortion,* ed. John Noonan (Cambridge, Mass.: Harvard University Press, 1970), 101–22.

56. James M. Gustafson, "Mongolism, Parental Desires, and the Right to Life," in *Bioethics*, 1st ed., ed. Thomas A. Shannon (New York: Paulist Press, 1976), 98.

57. Ibid., 115.

58. Ibid., 119.

59. Ibid., 120.

60. Ibid., 120–21.

61. Ramsey, "Curious Exception," 116–17, 125–26.

62. Gustafson, "Mongolism, Parental Desires, and the Right to Life," 112.

63. For Gustafson's more general discussion of what is normatively human, see his essay, "What Is the Normatively Human?" in Gustafson, *Theology and Christian Ethics* (Philadelphia: Pilgrim Press, 1974), 229–45.

64. As reported in Jonsen, *Birth of Bioethics*, 246–47.

65. Gustafson, "Mongolism, Parental Desires, and the Right to Life," 98.

66. Ibid., 114.

67. William F. May, *The Physician's Covenant: Images of the Healer in Medical Ethics* (Philadelphia: Westminster Press, 1983), 25.

68. Ibid., 20.

69. Ibid., 15.

70. William F. May, *Testing the Medical Covenant* (Grand Rapids: Wm. B. Eerdmans Publishing Co., 1996), 8.

71. Ibid.

72. Ibid., 8–9.

73. William F. May, "The Beleaguered Rulers: The Public Obligation of the Professional," *Kennedy Institute of Ethics Journal* 2 (1992): 38.

74. See, e.g, William M. Sullivan, *Work and Integrity: The Crisis and Promise of Professionalism in America* (New York: Basic Books, 1995).

75. May, "Beleaguered Rulers," 38.

76. Childress, *Who Should Decide?* 18.

77. May, *The Physician's Covenant*, 20.

78. See Charles Taylor, "To Follow a Rule," in Taylor, *Philosophical Arguments* (Cambridge, Mass.: Harvard University Press, 1995), 165–80.

79. William F. May, *The Patient's Ordeal* (Bloomington, Ind.: Indiana University Press, 1991), 2.

80. Ibid., 1–2.

81. Ibid., 6.

82. Ibid., 193.

83. Jonsen, *The Birth of Bioethics*, 50.

84. Chambliss, *Beyond Caring*, 6.

85. Kleinman, *Writing at the Margin*, 49–50.

86. May, *Testing the Medical Covenant*, 8–9.
87. Kleinman, *Writing at the Margin*, 51.
88. I have covered some of this ground in *Casuistry and Modern Ethics*, chaps. 1, 9.
89. Ramsey, Gustafson, and May were all students of H. Richard Niebuhr at Yale University. Niebuhr was keenly interested in the relation between theology and culture as well as the importance of description in moral analysis. See, e.g., H. Richard Niebuhr, *The Responsible Self: A Study in Christian Moral Philosophy*, with Introduction by James M. Gustafson (New York: Harper & Row, 1963).
90. About ethnographers, James Clifford writes, "The notion that literary procedures pervade any work of cultural representation is a recent idea in the discipline." In ethics, the idea that literary procedures pervade any work of moral representation has yet to take hold. See James Clifford, "Introduction," in *Writing Culture: The Poetics and Politics of Ethnography*, ed. James Clifford and George E. Marcus (Berkeley, Calif.: University of California Press, 1986), 4. I wish to add that my account of Ramsey, Gustafson, and May on moral authority and patterns of moral reasoning is informed in no small way by Clifford's survey of the methodologies and authority of participant-observation in cultural anthropology. See "On Ethnographic Authority" in James Clifford, *The Predicament of Culture: Twentieth Century Ethnography, Literature, and Art* (Cambridge: Harvard University Press, 1988), 21–54.
91. John Van Maanen, *Tales of the Field: On Writing Ethnography* (Chicago: University of Chicago Press, 1988), 28.
92. May, *The Patient's Ordeal*, 2.
93. See John Rawls, *The Theory of Justice* (Cambridge, Mass.: Harvard University Press, 1971), 20.
94. I began this chapter as a fellow in the Program in Ethics and the Professions at Harvard University in 1987–88, and I am grateful to Dennis Thompson for his intellectual support and leadership during that time. I also wish to thank members of the REPL seminar for comments on an earlier draft of this chapter, and Jennifer Girod, Terence Martin, Jr., Douglas Ottati, William Schweiker, and Lisa Sideris for their constructive suggestions.

Chapter 2: The Bios of Bioethics and the Bios of Autobiography

1. In addition to books and articles by many contributors to this volume, recent critics of bioethics who make these points include William May, *The Physician's Covenant* and *The Patient's Ordeal*, and many contributors to Edwin R. DuBose, Ronald P. Hamel, and Laurence J. O'Connell, eds., *A Matter of Principles? Ferment in U.S. Bioethics* (Valley Forge, Pa.: Trinity Press International, 1994). For an assessment of the proper place of princi-

ples in bioethics, see the first chapter of Gilbert Meilaender, *Body, Soul, and Bioethics* (Notre Dame, Ind.: University of Notre Dame Press, 1995).

2. Kleinman, *The Illness Narratives*, 3.

3. See especially Arthur Frank, *The Wounded Storyteller: Body, Illness, and Ethics* (Chicago: University of Chicago Press, 1995); and also Cheryl Mattingly, "The Concept of Therapeutic 'Emplotment,' " *Social Science and Medicine* 38 (1994): 811–22; Dena Davis, "Rich Cases: The Ethics of Thick Description," *Hastings Center Report* 21 (1991): 12–17; Howard Brody, *Stories of Sickness* (New Haven, Conn.: Yale University Press, 1987); and Barry Hoffmaster, "Can Ethnography Save the Life of Medical Ethics?" *Social Science and Medicine* 35 (1992): 1421–31. Another voice calling for more attention to narrative's role in medical ethics is Robert Coles, for instance in *The Call of Stories: Teaching and the Moral Imagination* (Boston: Houghton Mifflin Co., 1989).

4. Howard Brody, " 'My Story Is Broken; Can You Help Me Fix It?': Medical Ethics and the Joint Construction of Narrative," *Literature and Medicine* 13 (1994): 79–94.

5. Anne Hunsaker Hawkins, *Reconstructing Illness: Studies in Pathography* (West Lafayette, Ind.: Purdue University Press, 1993); Lucy Bregman and Sara Thiermann, *First Person Mortal: Personal Narratives of Illness, Dying and Grief* (New York: Paragon House, 1995); and Thomas Couser, *Recovering Bodies: Illness, Disability, and Life Writing* (Madison, Wisc.: University of Wisconsin Press, 1997).

6. Couser, *Recovering Bodies*, 115.

7. Frank, *Wounded Storyteller*, 10, 12.

8. Ibid., 17. I don't think Frank's ideas about a distinctive ethics of "the postmodern" are essential to his thesis and, in fact, undercut his insights into the role of storytelling in dealing with illness throughout human history.

9. Arthur Frank, *At the Will of the Body: Reflections on Illness* (Boston: Houghton Mifflin Co., 1991).

10. Frank, *Wounded Storyteller*, 160.

11. Arthur Frank, *At the Will of the Body;* William Styron, *Darkness Visible: A Memoir of Madness* (New York: Vintage Books, 1990); Nancy Mairs, *Waist-High in the World: Life Among the Nondisabled* (Boston: Beacon Press, 1996) and *Ordinary Time: Cycles in Marriage, Faith, and Renewal* (Boston: Beacon Press, 1993); and Reynolds Price, *A Whole New Life: An Illness and a Healing* (New York: Plume, 1995).

12. Couser, *Recovering Bodies*, 150. With improved treatments of AIDS, Couser's generalization is becoming less accurate.

13. Ibid., 5. Couser suggests (6) that a memoir by a family member or a diary by the ill person may better represent some illness conditions than autobiography because they do "not await the resolution—whether in recovery from or

accommodation to dysfunction—that seems to licence most retrospective autobiographical accounts of illness and disability."

14. Price, *A Whole New Life*, 188, 189.
15. St. Augustine, *Confessions*, trans. R. S. Pine-Coffin (Harmondsworth, England: Penguin, 1961), 112.
16. May, *Patient's Ordeal*, 5.
17. Ibid., 22.
18. Mairs, *Ordinary Time*, 101.
19. Mairs, *Waist-High*, 208–9.
20. Frank, *At the Will of the Body*, 138.
21. Couser, *Recovering Bodies*, 185.
22. Ibid., 198.
23. Ibid., 195.
24. Styron, *Darkness Visible*, 84.
25. Anatole Broyard, *Intoxicated by My Illness: and Other Writings on Life and Death* (New York: Clarkson Potter, 1992), 40.
26. Ibid., 42–43.
27. Styron, *Darkness Visible*, 52
28. Frank, *At the Will of the Body*, 14–15. However, Frank's later book, *The Wounded Storyteller*, vigorously pursues the suggestion that medicine should "reform itself" by dealing with "illness talk" as well as "disease talk."
29. Jerome Groopman, *The Measure of Our Days: New Beginnings at Life's End* (New York: Viking Penguin, 1997). This story appeared first as "The Last Deal" in *The New Yorker* on September 8, 1997. Numbers in parentheses in the rest of this essay refer to the pagination in *The Measure of Our Days*.
30. Joseph Conrad, *Heart of Darkness*, 2d ed. (New York: Norton, 1971), 72.

Chapter 3: Adequate Images and Evil Imaginations

1. John Steinbeck, *The Log from The Sea of Cortez: The Narrative Portion of the Book, Sea of Cortez, by John Steinbeck and E. F. Ricketts, 1941, Here Reissued with a Profile, "About Ed Ricketts"* (New York: Penguin Books, 1976), 2–3.
2. H. A. Prichard, "Does Moral Philosophy Rest on a Mistake?" in *Moral Obligation* (1912; reprint, London: Oxford University Press, 1949), 12.
3. H. Richard Niebuhr, *The Meaning of Revelation* (New York: Macmillan Co., 1960), 44.
4. Anne Hunsaker Hawkins, *Reconstructing Illness*, 14.
5. John Arras, "News from the Circuit Courts: How Not to Think About Physician-Assisted Suicide," *BioLaw Special Section* (July–August 1996): S171–S186.
6. Yale Kamisar, "The Reasons So Many People Support Physician-Assisted Suicide—And Why These Reasons Are Not Convincing," *Issues in Law and Medicine* 12 (1996): 113–131, at 113.

7. As quoted in *Vacco v. Quill*, 521 U.S. 793, 803 (1997).
8. James Rachels, "Active and Passive Euthanasia," *New England Journal of Medicine* 292 (January 1975): 78–80.
9. See *Cruzan v. Director, Missouri Department of Health*, 497 U.S. 261 (1990).
10. *Quill v. Vacco*, 80 F3d 716, 721 (2nd Cir. 1996).
11. *Quill v. Vacco*, at 728.
12. *Quill v. Vacco*, at 728.
13. *Vacco v. Quill*, at 800.
14. *Vacco v. Quill*, at 807.
15. Timothy Quill, *A Midwife Through the Dying Process: Stories of Healing and Hard Choices at the End of Life* (Baltimore: Johns Hopkins University Press, 1996).
16. Ira Byock, *Dying Well: Peace and Possibilities at the End of Life* (New York: Riverhead Books, 1997).
17. Quill, *Midwife*, 205.
18. Ibid., 207.
19. Ibid., 163.
20. Ibid., 208.
21. Ibid., 210.
22. Byock, *Dying Well*, 60; emphasis in original.
23. Quill, *Midwife*, 210–11.
24. Wayne Booth, *The Company We Keep* (Berkeley, Calif.: University of California Press, 1988), 72–73.
25. Byock, *Dying Well*, 180.
26. Ibid., 183.
27. Quill, *Midwife*, 151.
28. Niebuhr, *The Meaning of Revelation*, 79.

Chapter 4: "It's What Pediatricians Are Supposed to Do"

1. Eric J. Cassell, *Doctoring: The Nature of Primary Care Medicine* (New York: Oxford University Press, 1997).
2. Harmon L. Smith and Larry R. Churchill, *Professional Ethics and Primary Care Medicine: Beyond Dilemmas and Decorum* (Durham, N.C.: Duke University Press, 1986), 5. Another, related approach to primary care ethics, also published in 1986, is found in Ronald J. Christie and C. Barry Hoffmaster, *Ethical Issues in Family Medicine* (New York: Oxford University Press, 1986), which argues for a more casuistic approach to ethics and raises issues characteristic of family medicine, but does not consider moral premises and contexts that distinguish primary care from other forms of medical practice.
3. In addition to the works already cited, there are numerous attestations to and analyses of the importance of the physician-patient relationship for effective

health care. Selected references, which directly or indirectly inform the discussion in this chapter, include the following: Francis W. Peabody, "The Care of the Patient," *Journal of the American Medical Association* 88 (1927): 877–82; Anthony L. Suchman and Dale A. Matthews, "What Makes the Patient-Doctor Relationship Therapeutic? Exploring the Connexional Dimension of Medical Care," *Annals of Internal Medicine* 108 (1988): 125–30; Howard Brody, *Placebos and the Philosophy of Medicine* (Chicago: University of Chicago Press, 1977) and *The Healer's Power* (New Haven, Conn.: Yale University Press, 1992); and the text and citations in Felicia G. Cohn's thoughtful and well-researched doctoral dissertation, *Dialogue in Medicine: Martin Buber and the Physician-Patient Relationship* (University of Virginia, 1996), 176–216.

4. Brody, *Placebos and the Philosophy of Medicine;* Cohn, *Dialogue in Medicine,* 189–200.

5. Smith and Churchill, *Professional Ethics and Primary Care Medicine,* 5.

Chapter 5: Ethics, Faith, and Healing

1. I wish to thank the Poynter Center for the Study of Ethics and American Institutions at Indiana University, and especially its director, David H. Smith, for enabling me to participate in the collaborative project on Religion, Ethnography, and Professional Life. In addition to all that I learned from the other participants in that project, I gratefully acknowledge the help that I received throughout this project from two consultants. Sheldon Berkowitz, a close friend and a pediatrician, has strong interests in medical ethics and has served for many years on the ethics committee of Minneapolis Children's Medical Center. Laurence Savett, a recently retired internist, has taught courses to undergraduates and to medical students on humanistic values in medicine. Both contributed in significant ways to my conceptualization of the issues addressed here. I also wish to thank the six physicians who gave so generously of their time in responding to my questions. I learned a great deal from each of them and hope that this paper, in addition to representing their views accurately, succeeds in conveying the admiration I have for each of them.

2. Of course, shamans in native cultures in both the Americas and Africa provide evidence of the widespread belief that the power to heal is supernatural in origin.

3. See Numbers 12:1–15.

4. 1 Kings 17:17–24.

5. See John 5:3–9; Matthew 9:27–31; 20:17–19; Mark 10:46–52; Luke 13:10–17, among many such examples. It should be noted that stories of holy men capable of healing circulated in rabbinic literature of the same period. See, for example, the two healing stories of Rabbi Hanina and Rabbi Yohanan; *Babylonian Talmud Berakhot* 5b.

6. See Claude Levi-Strauss, *Structural Anthropology* (New York: Basic Books, 1963), especially chapter 10, "The Effectiveness of Symbols." For more recent illustrations of the close connection between religious authority and the power to heal, see Dwight Conquergood and Paga Thao, *I Am a Shaman: A Hmong Life Story with Ethnographic Commentary,* Southeast Asia Refugee Studies, Occasional Papers Number 8 (Minneapolis: Center for Urban and Regional Affairs, 1989) and Anne Fadiman, *The Spirit Catches You and You Fall Down* (New York: Farrar, Straus & Giroux, 1997).

7. Anatole Broyard, *Intoxicated by My Illness,* excerpted in *On Doctoring,* ed. Richard Reynolds and John Stone (New York: Simon & Schuster, 1995), 178.

8. There was nothing scientific or random about the process of selecting physicians to interview. I began by questioning a couple of close physician friends about individuals who might be interested in discussing these issues with me. My initial screening of ten to twelve candidates enabled me to select a half dozen who appeared to have reflected most seriously on the intersection of their personal and professional lives. I settled on three pediatricians in general practice and three pediatric specialists in separate fields. I chose not to interview physicians who now work as administrators rather than clinicians on the assumption that those whose experience was current would offer me the freshest and most detailed answers to my inquiries.

9. I recognize that physicians who work with pediatric patients are often regarded as a self-selected group, perhaps more concerned with humanistic dimensions of medical care and less concerned with professional status and the financial rewards of medicine than those attracted to other areas of medicine. In some respects, the responses of these physicians confirmed those characterizations. Of course, without comparative data, it is not possible to draw conclusions about whether the values of those interviewed for this study were unique, either among those providing pediatric care or among physicians in general.

10. In the end, all those who agreed to participate in this study were male, although it was not my original intent to restrict the study in this way. The group was also somewhat more homogeneous than I intended in terms of professional experience, in that all the participants have been in practice at least fourteen years. I cannot say the extent to which either of these factors may have skewed the responses I received.

11. I met with each physician two or three times for a total of three to five hours. While I have no way of knowing the extent to which they were completely candid with me about frequently sensitive matters, each of them shared with me things that did not reflect positively on their professional lives, a sign of genuine and significant self-disclosure. It should also be noted that each of the participants in this study reviewed an earlier draft of this paper and had an opportunity to suggest additions or corrections. Several of them also participated in a group discussion of the paper, which helped me to clarify their views considerably.

12. I have attempted here to capture as accurately as possible the views and values of the participants in this study as they reported them to me; hence, the substantial quantity of direct quotation, drawn from tape recordings of these interviews. Of course, the organization and conceptualization, as well as the interpretation of this material, is my own.

13. This concept is taken from Alisdair MacIntyre, *After Virtue: A Study in Moral Theory* (Notre Dame, Ind.: University of Notre Dame, 1981).

14. Given the limited nature of this study, I make no claims that these are exhaustive, only that they were most salient in my conversations with this group of physicians about the ways in which they meet the challenges inherent in their practice.

15. Rachel Naomi Remen, *Kitchen Table Wisdom* (New York: Riverhead Books, 1996), 164.

16. This point is made with particular eloquence by Anatole Broyard in his book, *Intoxicated by My Illness*, excerpted in Reynolds and Stone, *On Doctoring*, 178: "To most physicians, my illness is a routine incident in their rounds, while for me it's the crisis of my life. I would feel better if I had a doctor who at least perceived this incongruity."

17. See Ramsey, *Patient as Person* (New Haven: Yale University Press, 1970).

18. In a group conversation with several of the physicians long after the individual interviews had been completed, this distinction between "compassion" as a feeling and "caring" as compassion translated into action received a good deal of attention. Some felt that through medical education one could learn certain techniques (the value of touch, listening skills, etc.) that are indicative of caring, but that compassion is a personal trait that one cannot be taught (at least not in any formal way). Others voiced the belief that caring without compassion was the equivalent of "going through the motions" without real conviction or feeling, and so was disingenuous (and would be recognized as such by patients). Despite these differences, they agreed that when they identified compassion as a virtue of medical practice, they meant to include the willingness and ability to communicate that compassion to patients through actions.

19. Remen, *Kitchen Table Wisdom*, 225.

20. Dr. Sheldon Berkowitz, personal communication, July 22, 1998.

21. I use the term "religious," as scholars of religion often do, to refer to the attitudes of awe and reverence in response to the transcendent dimensions of human life. The physicians themselves, in keeping with contemporary parlance, might refer to these experiences or attitudes as "spiritual," reserving the term "religious" for things connected to organized religious groups and established religious traditions. The difference, in this instance, is strictly semantic.

22. Arthur Kleinman, *The Illness Narratives* (New York: Basic Books, 1988), 210.

23. Indeed, Laurence Savett, who served as a consultant on this project, suggested that each of the influences on these physicians (personal experience, role models, the communities to which they belong) was a source of values for their practice, and, moreover, that each of these factors influenced the others. At different times, different influences might come to the fore, but no one of them is decisive, nor could it be. In that sense, any attempt to isolate the "Jewish" influence on these physicians' practice as distinct from the other factors that play a role in their professional lives is futile from the start.

24. Abraham Joshua Heschel, *God in Search of Man* (New York: Farrar, Straus & Giroux, 1955).

25. One does find this perspective represented in the works, both autobiographical and fictional, of physicians themselves, as in Reynolds and Stone, *On Doctoring*.

26. An important exception to this is Margaret E. Mohrmann, *Medicine as Ministry: Reflections on Suffering, Ethics and Hope* (Cleveland: Pilgrim Press, 1995). See also her article, "The Practice of the Ministry of Medicine," in *Update, Loma Linda University Center for Christian Bioethics* 14 (October 1998): 3.

27. By way of example, see Alan H. Goldman, *The Moral Foundations of Professional Ethics* (Totowa, N.J.: Rowman & Littlefield, 1980), and Michael D. Bayles, *Professional Ethics*, 2d ed. (Belmont, Calif.: Wadsworth, 1989).

28. Arguably, had our conversations gone on much longer, these things might have come up. But questions about "how being Jewish affects the kind of doctor you are" and "has Judaism helped you in any way to deal with the challenges of caring for sick children and their families" evoked only rather general answers.

29. Some of these physicians indicated that their practice of medicine was indeed influenced by their Jewishness, but "not directly." When asked to spell out what this meant, Kohen noted that his practice is "driven by values that come from my family and those are very clearly Jewish values, but they're home, ethnocultural values, not shul [synagogue], scripture-based values." To the extent that this sentiment is shared, it reinforces two important points—that traditional Jewish texts and beliefs are not a major factor in shaping the values of these practitioners, and that, nonetheless, Jewish cultural and social mores may be an important influence on them.

30. Again, Breningstall may be an exception here. Given his Orthodox Jewish practice, he seems most able to articulate the connections between these aspects of his life: "The whole practice of Judaism . . . becomes a sort of affirming way of life that carries over when things get difficult in medical practice. As I'm involved in Jewish learning or religious practice, various aspects of religious living, it all seems to make a coherent whole that helps everything else fit together too." And later he commented, "Jewish learning

is clearly the most complicated kind of intellectual discipline in which I've ever been involved. The difficulties in undertaking the study of medicine pale in comparison to studying gemara [Talmud]. Just like medical practice is an encounter with a much greater intelligence, this is also an encounter with a greater intelligence." His integration of religious and medical practice is also evident in his acknowledgment that "saying tehilim [psalms] for someone who is ill [which is a traditional Jewish practice] is as potent a healing endeavor as medical practice."

Chapter 6: Organ Transplants

1. Richard Selzer, *Imagine a Woman and Other Tales* (New York: Random House, 1990), 3–28.
2. Ibid., 4.
3. Ibid.
4. Ibid., 6.
5. Ibid., 7.
6. Ibid.
7. Ibid., 7–8.
8. Ibid., 8–9.
9. Ibid., 10.
10. Ibid.
11. Ibid., 19.
12. Ibid.
13. Ibid., 20.
14. Ibid., 23.
15. Ibid., 27.
16. Ibid., 28.
17. S. J. Youngner, S. Landefeld, C. J. Coulton et al., "'Brain Death' and Organ Retrieval: A Cross-sectional Survey of Knowledge and Concepts among Health Professionals," *Journal of the American Medical Association* 261 (21 April 1989): 2205–2210.
18. D. Wikler and A. J. Weisbard, "Appropriate Confusion over 'Brain Death,'" *Journal of the American Medical Association* 261 (21 April 1989): 2246.
19. Joseph Fins, "When Brain Death Pulls at the Heart Strings," in *Personal Narratives on Caring for the Dying*, 2d ed. (American Board of Internal Medicine, forthcoming), 21–22.
20. Hans Jonas, "Against the Stream: Comments on the Definition and Redefinition of Death," in *Philosophical Essays: From Ancient Creed to Technological Man* (Englewood Cliffs, N.J.: Prentice-Hall, 1974). Reprinted in *Contemporary Issues in Bioeethics,* ed. Tom L. Beauchamp and LeRoy Walters (Encino, Calif.: Dickenson Publishing Co., 1978), 263.
21. Ibid., 264.
22. Ibid., 266.
23. Ibid.

24. Ibid.

25. The image of physician as crusader helps to clarify, I think, why so much of medical ethics and public discourse about medical ethics focuses on the "rights" of patients. It also helps us to understand what is good and what is bad about that focus. It is good because the language of "rights" is the most powerful language we have to constrain and restrain the powerful do-gooder. It is bad because it is essentially adversarial—it will not (cannot) nurture or sustain the loyalty and trust that are essential not only to healing but to the effort to procure organs for transplant. Adversarial relationships and distrust are serious barriers to procuring organs for transplant. Legalistic attention to the "rights" of patients and their families will not nurture the necessary trust, and any actions that are seen as compromising the loyalty physicians owe patients and their families will threaten that trust. Medical ethics could contribute to alleviating suspicion by developing alternative ways to talk about these issues. And religious communities have access to other ways of talking about professional obligations, like the image of "covenant" that William F. May has used so compellingly.

26. Task Force on Organ Transplantation, *Organ Transplantation: Issues and Recommendations* (Washington, D.C.: U.S. Department of Health and Human Services, 1986), 31.

27. The Partnership for Organ Donation, *The American Public's Attitudes toward Organ Donation and Transplantation: Summary Results of a Gallup Survey Prepared for The Partnership for Organ Donation* (Boston: The Partnership for Organ Donation, 1993), 3, 6.

28. Task Force on Organ Transplantation, *Organ Transplantation*, 31.

29. Partnership for Organ Donation, *American Public's Attitudes*, 3, 6.

30. Task Force on Organ Transplantation, *Organ Transplantation*, 31.

31. May, *The Patient's Ordeal*, 176–77.

32. Gil Meilaender, "Case Studies: The Anencephalic Newborn as Donor," *Hastings Center Report* 16 (April 1986): 23.

33. Alexander Capron, "Anencephalic Donors: Separate the Dead from the Dying," *Hastings Center Report* 17 (February 1987); see also Arthur Caplan, "Fragile Trust," in *Pediatrics, Brain Death, and Organ Transplantation*, ed. H. Kaufman (New York: Plenum Press, 1989), 299–307.

34. Selzer, *Imagine a Woman*, 7.

35. Leon Kass, *Toward a More Natural Science* (New York: Free Press, 1985), 277–78.

36. May, *The Patient's Ordeal*, 182–87.

37. Arthur Caplan, "Professional Arrogance and Public Misunderstanding," *Hastings Center Report* 18 (April–May 1988): 34–37.

38. Susan Martyn, Richard Wright, and Leo Clark, "Required Request for Organ Donation: Moral, Clinical, and Legal Problems," *Hastings Center Report* 18 (April–May 1988): 27–33.

39. Caplan, "Professional Arrogance," 36.

40. James Childress, "Ethical Criteria for Procuring and Distributing Organs for Transplantation," *Journal of Health Policies, Policy and Law* 14 (1989): 87–113.
41. Renee C. Fox and Judith P. Swazey, *Spare Parts: Organ Replacement in American Society* (New York: Oxford University Press, 1992), 40.
42. Selzer, *Imagine a Woman*, 8–9.
43. Cheryl J. Sanders, "African Americans and Organ Donation: Reflections on Religion, Ethics and Embodiment," in *Embodiment, Morality, and Medicine,* ed. L. Sowle Cahill and M. A. Farley (Dordrecht: Kluwer, 1995), 141–53.
44. Catherine Bell, *Ritual Theory, Ritual Practice* (New York: Oxford University Press, 1992), 74.
45. Cited in Fox and Swazey, *Spare Parts*, 63.
46. For a brief summary of several rituals, see Kenneth Kramer, *The Sacred Art of Dying: How World Religions Understand Death* (New York: Paulist Press, 1988).
47. Laurence J. O'Connell, "Ritual Practice and End-of-Life Care," *The Park Ridge Center Bulletin* 5 (August/September 1988): 14.
48. Andrew Lustig, ed., *Bioethics Yearbook,* Vol. 1: *Theological Developments in Bioethics, 1988–1990* (Dordrecht: Kluwer, 1991), 193.
49. Ibid., 194.
50. Andrew Lustig, ed., *Bioethics Yearbook,* Vol. 3: *Theological Developments in Bioethics, 1990–92.* (Dordrecht: Kluwer, 1995).
51. Cited in Lustig, *Bioethics Yearbook,* Vol. 1, 158.
52. Lustig, *Bioethics Yearbook,* Vol. 3.
53. Lustig, *Bioethics Yearbook,* Vol. 1, 36–38.
54. Ibid., 139.
55. Ibid., 158.
56. Ibid., 89–90.
57. Ibid., 114–16.
58. Ibid., 66–67.

Chapter 7: Giving in Grief

1. Data from the United Network for Organ Sharing (UNOS). These data reflect transplants completed in 1998 and one-year survival rates for transplants completed in 1997.
2. Ibid.
3. Ongoing disputes include the process for coding the medical condition of transplant patients; the relative weights of medical urgency and likely medical benefit in allocation algorithms; geographic variation in average waiting time for transplant; geographic allocation of transplant organs, including the relative allocation of organs to high-volume urban transplant centers vs. regional transplant programs.
4. In late 1997, Vice President Al Gore launched a new public-private partnership for organ donation. Administered by the U.S. Department of Health and

Human Services (DHHS), the partnership includes governmental, nonprofit, religious, business, and community organizations in a cooperative attempt to encourage organ donation. DHHS has also increased its internal research, assessing factors affecting organ donation and reviewing the results of various efforts to promote donation.

5. Other reasons given for the common rejection of physicians as primary approachers were as follows: "It is a bother for them"; it is hard for them to take the time necessary to do it well; it can become a control issue for them—"This is my case or my E.R."; they may undertake approach out of a sincere sense of responsibility to see a case through even if they are not very comfortable talking to families in such situations, and "that can be unhelpful" although well-intentioned.

6. This phenomenon might explain disparities in support rates for organ donation in public opinion polls (about 80 percent) and actual approach-acceptance rates (about 50 percent). Partnership for Organ Donation, Boston, Mass. See, e.g., S. L. Gortmaker et al., "Improving the Request Process to Increase Family Consent for Organ Donation," *Journal of Transplant Coordination* 8 (December 1998):210–17.

7. The issue of next-of-kin was addressed in a complex way at a regional OPO training session I attended in the spring of 1999. The session was designed to train designated approachers, consistent with the new federal legislation dictating that all primary approachers be OPO-trained. The other attendees were nurses and social workers at the hospital where the training occurred, all of whom were volunteering to be designated primary approachers.

Certainly the instructor emphasized the need to be sensitive to family dynamics and to try to facilitate productive family discourse. He even specifically described cases in which he had suggested that families stop considering donation when it became clear they were so divided on the issue that it was fraying the family in ways unlikely to be resolved. Yet his emphases were subtly different from those of all the chaplains interviewed. First, he repeatedly raised a concern with numbers that the chaplains never articulated, urging approachers to limit the number of family members involved in the decision making. He warned that the more people involved, the more chance for friction, noting that dissonance often weighs toward refusal to donate. He lamented cases he had witnessed in which a minority view stymied donation as other family members relinquished their desire for donation in order to relieve family stress. (Several chaplains noted similar cases, but in the context of describing frustrations to be accepted.) At times he seemed simply to be urging that only family members truly close to the deceased be included in discussions. But at other times his concern seemed to be with numbers per se, suggesting that facilitating discussions with larger or extended families might be problematic because of predicted adverse affect on consent rates.

Moreover, in contrast to the chaplains he emphasized the legal right of the next-of-kin to make donation decisions. He urged approachers to be sure next-of-kin knew that legally the decision is theirs and that it will be a confidential decision. One of the cases he described as a heroic, positive case was one in which a decedent's spouse favored donation while his natal family opposed it. The spouse seemingly acquiesced to the natal family. Then, minutes after the family had left, she ran back and told the OPO coordinator that she definitely wanted to donate because she knew her husband would have wanted that, and she didn't want his family to know of the donation. The donation proceeded, and the confidentiality of her decision was maintained. I do not know how any of the chaplains interviewed would comment on this case. But the difference between this "ideal" case and their "ideal" cases is striking.

8. Ramsey, *Patient as Person*, especially 64–74.
9. Ramsey's concern expresses the Kantian categorical imperative never to treat people solely as a means to an end. It could also be understood as a bioethical permutation of the doctrine of double effect. Originally articulated by medieval Roman Catholic casuists, the doctrine of double effect addresses situations in which the same action could result in both morally desirable and undesirable effects. This doctrine precludes intending evil that good may come of it.

Chapter 8: Boundary Crossings

1. Cicely Saunders, "The Evolution of the Hospices," *Free Inquiry* (Winter 1991/92): 19.
2. Cf. C. Morgan, *Hospice: A Special Kind of Caring* (n.p., n.d.).
3. L. Shiner, "The Meanings of Secularization," in *Secularization and the Protestant Prospect,* ed. J. F. Childress and D. B. Harned (Philadelphia: Westminster Press, 1970), 38–40.
4. J. D. Cushman, "Hospice Penetration: The Use of Public Data to Measure Hospice Performance," National Hospice Organization Senior Management and Leadership Conference, 1998; A. Jackson, personal communication, 1998.
5. E. Kubler-Ross, "On Death and Dying," in *The Phenomenon of Death,* ed. E. Wyschogrod (New York: Harper & Row, 1973), 14–39.
6. G. Meilaender, "On Removing Food and Water: Against the Stream," *Hastings Center Report* 14 (December 1984): 11–13.
7. Cf. Kubler-Ross, "On Death and Dying."
8. A. Chin, K. Hedberg, G. Higginson, and D. Fleming, "Legalized Physician-Assisted Suicide in Oregon—The First Year's Experience," *New England Journal of Medicine* 340 (February 18, 1999): 577–83.
9. C. Campbell, J. Hare, and P. Matthews, "Conflicts of Conscience: Hospice and Assisted Suicide," *Hastings Center Report* 25 (May–June 1995): 36–43.
10. H. Bouma, III, et al., *Christian Faith, Health, and Medical Practice* (Grand Rapids: Wm. B. Eerdmans Publishing Co., 1989), 95–102.

11. Ibid., 97–98.
12. Chin, Hedberg, Higginson, and Fleming, "Legalized Physician-Assisted Suicide," 582.
13. J. F. Childress, *Who Should Decide? Paternalism in Health Care* (New York: Oxford University Press, 1982), 16–21.
14. C. Campbell, "Give Me Liberty and Give Me Death: Physician-Assisted Suicide in Oregon" (MS in review).

Chapter 9: Professional Commitment to Personal Care

1. Interviews were conducted by my colleague Judith A. Granbois and me over a period of over a year. I am very grateful for Ms. Granbois's invaluable assistance in this process.
2. Daniel F. Chambliss, *Beyond Caring: Hospitals, Nurses, and the Social Organization of Ethics* (Chicago: University of Chicago Press, 1996). (References will be given by page number in parentheses within the body of the text.)

Chapter 10: "Apart and Not a Part"

1. Dietrich Bonhoeffer, *Letters and Papers from Prison*, enlarged edition, ed. Eberhard Bethge (New York: Macmillan Publishing Co., 1972), 240.
2. Felix Salten, *Bambi* (New York: Grosset & Dunlap, 1929), 110–15 passim.
3. Felicia Ackerman, "Goldilocks and Mrs. Ilych: A Critical Look at the 'Philosophy of Hospice,'" *Cambridge Quarterly of Healthcare Ethics* 6 (1997): 314f. As the passage from Bonhoeffer used as an epigraph for this essay may indicate, we should not too readily suppose that religious belief will incline one toward acceptance of death. It is Socrates, not Jesus in Gethsemane, who more closely approximates the "ideology" that Ackerman rejects.
4. Ira Byock, *Dying Well* (New York: Riverhead Books, 1997). (References will be given by page number in parentheses within the body of the text.)
5. Both were published in the *Hastings Center Studies* 2 (May 1974). Ramsey's essay covers pp. 47–62; Kass's, pp. 67–80. (References will be given by page number in parentheses within the body of the text.)
6. C. S. Lewis, *A Grief Observed* (London: Faber & Faber, 1961), 24.
7. We should not overlook the fact that there may also be a kind of empirical evidence for the perception of death as hostile power. Several recent studies have concluded that seriously ill people may struggle far more to stay alive than the healthy think sensible—or than the ill themselves would have thought reasonable prior actually to facing death. See the studies cited by Ackerman in her footnotes 28, 29, and 30.
8. The title of chapter 10 is "Facing Unbearable Pain, Unspeakable Losses: Terry Matthews." Even in this case, however, pain relief was provided, though it could be achieved only by means of permanent sedation. Indeed, Byock emphasizes throughout the book his conviction that "physical suffering

can always be alleviated"—and "always" is always italicized when he makes this point. Cf. xiv, 44, 60, 215, 245.

9. Byock does, in fact, provide the obligatory (!) citation of Dylan Thomas. Cf. 193.

10. Although Byock himself is Jewish, I think that any reader of *Dying Well* would conclude that his religious views or, perhaps more accurately, his "spirituality," are decidedly eclectic.

11. Lewis Thomas, "The Deacon's Masterpiece," in *The Medusa and the Snail* (New York: Viking Press, 1979), 130–36 .

12. C. S. Lewis, *Miracles* (New York: Macmillan Co., 1947), 129–30.

13. St. Augustine, *Confessions* 4.7. It was Richard Miller who first pointed out the relevance for my analysis of Augustine's treatment of the proper way to love temporal goods, and I thank him for the insight.

14. St. Augustine, *Confessions* 4.12.

15. Ramsey, *Patient as Person,* 144–57.

AUTHOR INDEX